Garfield

WEIGHS HIS OPTIONS

BY JIM DAVIS

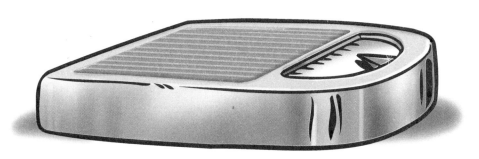

Ballantine Books • New York

A Ballantine Books Trade Paperback Original

Copyright © 2010 by PAWS, Inc. All rights reserved.
"GARFIELD" and the GARFIELD characters are trademarks of PAWS, Inc.

Published in the United States by Ballantine Books, an imprint of The Random House Publishing Group,
a division of Random House, Inc., New York.

BALLANTINE and colophon are registered trademarks of Random House, Inc.

ISBN 978-0-345-49181-7

Printed in the United States of America

www.ballantinebooks.com

9 8 7 6 5 4 3

GARFIELD FROM THE TRASH BIN

One cat's trash is another cat's treasure, and in the all-new Ballantine book, Garfield creator Jim Davis has collected the best of the worst: never-before-seen rejected comic strips, questionable covers, silly sketches, and over-the-top outtakes sure to amuse–or offend–just about everyone. So hold your nose and dive in!

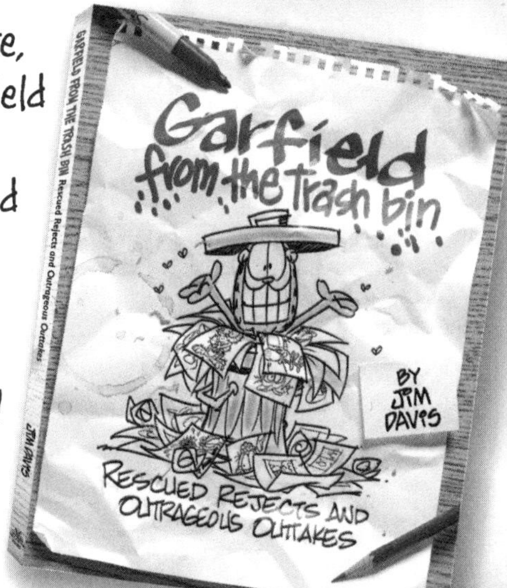
Garfield from the Trash bin
BY JIM DAVIS
RESCUED REJECTS AND OUTRAGEOUS OUTTAKES
GARFIELD FROM THE TRASH BIN Rescued Rejects and Outrageous Outtakes
JIM DAVIS

BUY THE BOOK FEBRUARY 2010!

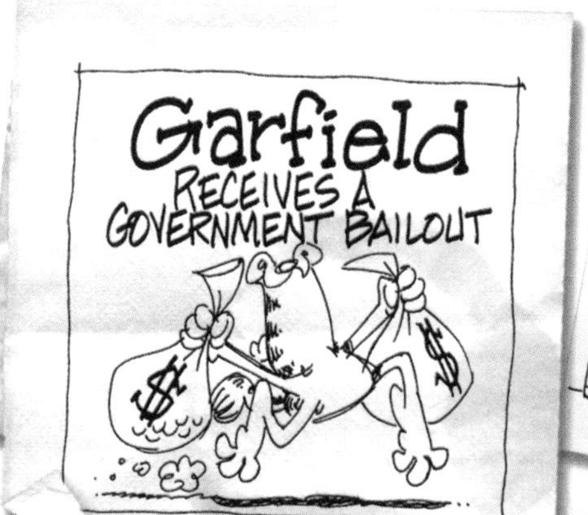
Garfield
RECEIVES A GOVERNMENT BAILOUT

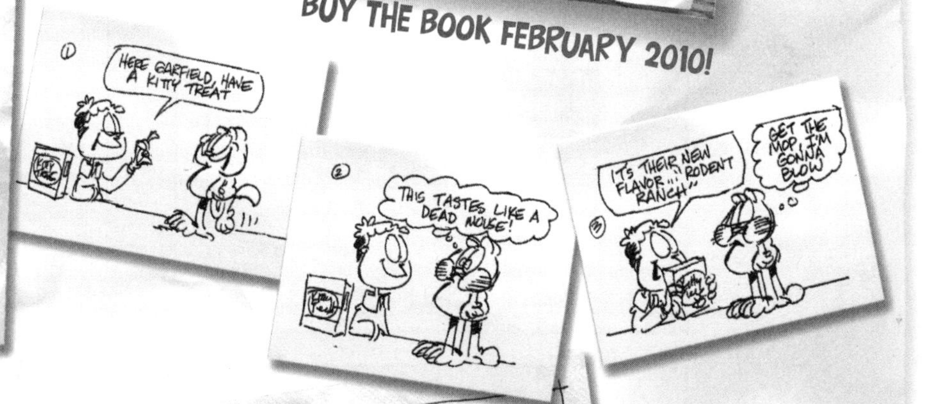
HERE GARFIELD, HAVE A KITTY TREAT
THIS TASTES LIKE A DEAD MOUSE!
IT'S THEIR NEW FLAVOR... RODENT RANCH
GET THE MOP, I'M GONNA BLOW

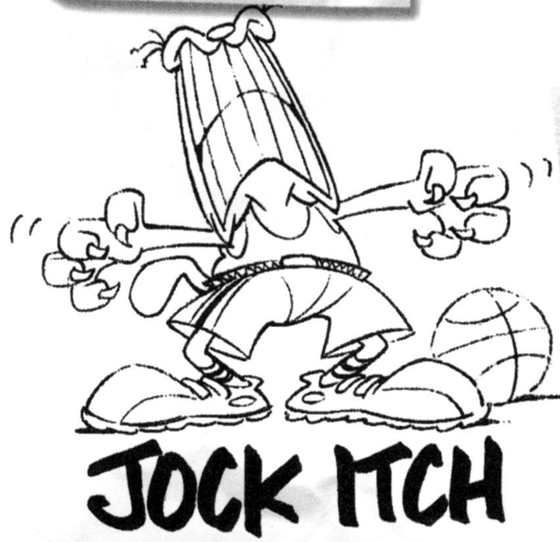
JOCK ITCH

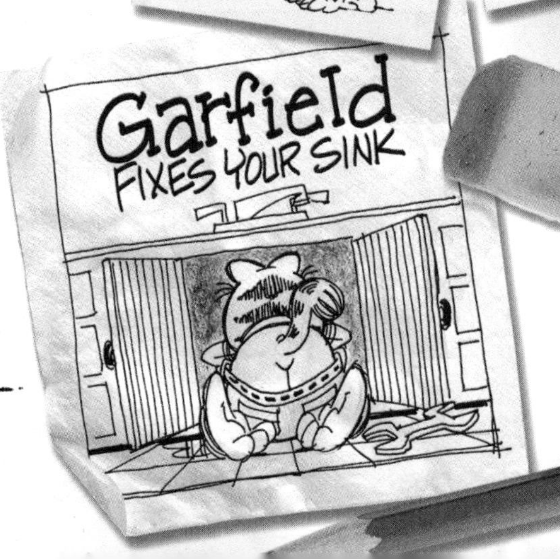
Garfield
FIXES YOUR SINK

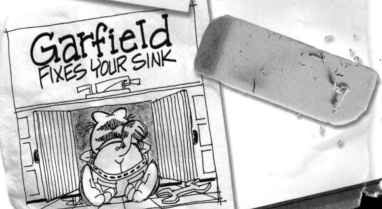

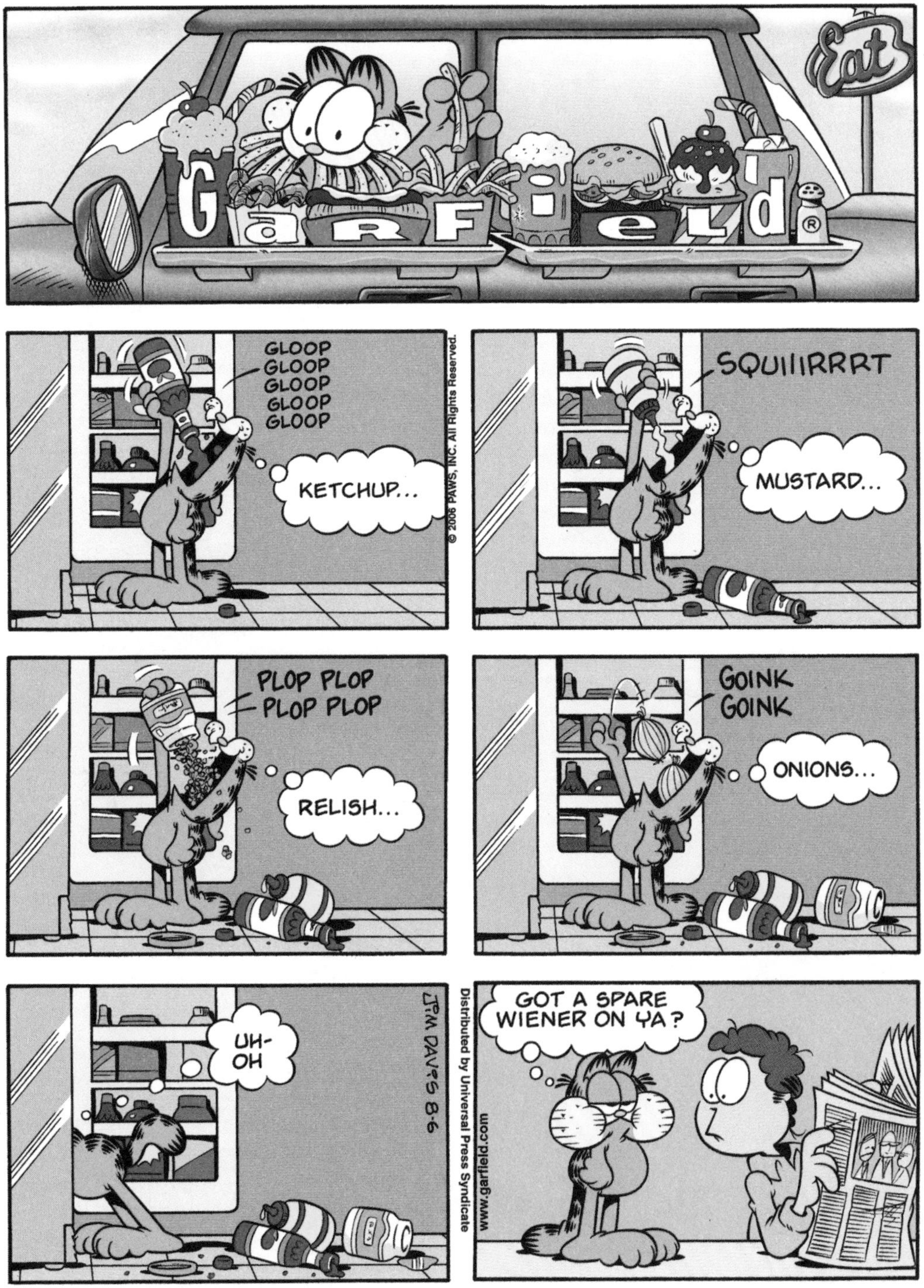
Garfield®
Eat
GLOOP GLOOP GLOOP GLOOP GLOOP
KETCHUP...
© 2006 PAWS, INC. All Rights Reserved.
SQUIIIRRRT
MUSTARD...
PLOP PLOP PLOP PLOP
RELISH...
GOINK GOINK
ONIONS...
UH-OH
JIM DAVIS 8-6
Distributed by Universal Press Syndicate
www.garfield.com
GOT A SPARE WIENER ON YA?

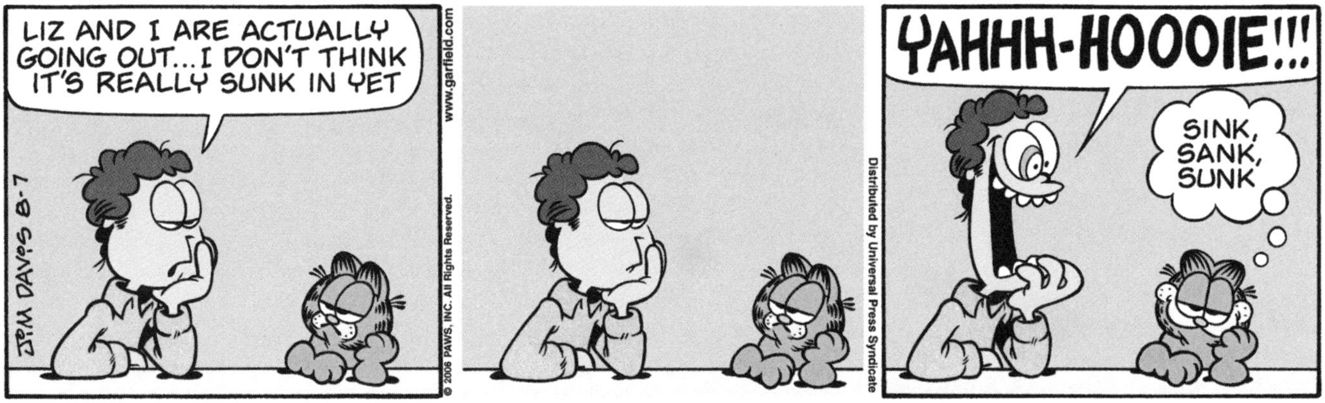
LIZ AND I ARE ACTUALLY GOING OUT...I DON'T THINK IT'S REALLY SUNK IN YET
JIM DAVIS 8-7
© 2006 PAWS, INC. All Rights Reserved.
www.garfield.com
Distributed by Universal Press Syndicate
YAHHH-HOOOIE!!!
SINK, SANK, SUNK

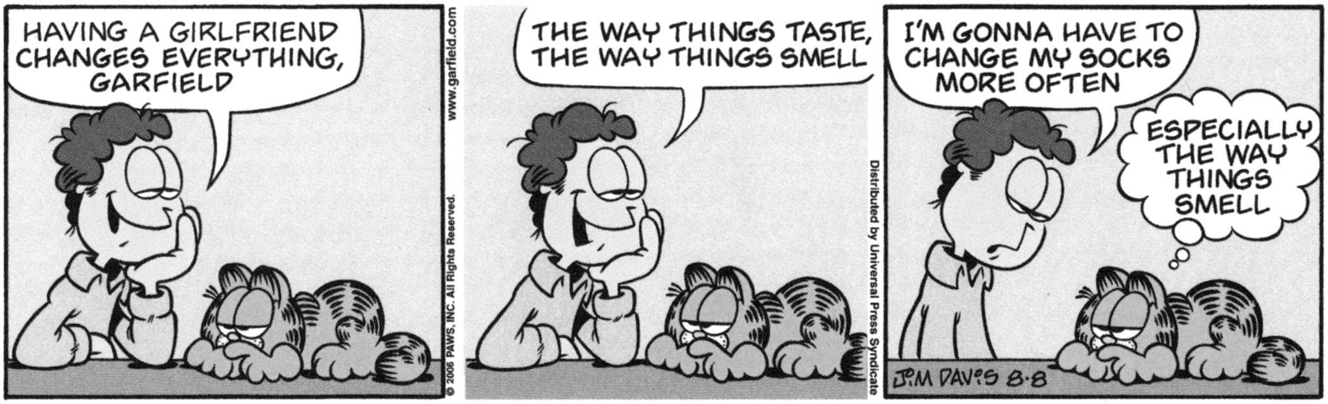
HAVING A GIRLFRIEND CHANGES EVERYTHING, GARFIELD
© 2006 PAWS, INC. All Rights Reserved.
www.garfield.com
THE WAY THINGS TASTE, THE WAY THINGS SMELL
Distributed by Universal Press Syndicate
I'M GONNA HAVE TO CHANGE MY SOCKS MORE OFTEN
ESPECIALLY THE WAY THINGS SMELL
JIM DAVIS 8-8

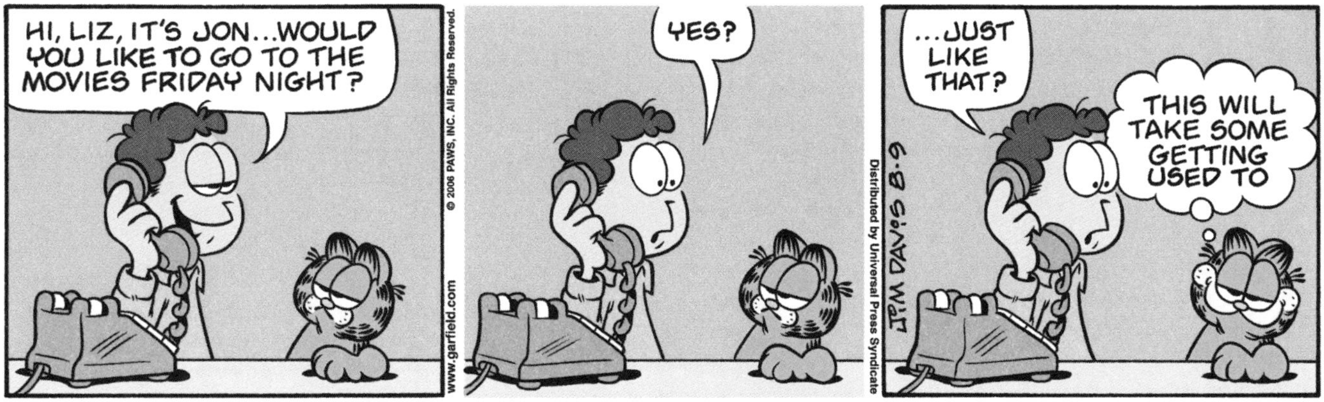
HI, LIZ, IT'S JON...WOULD YOU LIKE TO GO TO THE MOVIES FRIDAY NIGHT?
© 2006 PAWS, INC. All Rights Reserved.
www.garfield.com
YES?
Distributed by Universal Press Syndicate
JIM DAVIS 8-9
...JUST LIKE THAT?
THIS WILL TAKE SOME GETTING USED TO

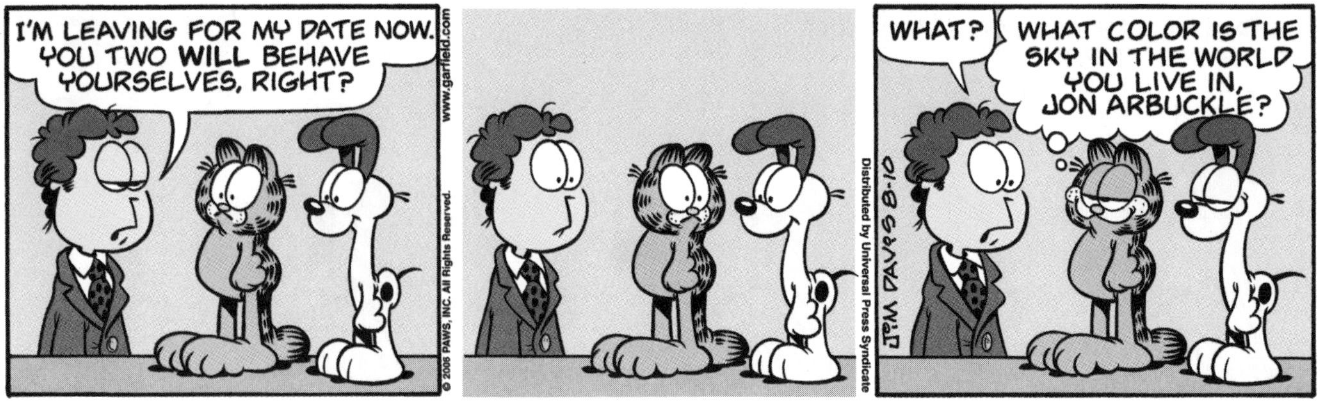
I'M LEAVING FOR MY DATE NOW. YOU TWO WILL BEHAVE YOURSELVES, RIGHT?
WHAT?
WHAT COLOR IS THE SKY IN THE WORLD YOU LIVE IN, JON ARBUCKLE?
www.garfield.com
© 2006 PAWS, INC. All Rights Reserved.
Distributed by Universal Press Syndicate
JIM DAVIS 8-10

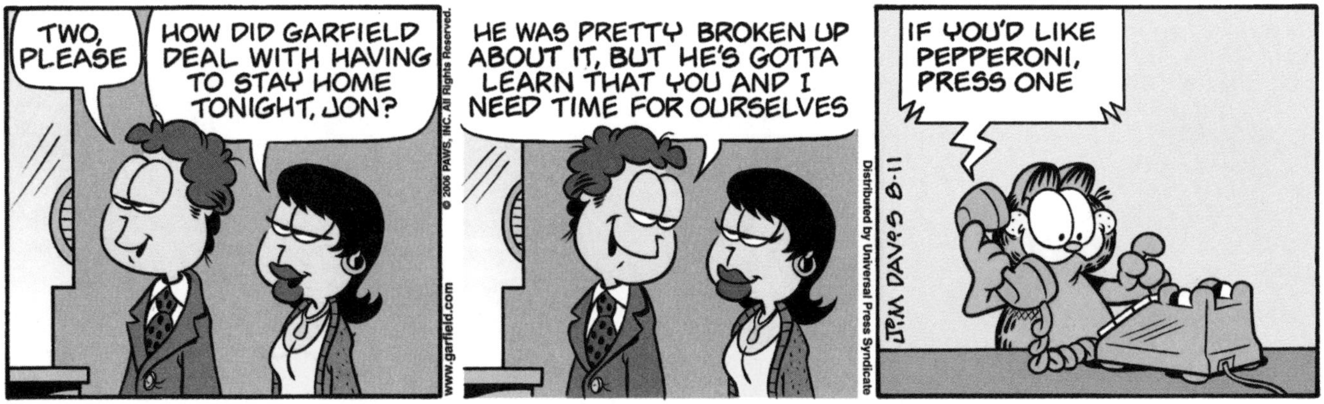
TWO, PLEASE
HOW DID GARFIELD DEAL WITH HAVING TO STAY HOME TONIGHT, JON?
HE WAS PRETTY BROKEN UP ABOUT IT, BUT HE'S GOTTA LEARN THAT YOU AND I NEED TIME FOR OURSELVES
IF YOU'D LIKE PEPPERONI, PRESS ONE
© 2006 PAWS, INC. All Rights Reserved.
www.garfield.com
Distributed by Universal Press Syndicate
JIM DAVIS 8-11

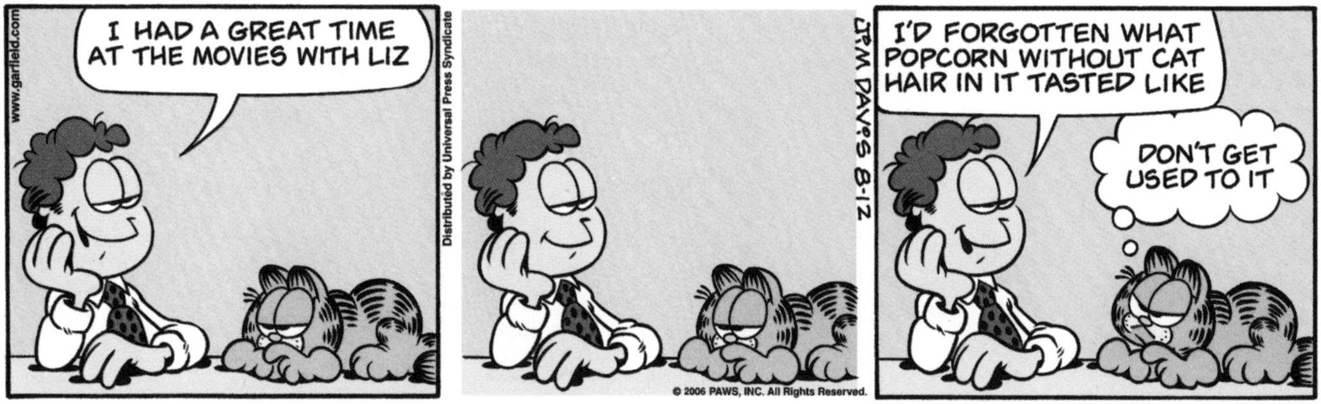
I HAD A GREAT TIME AT THE MOVIES WITH LIZ
I'D FORGOTTEN WHAT POPCORN WITHOUT CAT HAIR IN IT TASTED LIKE
DON'T GET USED TO IT
www.garfield.com
Distributed by Universal Press Syndicate
JIM DAVIS 8-12
© 2006 PAWS, INC. All Rights Reserved.

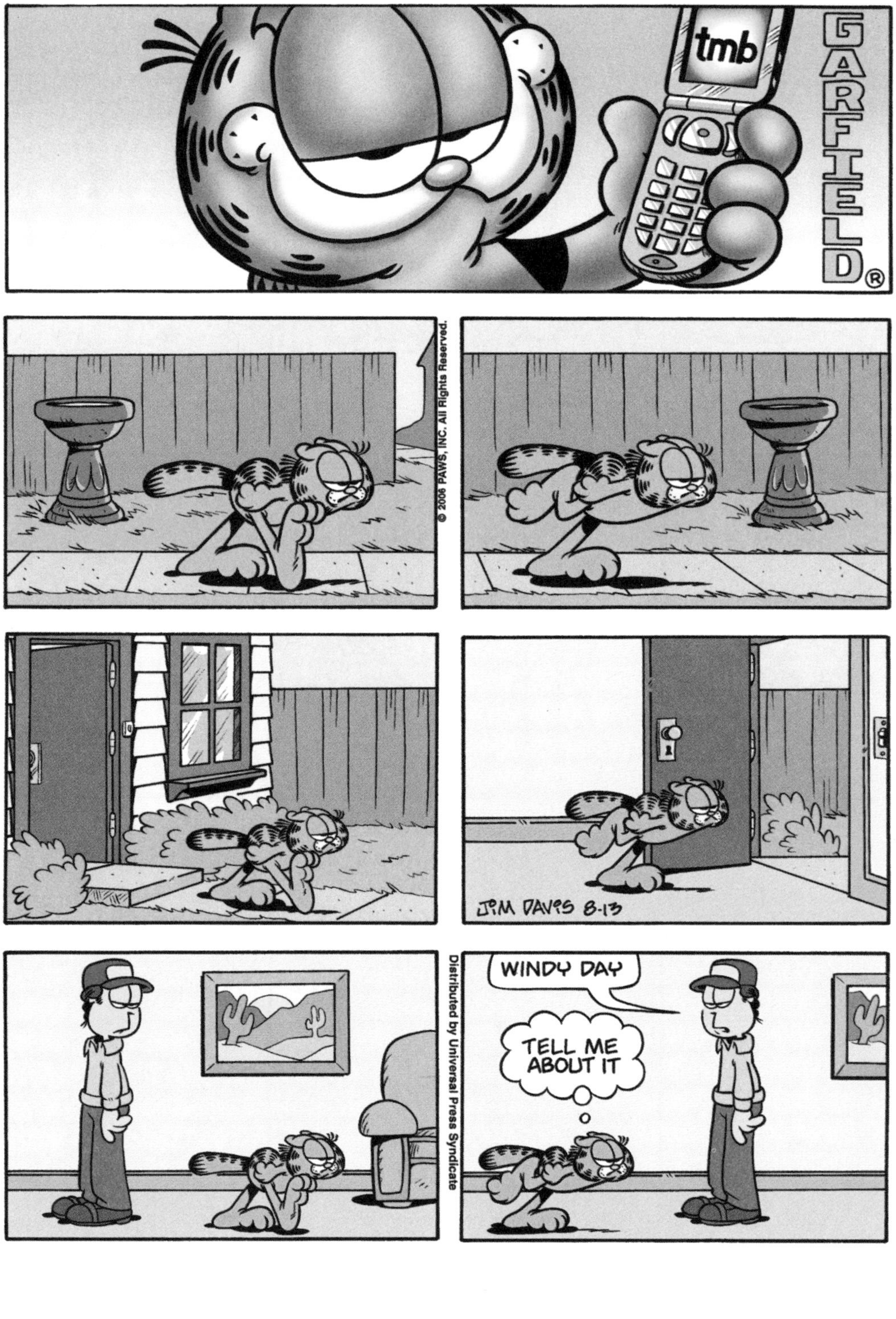
tmb
GARFIELD®
© 2006 PAWS, INC. All Rights Reserved.
JIM DAVIS 8-13
Distributed by Universal Press Syndicate
WINDY DAY
TELL ME ABOUT IT

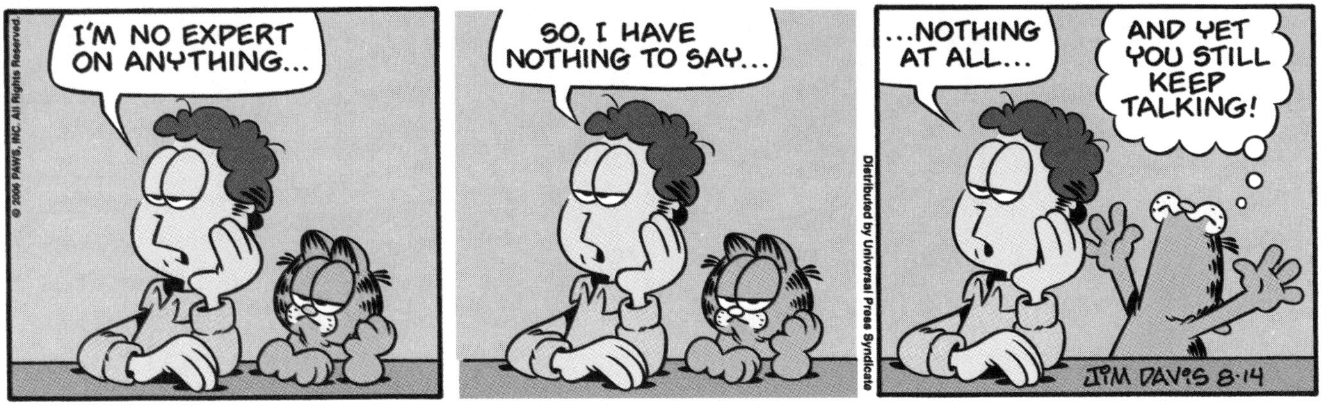
© 2006 PAWS, INC. All Rights Reserved.
I'M NO EXPERT ON ANYTHING...
SO, I HAVE NOTHING TO SAY...
Distributed by Universal Press Syndicate
...NOTHING AT ALL...
AND YET YOU STILL KEEP TALKING!
JIM DAVIS 8-14

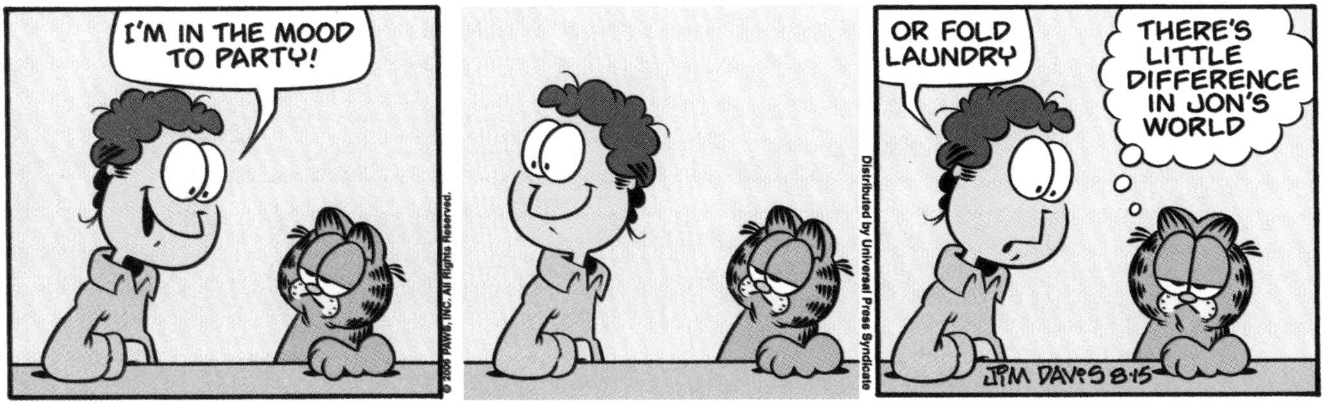
I'M IN THE MOOD TO PARTY!
© 2006 PAWS, INC. All Rights Reserved.
Distributed by Universal Press Syndicate
OR FOLD LAUNDRY
THERE'S LITTLE DIFFERENCE IN JON'S WORLD
JIM DAVIS 8-15

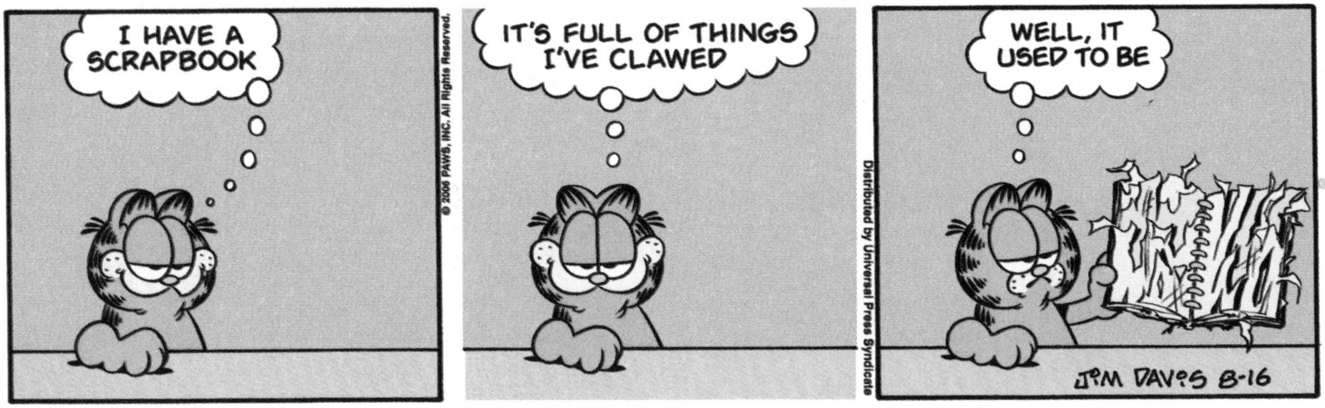
I HAVE A SCRAPBOOK
© 2006 PAWS, INC. All Rights Reserved.
IT'S FULL OF THINGS I'VE CLAWED
Distributed by Universal Press Syndicate
WELL, IT USED TO BE
JIM DAVIS 8-16

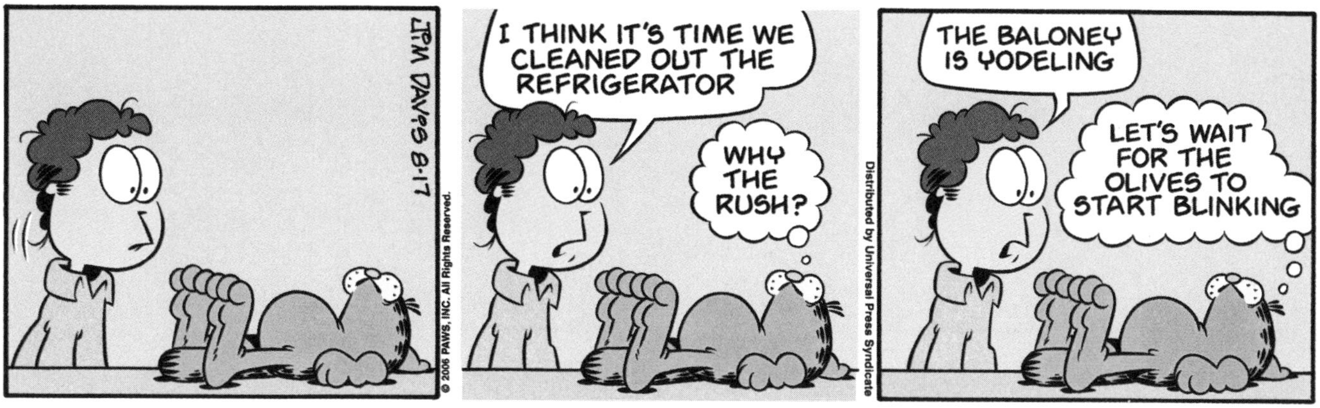
JIM DAVIS 8-17
© 2006 PAWS, INC. All Rights Reserved.
I THINK IT'S TIME WE CLEANED OUT THE REFRIGERATOR
WHY THE RUSH?
Distributed by Universal Press Syndicate
THE BALONEY IS YODELING
LET'S WAIT FOR THE OLIVES TO START BLINKING

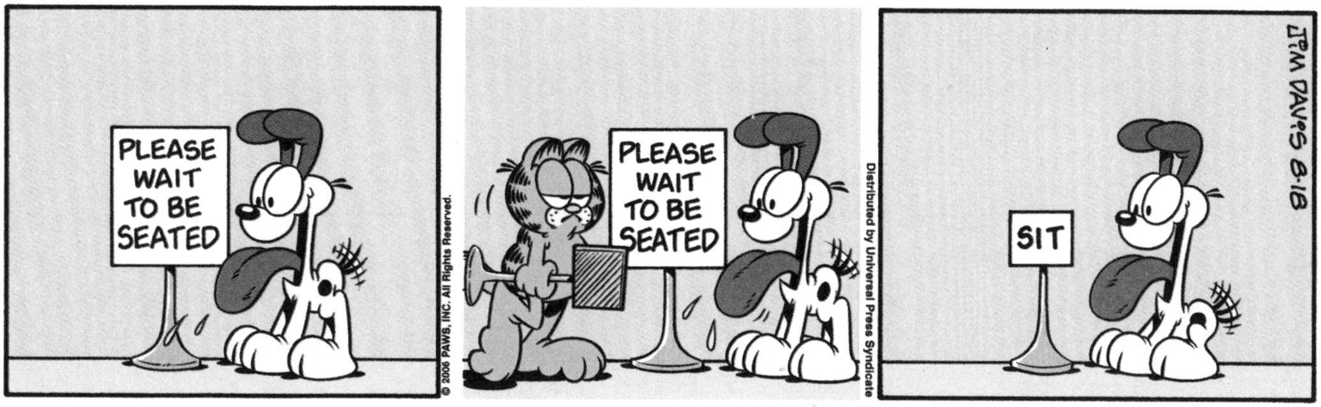
PLEASE WAIT TO BE SEATED
© 2006 PAWS, INC. All Rights Reserved.
PLEASE WAIT TO BE SEATED
Distributed by Universal Press Syndicate
SIT
JIM DAVIS 8-18

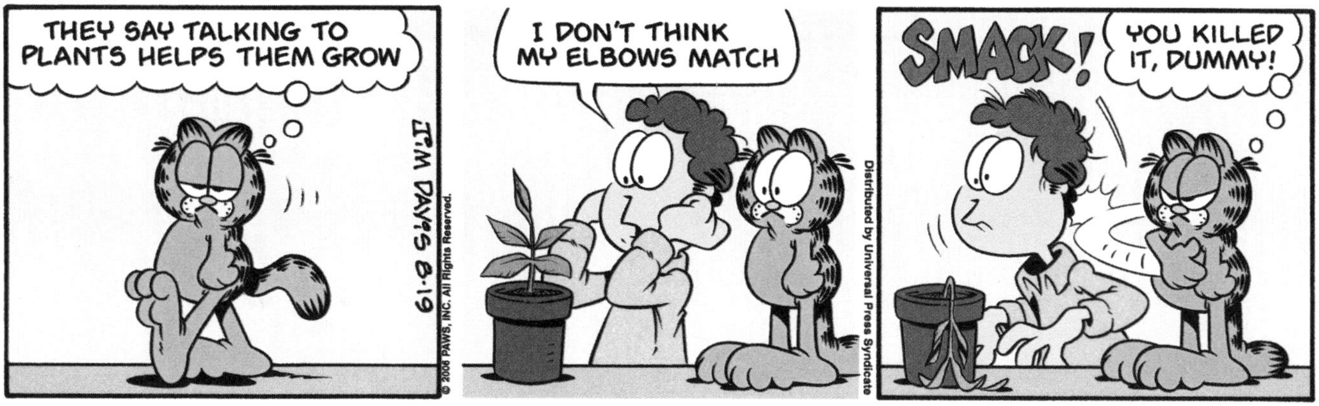
THEY SAY TALKING TO PLANTS HELPS THEM GROW
JIM DAVIS 8-19
© 2006 PAWS, INC. All Rights Reserved.
I DON'T THINK MY ELBOWS MATCH
Distributed by Universal Press Syndicate
SMACK!
YOU KILLED IT, DUMMY!

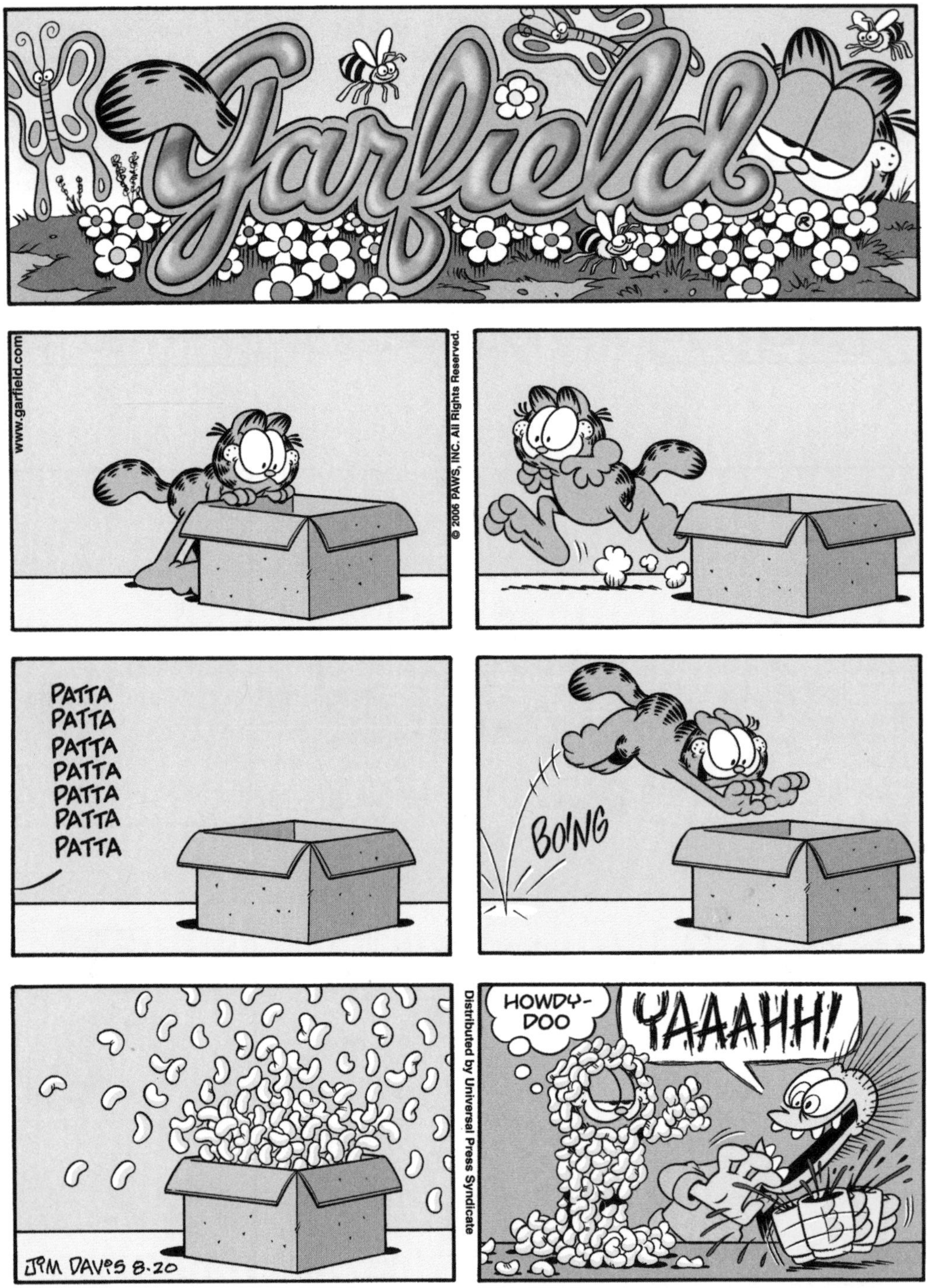
Garfield
www.garfield.com
© 2006 PAWS, INC. All Rights Reserved.
PATTA PATTA PATTA PATTA PATTA PATTA PATTA PATTA
BOING
JIM DAVIS 8-20
Distributed by Universal Press Syndicate
HOWDY-DOO
YAAAHH!

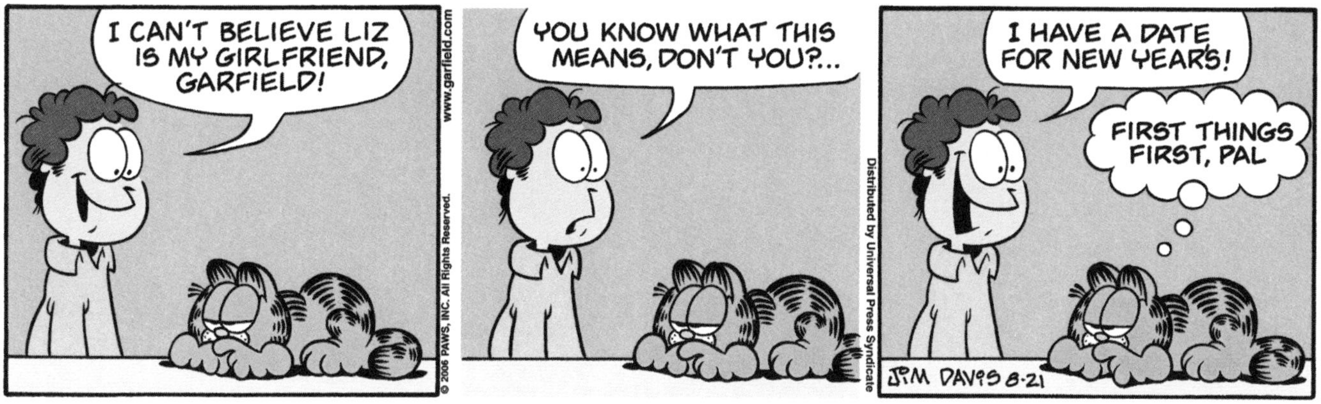
I CAN'T BELIEVE LIZ IS MY GIRLFRIEND, GARFIELD!
© 2006 PAWS, INC. All Rights Reserved. www.garfield.com
YOU KNOW WHAT THIS MEANS, DON'T YOU?...
Distributed by Universal Press Syndicate
I HAVE A DATE FOR NEW YEAR'S!
FIRST THINGS FIRST, PAL
JIM DAVIS 8-21

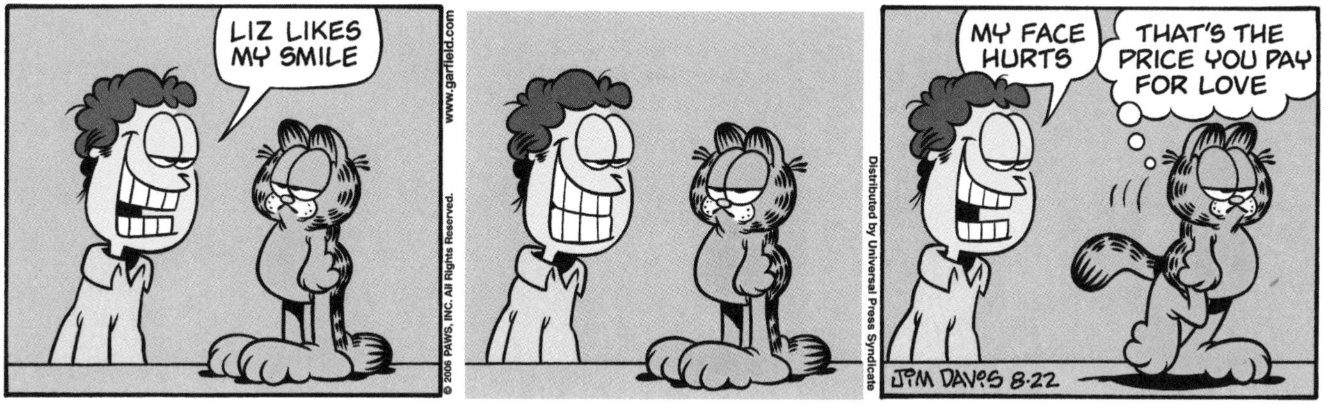
LIZ LIKES MY SMILE
© 2006 PAWS, INC. All Rights Reserved. www.garfield.com
Distributed by Universal Press Syndicate
MY FACE HURTS
THAT'S THE PRICE YOU PAY FOR LOVE
JIM DAVIS 8-22

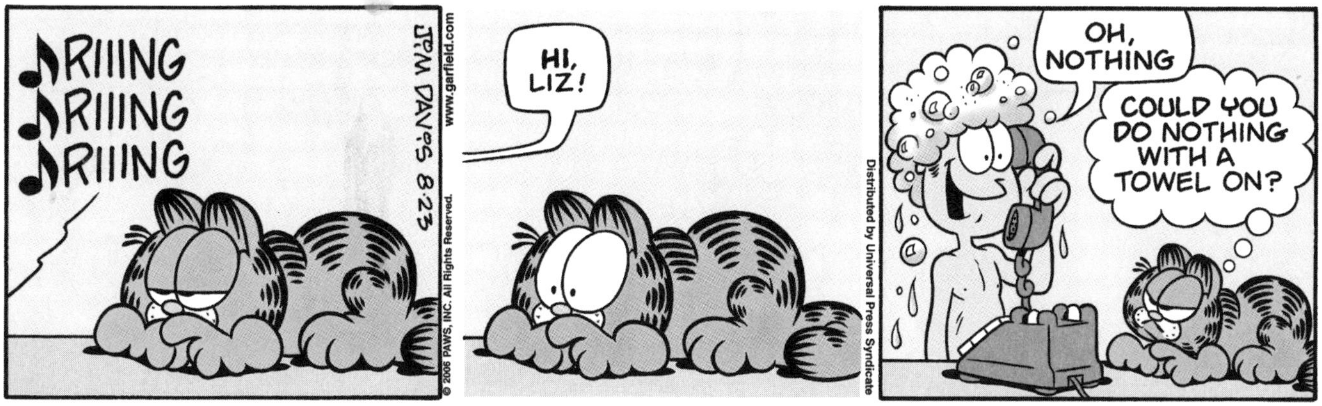
RIIING
RIIING
RIIING
JIM DAVIS 8-23
© 2006 PAWS, INC. All Rights Reserved. www.garfield.com
HI, LIZ!
Distributed by Universal Press Syndicate
OH, NOTHING
COULD YOU DO NOTHING WITH A TOWEL ON?

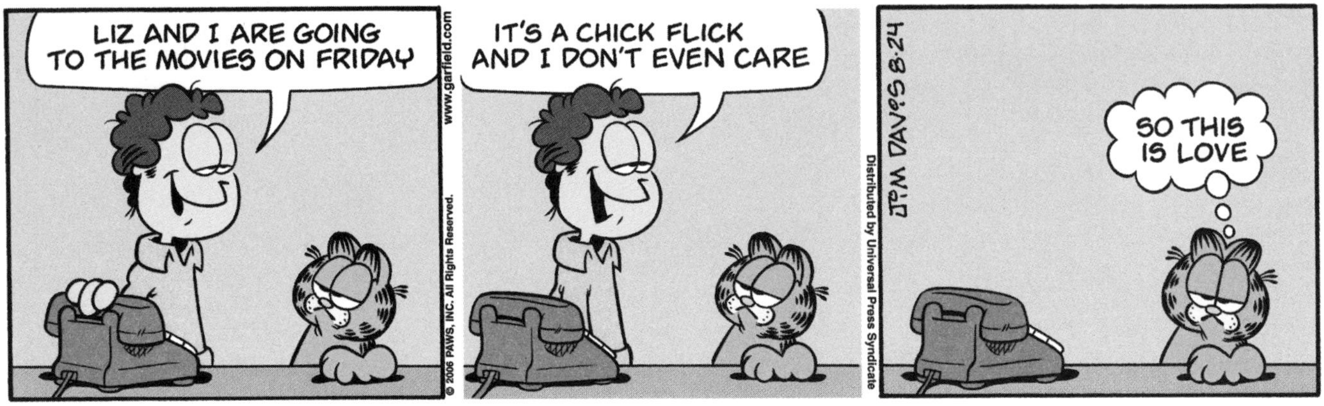
LIZ AND I ARE GOING TO THE MOVIES ON FRIDAY
IT'S A CHICK FLICK AND I DON'T EVEN CARE
SO THIS IS LOVE
JIM DAVIS 8·24
© 2006 PAWS, INC. All Rights Reserved.
www.garfield.com
Distributed by Universal Press Syndicate

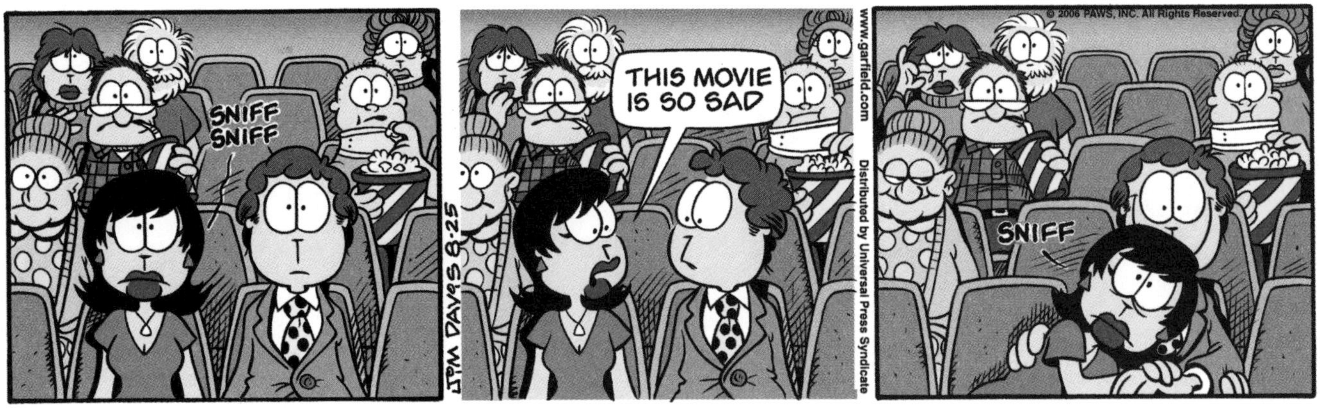
SNIFF SNIFF
THIS MOVIE IS SO SAD
SNIFF
JIM DAVIS 8·25
www.garfield.com
Distributed by Universal Press Syndicate
© 2006 PAWS, INC. All Rights Reserved.

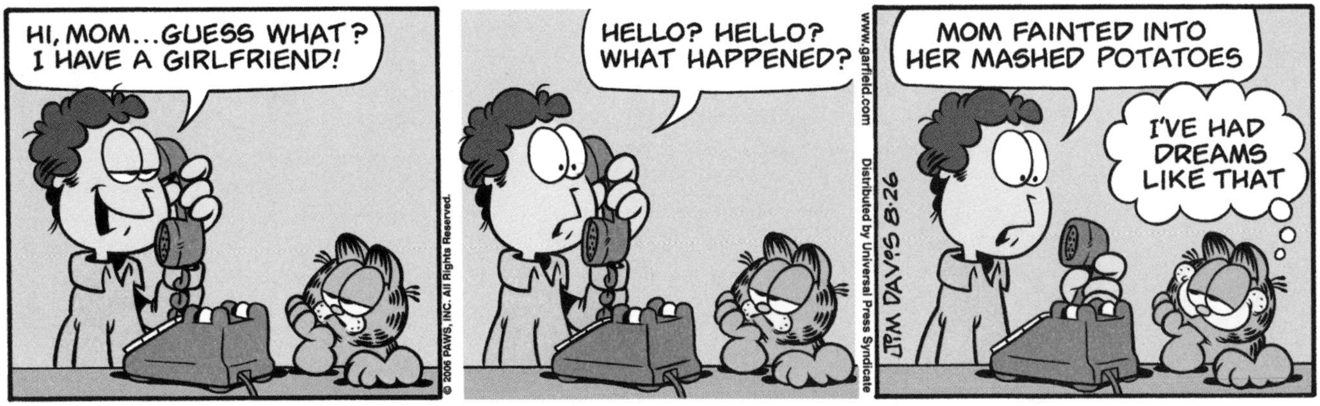
HI, MOM...GUESS WHAT? I HAVE A GIRLFRIEND!
HELLO? HELLO? WHAT HAPPENED?
MOM FAINTED INTO HER MASHED POTATOES
I'VE HAD DREAMS LIKE THAT
JIM DAVIS 8·26
© 2006 PAWS, INC. All Rights Reserved.
www.garfield.com
Distributed by Universal Press Syndicate

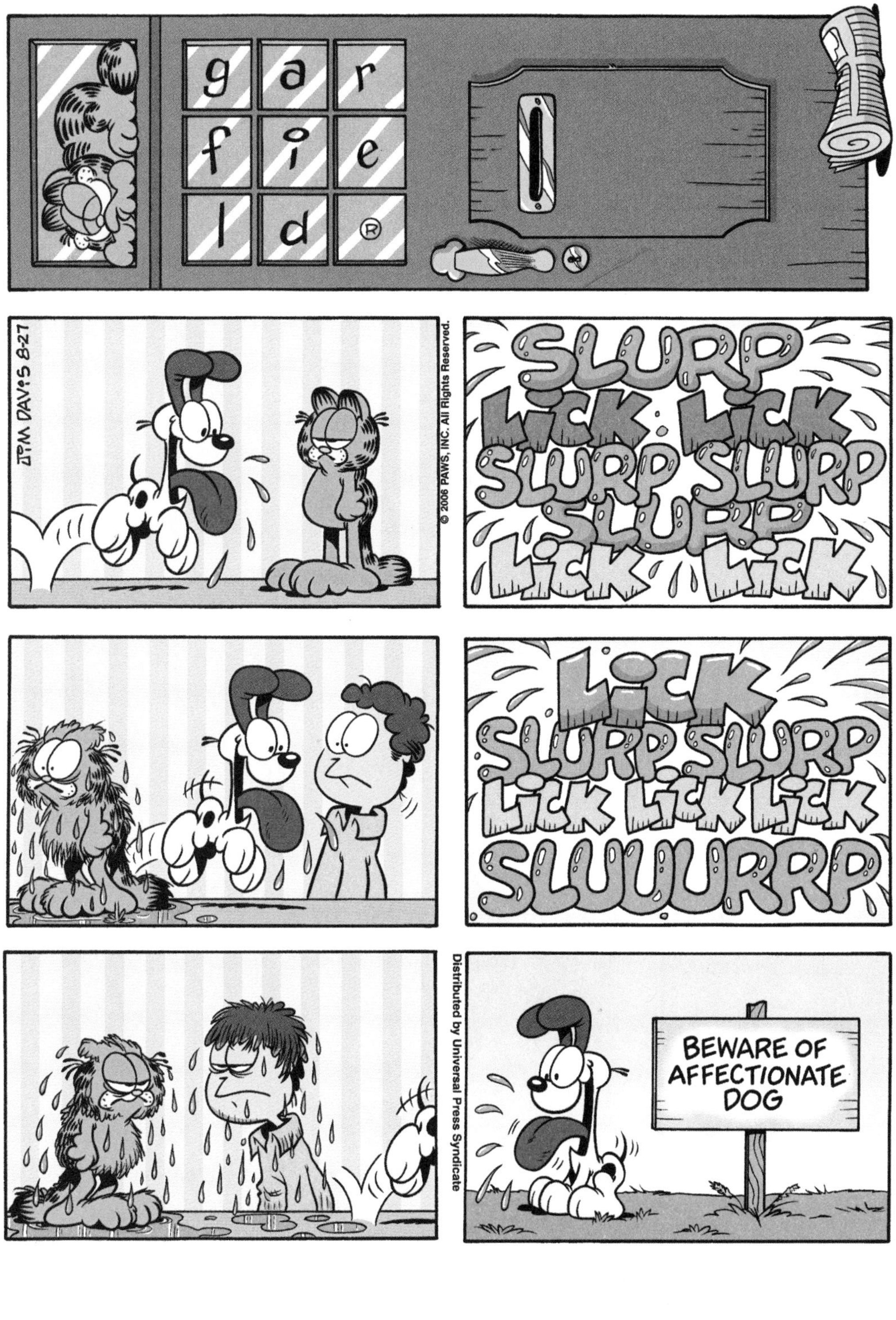
garfield®
JPM DAVPS 8-27
© 2006 PAWS, INC. All Rights Reserved.
SLURP
LICK LICK
SLURP SLURP
SLURP
LICK LICK
LICK
SLURP SLURP
LICK LICK LICK
SLUUURRP
Distributed by Universal Press Syndicate
BEWARE OF
AFFECTIONATE
DOG

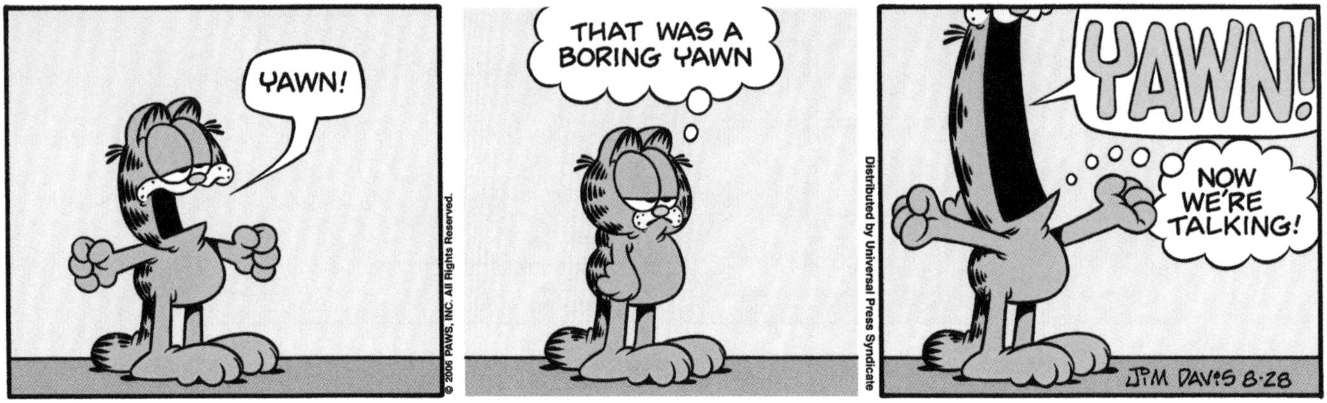
YAWN!
THAT WAS A BORING YAWN
YAWN!
NOW WE'RE TALKING!
JIM DAVIS 8-28
© 2006 PAWS, INC. All Rights Reserved.
Distributed by Universal Press Syndicate

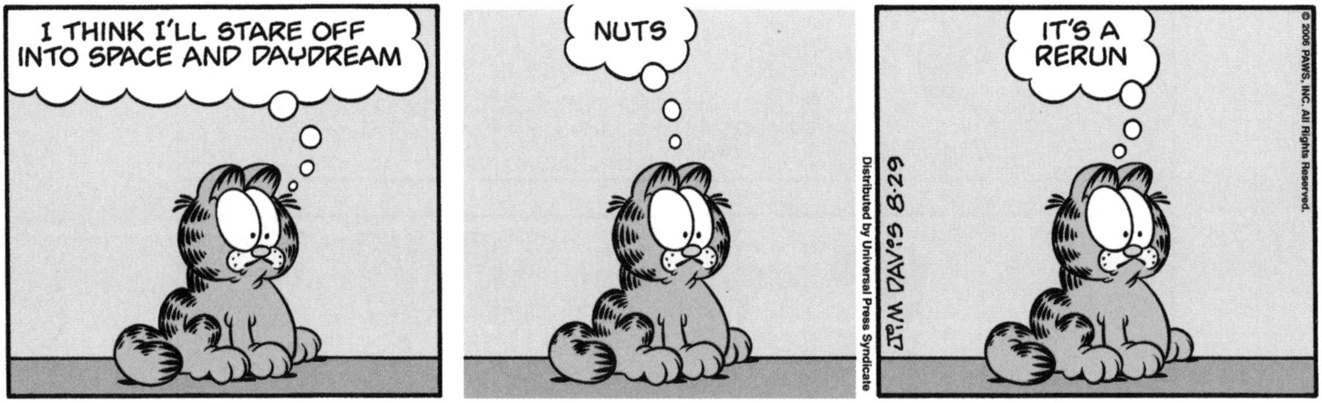
I THINK I'LL STARE OFF INTO SPACE AND DAYDREAM
NUTS
IT'S A RERUN
JIM DAVIS 8-29
Distributed by Universal Press Syndicate
© 2006 PAWS, INC. All Rights Reserved.

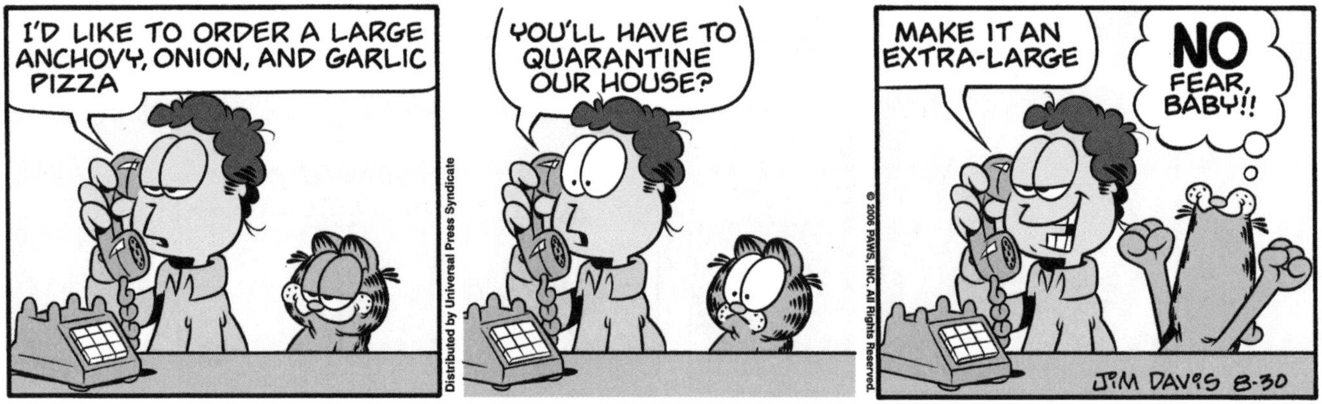
I'D LIKE TO ORDER A LARGE ANCHOVY, ONION, AND GARLIC PIZZA
YOU'LL HAVE TO QUARANTINE OUR HOUSE?
MAKE IT AN EXTRA-LARGE
NO FEAR, BABY!!
JIM DAVIS 8-30
Distributed by Universal Press Syndicate
© 2006 PAWS, INC. All Rights Reserved.

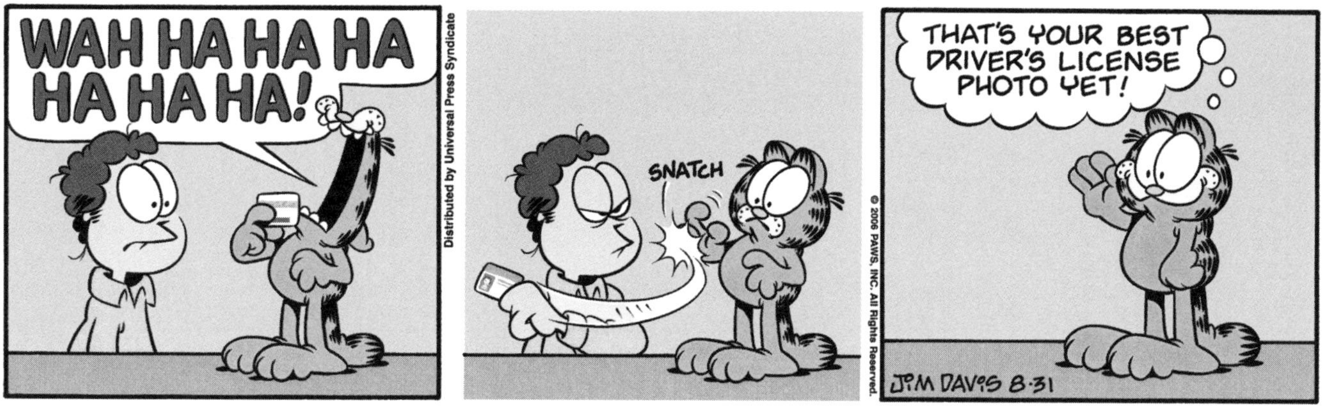
WAH HA HA HA HA HA HA!
Distributed by Universal Press Syndicate
SNATCH
© 2006 PAWS, INC. All Rights Reserved.
THAT'S YOUR BEST DRIVER'S LICENSE PHOTO YET!
JIM DAVIS 8-31

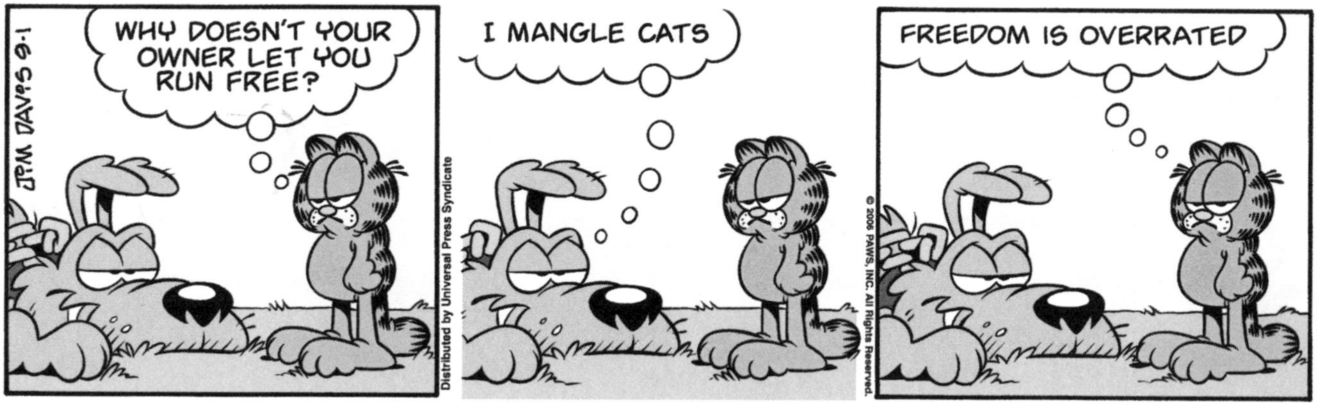
JIM DAVIS 9-1
WHY DOESN'T YOUR OWNER LET YOU RUN FREE?
Distributed by Universal Press Syndicate
I MANGLE CATS
© 2006 PAWS, INC. All Rights Reserved.
FREEDOM IS OVERRATED

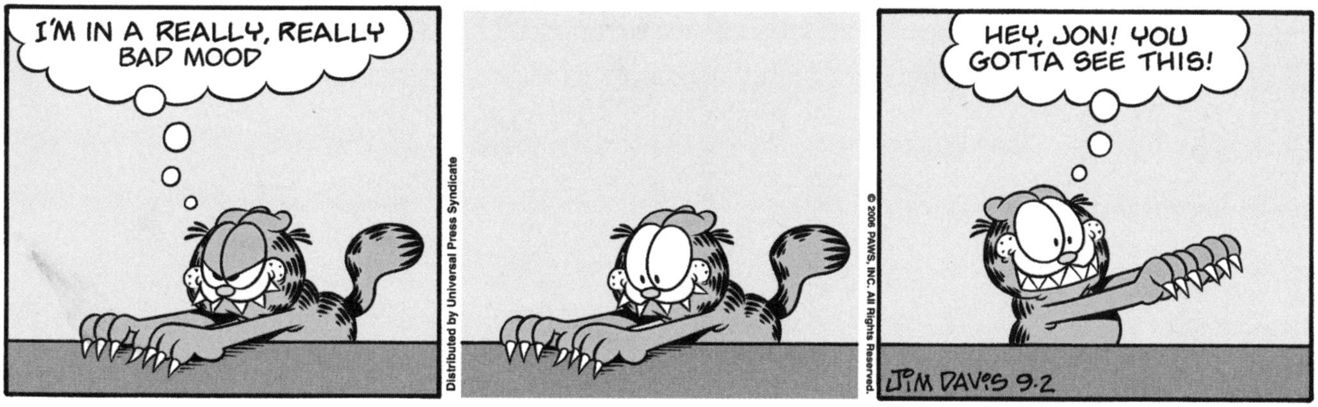
I'M IN A REALLY, REALLY BAD MOOD
Distributed by Universal Press Syndicate
© 2006 PAWS, INC. All Rights Reserved.
HEY, JON! YOU GOTTA SEE THIS!
JIM DAVIS 9-2

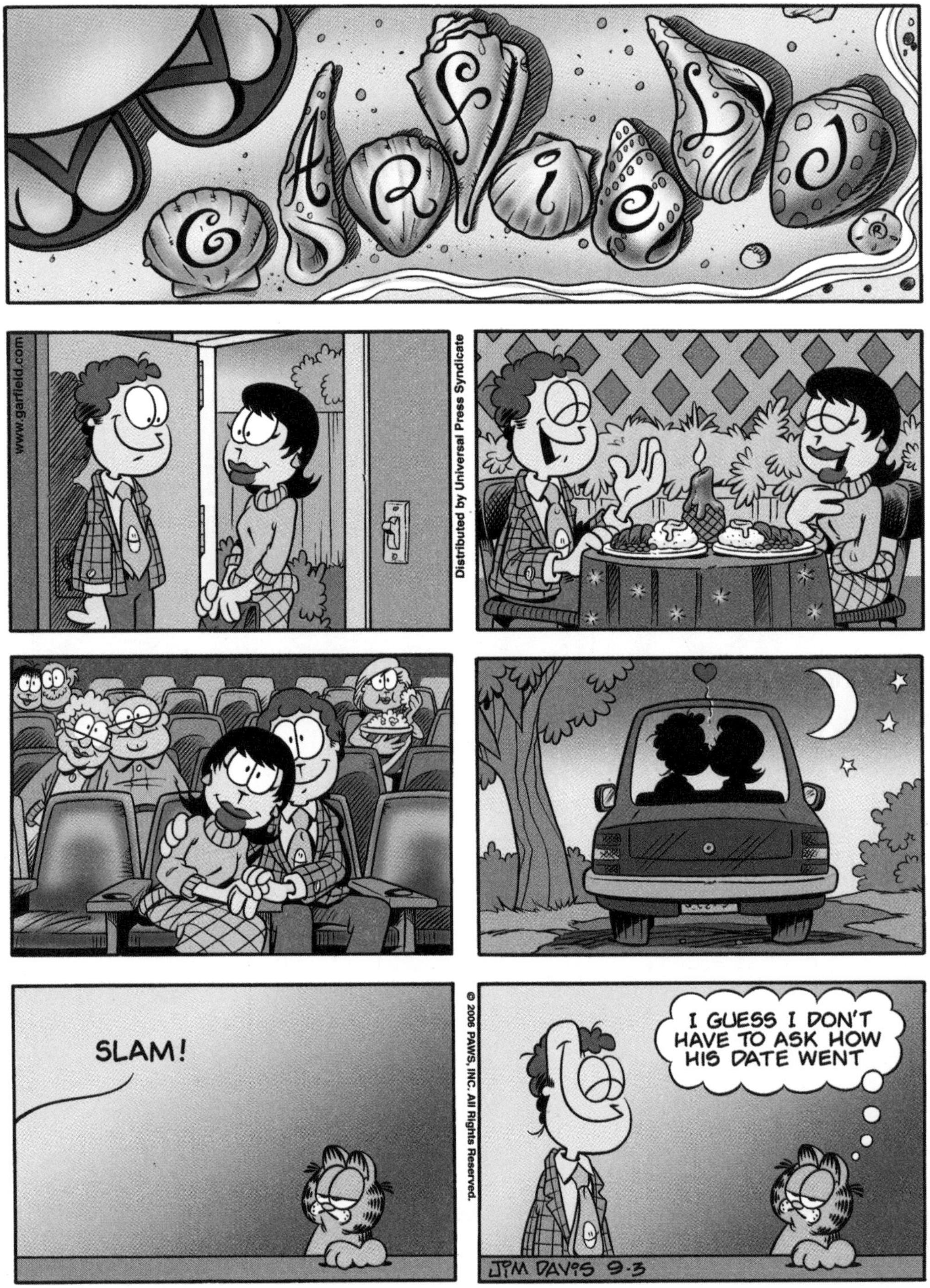
GARFIELD
www.garfield.com
Distributed by Universal Press Syndicate
SLAM!
I GUESS I DON'T HAVE TO ASK HOW HIS DATE WENT
© 2006 PAWS, INC. All Rights Reserved.
JIM DAVIS 9-3

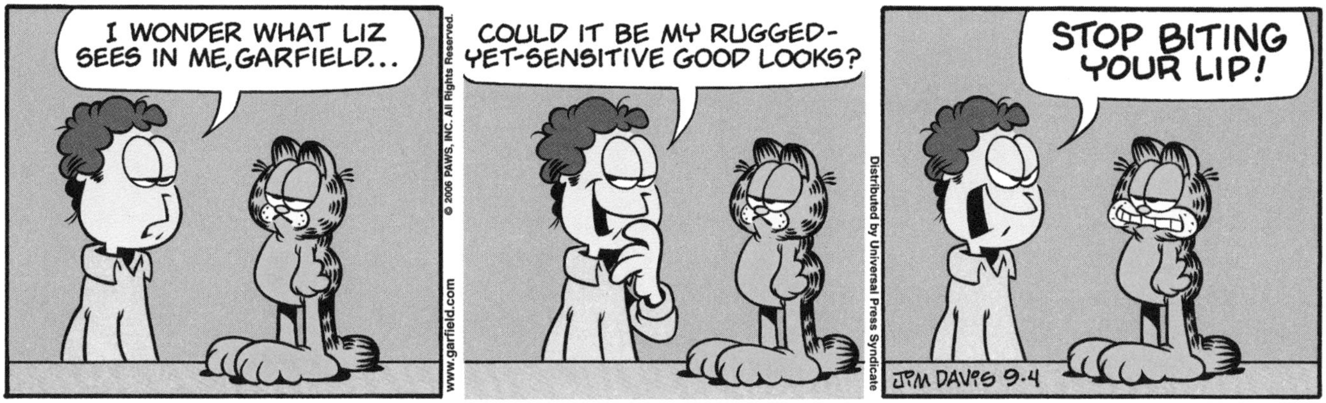
I WONDER WHAT LIZ SEES IN ME, GARFIELD...
COULD IT BE MY RUGGED-YET-SENSITIVE GOOD LOOKS?
STOP BITING YOUR LIP!
JIM DAVIS 9-4
© 2006 PAWS, INC. All Rights Reserved.
www.garfield.com
Distributed by Universal Press Syndicate

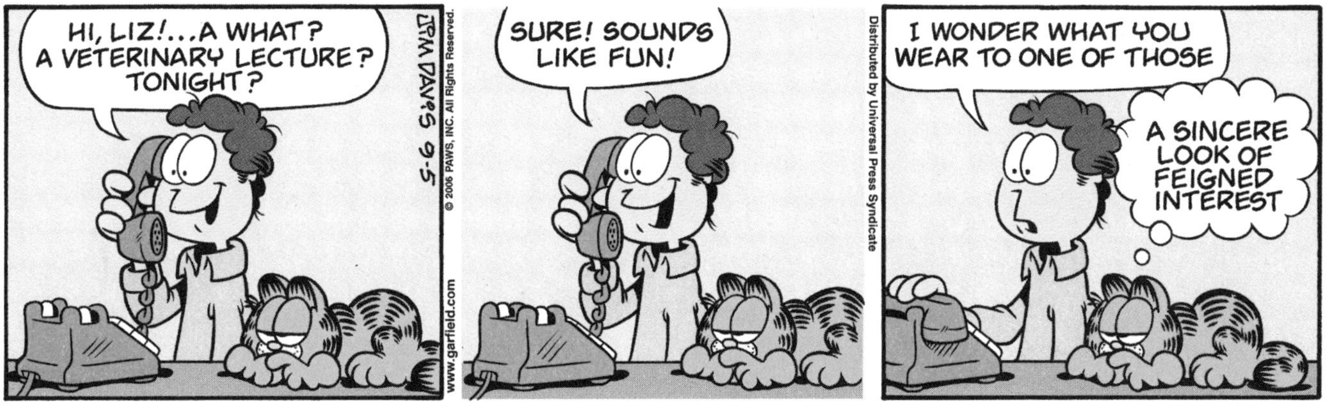
HI, LIZ!...A WHAT? A VETERINARY LECTURE? TONIGHT?
SURE! SOUNDS LIKE FUN!
I WONDER WHAT YOU WEAR TO ONE OF THOSE
A SINCERE LOOK OF FEIGNED INTEREST
JIM DAVIS 9-5
© 2006 PAWS, INC. All Rights Reserved.
www.garfield.com
Distributed by Universal Press Syndicate

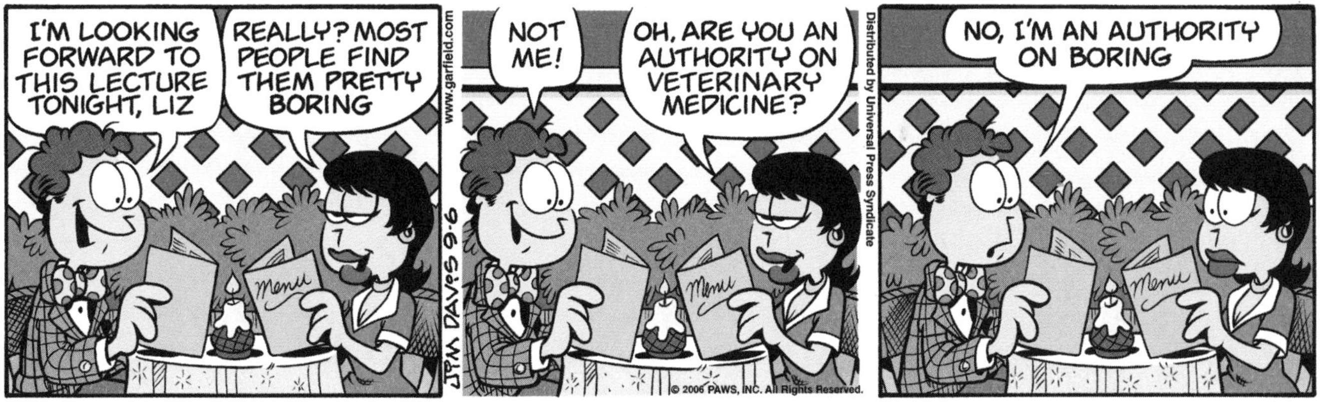
I'M LOOKING FORWARD TO THIS LECTURE TONIGHT, LIZ
REALLY? MOST PEOPLE FIND THEM PRETTY BORING
NOT ME!
OH, ARE YOU AN AUTHORITY ON VETERINARY MEDICINE?
NO, I'M AN AUTHORITY ON BORING
Menu
JIM DAVIS 9-6
www.garfield.com
© 2006 PAWS, INC. All Rights Reserved.
Distributed by Universal Press Syndicate

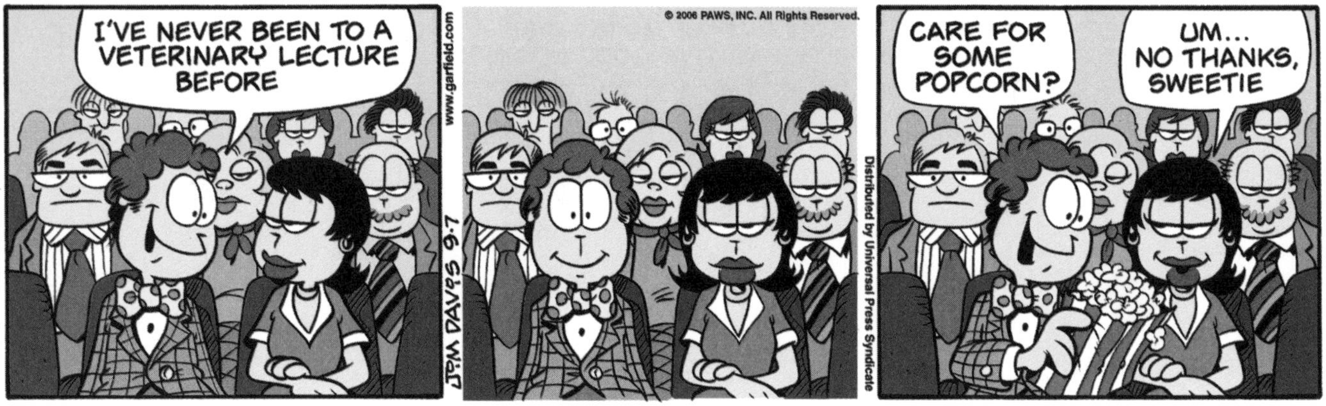
I'VE NEVER BEEN TO A VETERINARY LECTURE BEFORE
www.garfield.com
JIM DAVIS 9-7
© 2006 PAWS, INC. All Rights Reserved.
Distributed by Universal Press Syndicate
CARE FOR SOME POPCORN?
UM... NO THANKS, SWEETIE

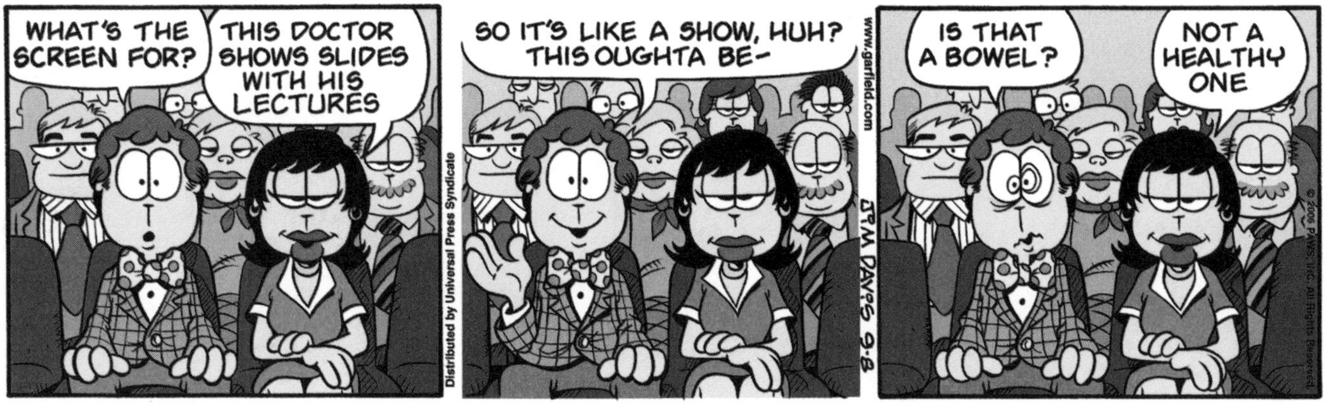
WHAT'S THE SCREEN FOR?
THIS DOCTOR SHOWS SLIDES WITH HIS LECTURES
Distributed by Universal Press Syndicate
SO IT'S LIKE A SHOW, HUH? THIS OUGHTA BE-
www.garfield.com
JIM DAVIS 9-8
IS THAT A BOWEL?
NOT A HEALTHY ONE
© 2006 PAWS, INC. All Rights Reserved.

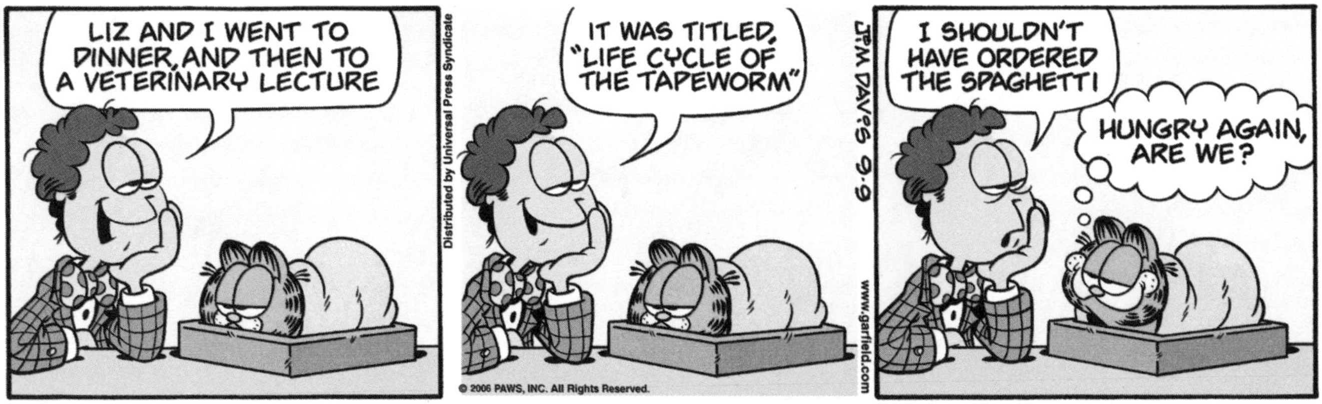
LIZ AND I WENT TO DINNER, AND THEN TO A VETERINARY LECTURE
Distributed by Universal Press Syndicate
IT WAS TITLED, "LIFE CYCLE OF THE TAPEWORM"
© 2006 PAWS, INC. All Rights Reserved.
JIM DAVIS 9-9
www.garfield.com
I SHOULDN'T HAVE ORDERED THE SPAGHETTI
HUNGRY AGAIN, ARE WE?

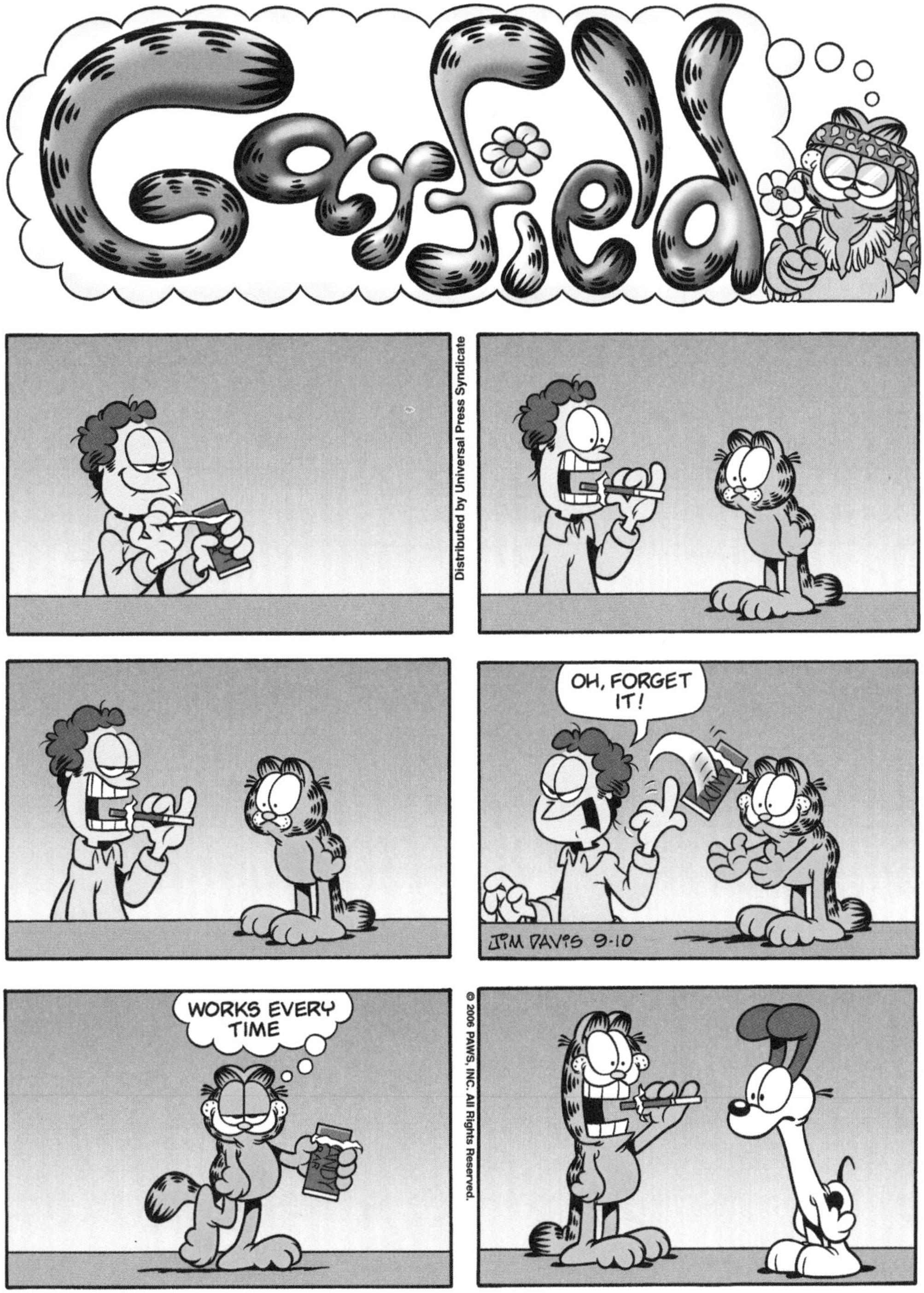
Garfield
Distributed by Universal Press Syndicate
OH, FORGET IT!
JIM DAVIS 9-10
© 2006 PAWS, INC. All Rights Reserved.
WORKS EVERY TIME

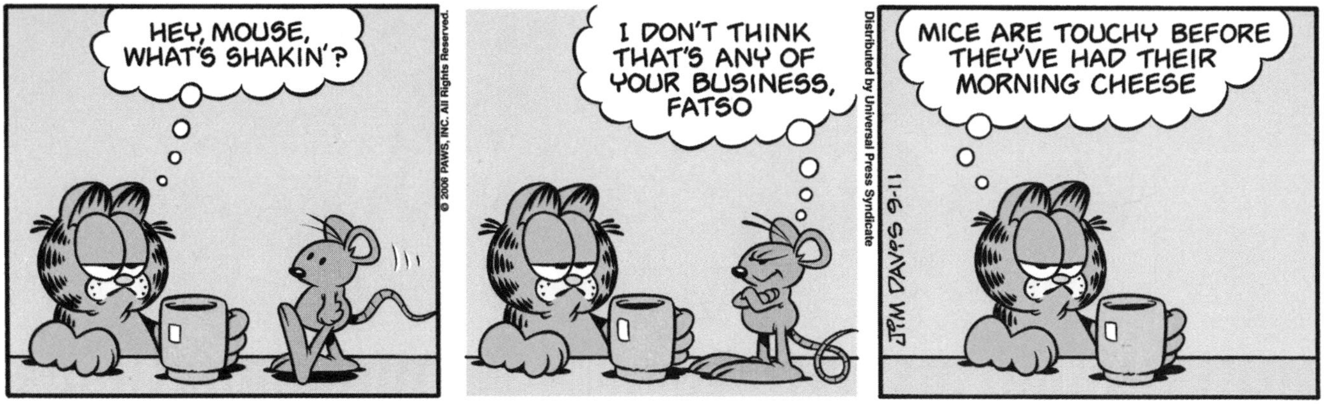
HEY, MOUSE, WHAT'S SHAKIN'?
I DON'T THINK THAT'S ANY OF YOUR BUSINESS, FATSO
MICE ARE TOUCHY BEFORE THEY'VE HAD THEIR MORNING CHEESE
© 2006 PAWS, INC. All Rights Reserved.
Distributed by Universal Press Syndicate
JIM DAVIS 9-11

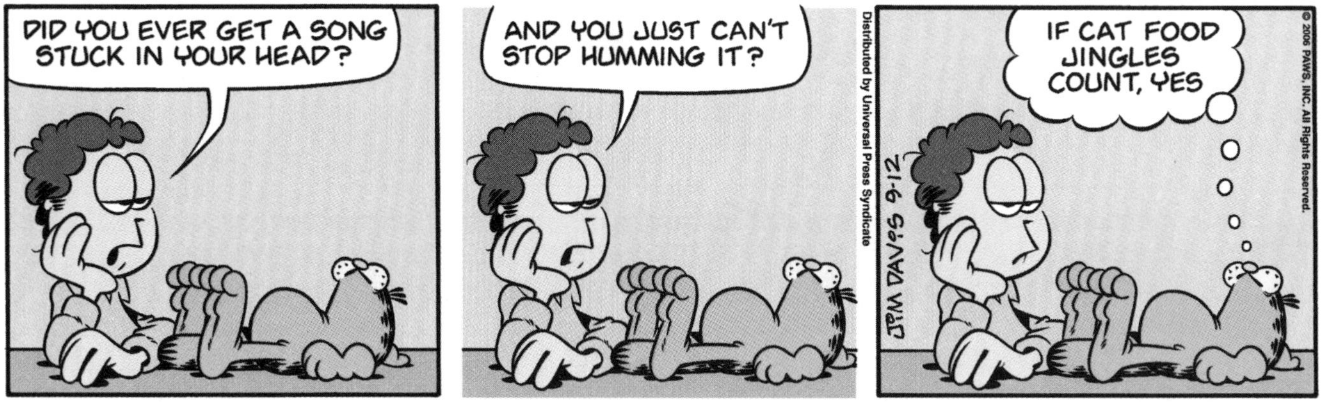
DID YOU EVER GET A SONG STUCK IN YOUR HEAD?
AND YOU JUST CAN'T STOP HUMMING IT?
IF CAT FOOD JINGLES COUNT, YES
Distributed by Universal Press Syndicate
JIM DAVIS 9-12
© 2006 PAWS, INC. All Rights Reserved.

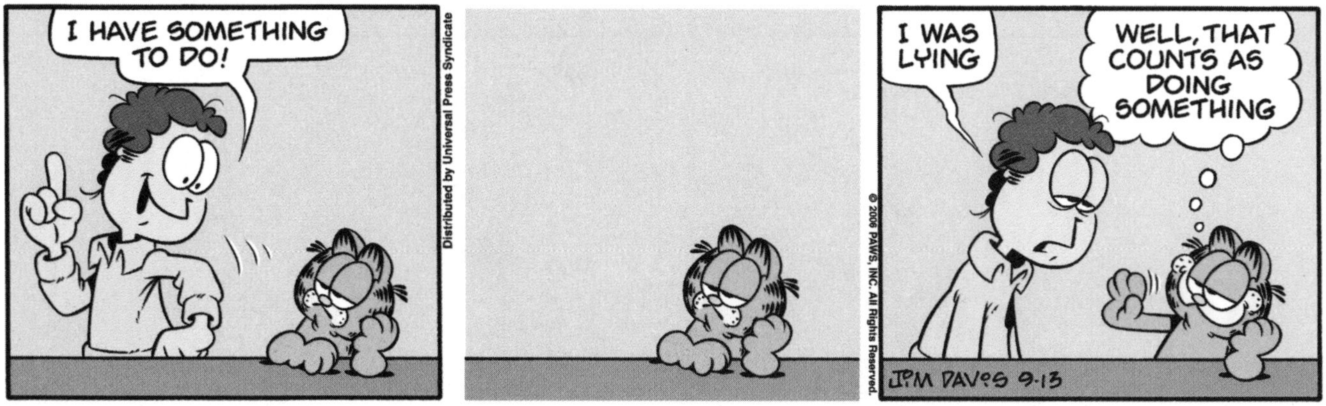
I HAVE SOMETHING TO DO!
I WAS LYING
WELL, THAT COUNTS AS DOING SOMETHING
Distributed by Universal Press Syndicate
© 2006 PAWS, INC. All Rights Reserved.
JIM DAVIS 9-13

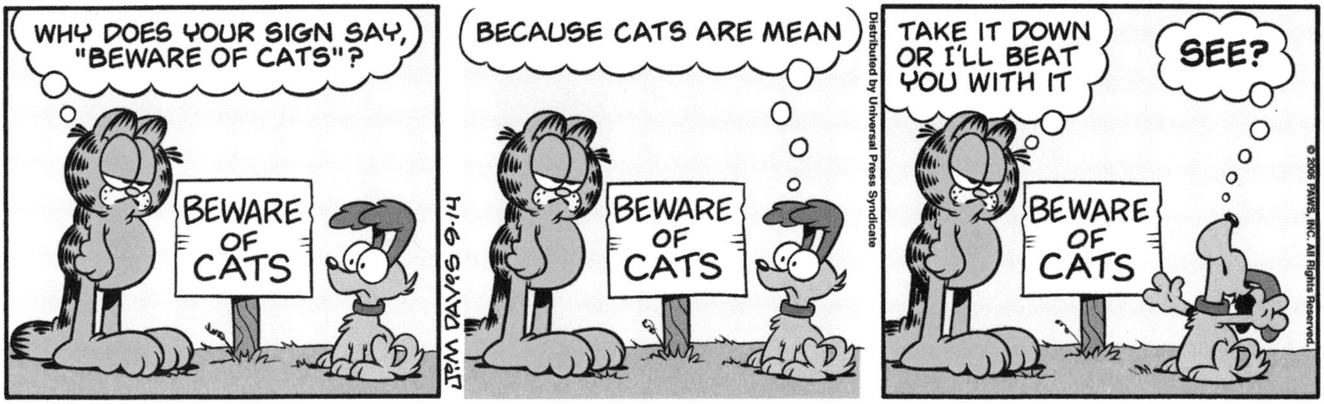
WHY DOES YOUR SIGN SAY, "BEWARE OF CATS"?
BEWARE OF CATS
JIM DAVIS 9-14
BECAUSE CATS ARE MEAN
Distributed by Universal Press Syndicate
TAKE IT DOWN OR I'LL BEAT YOU WITH IT
SEE?
© 2006 PAWS, INC. All Rights Reserved.

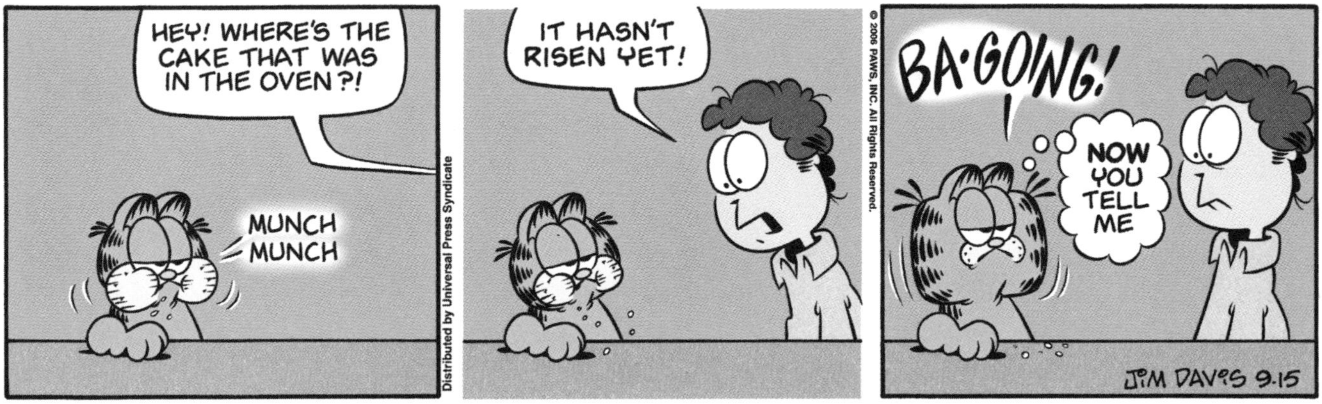
HEY! WHERE'S THE CAKE THAT WAS IN THE OVEN?!
MUNCH MUNCH
Distributed by Universal Press Syndicate
IT HASN'T RISEN YET!
© 2006 PAWS, INC. All Rights Reserved.
BA·GOING!
NOW YOU TELL ME
JIM DAVIS 9-15

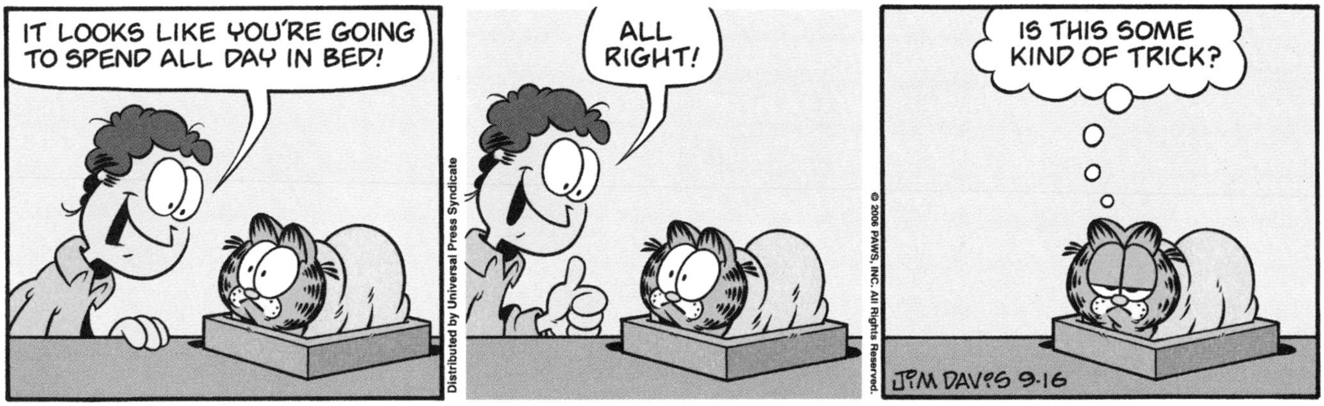
IT LOOKS LIKE YOU'RE GOING TO SPEND ALL DAY IN BED!
Distributed by Universal Press Syndicate
ALL RIGHT!
© 2006 PAWS, INC. All Rights Reserved.
IS THIS SOME KIND OF TRICK?
JIM DAVIS 9-16

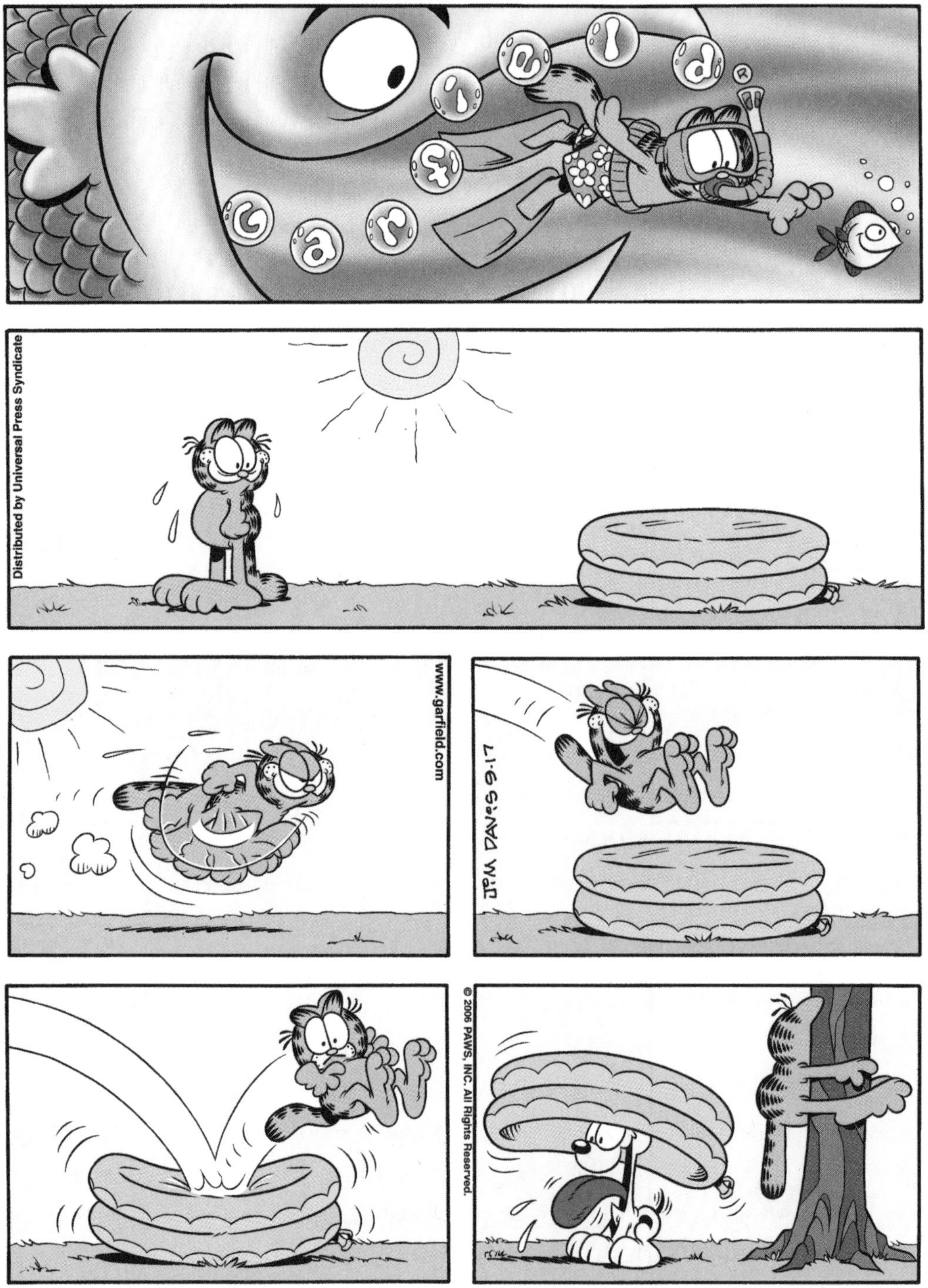
garfield®
Distributed by Universal Press Syndicate
www.garfield.com
JIM DAVIS 9-17
© 2006 PAWS, INC. All Rights Reserved.

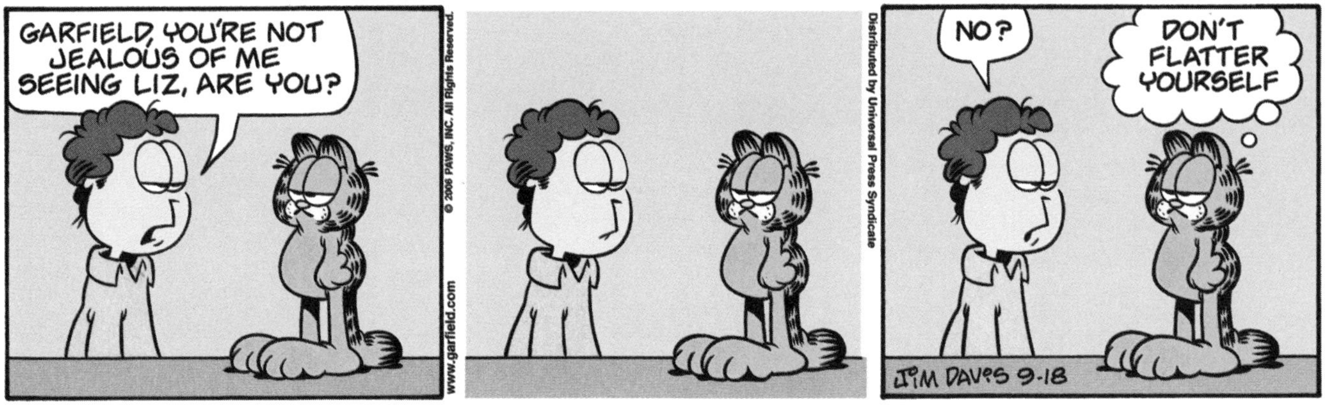
GARFIELD, YOU'RE NOT JEALOUS OF ME SEEING LIZ, ARE YOU?
www.garfield.com © 2006 PAWS, INC. All Rights Reserved.
Distributed by Universal Press Syndicate
NO?
DON'T FLATTER YOURSELF
JIM DAVIS 9-18

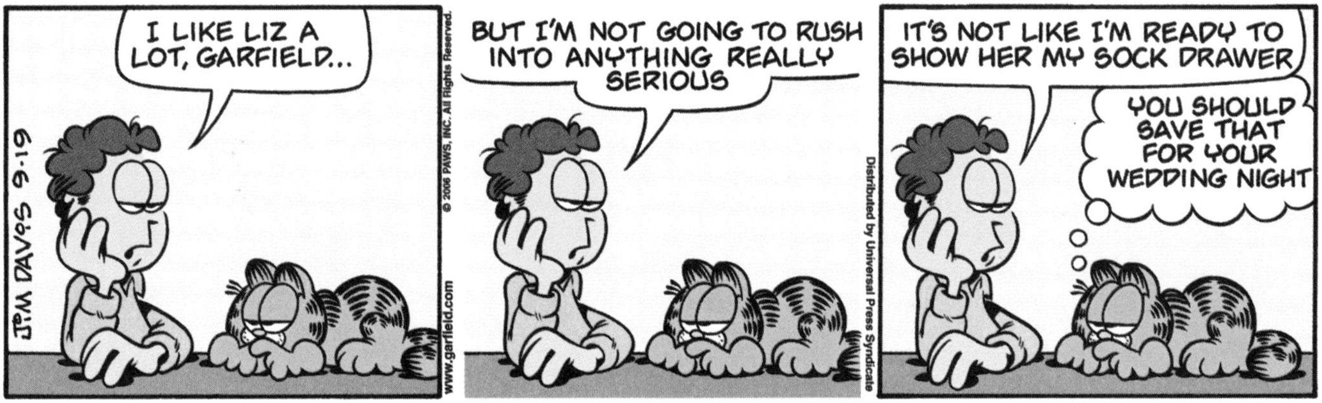
JIM DAVIS 9-19
I LIKE LIZ A LOT, GARFIELD...
www.garfield.com © 2006 PAWS, INC. All Rights Reserved.
BUT I'M NOT GOING TO RUSH INTO ANYTHING REALLY SERIOUS
Distributed by Universal Press Syndicate
IT'S NOT LIKE I'M READY TO SHOW HER MY SOCK DRAWER
YOU SHOULD SAVE THAT FOR YOUR WEDDING NIGHT

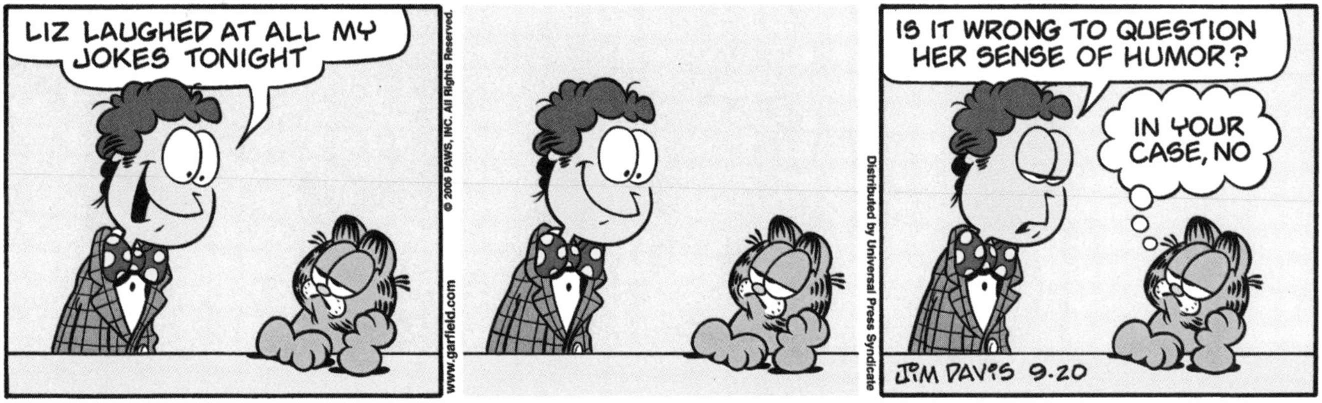
LIZ LAUGHED AT ALL MY JOKES TONIGHT
www.garfield.com © 2006 PAWS, INC. All Rights Reserved.
Distributed by Universal Press Syndicate
IS IT WRONG TO QUESTION HER SENSE OF HUMOR?
IN YOUR CASE, NO
JIM DAVIS 9-20

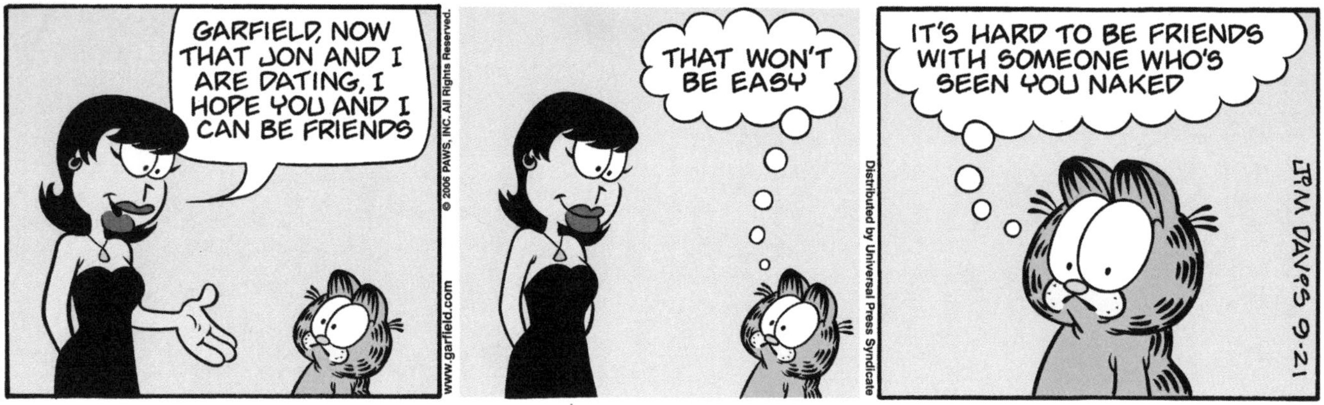
GARFIELD, NOW THAT JON AND I ARE DATING, I HOPE YOU AND I CAN BE FRIENDS
© 2006 PAWS, INC. All Rights Reserved.
www.garfield.com
THAT WON'T BE EASY
Distributed by Universal Press Syndicate
IT'S HARD TO BE FRIENDS WITH SOMEONE WHO'S SEEN YOU NAKED
JIM DAVIS 9-21

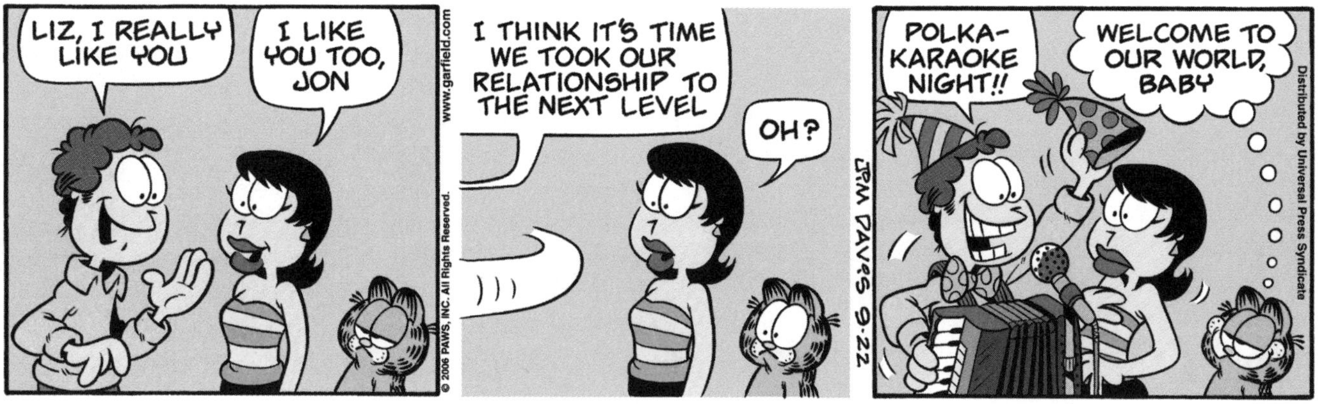
LIZ, I REALLY LIKE YOU
I LIKE YOU TOO, JON
www.garfield.com
© 2006 PAWS, INC. All Rights Reserved.
I THINK IT'S TIME WE TOOK OUR RELATIONSHIP TO THE NEXT LEVEL
OH?
JIM DAVIS 9-22
POLKA-KARAOKE NIGHT!!
WELCOME TO OUR WORLD, BABY
Distributed by Universal Press Syndicate

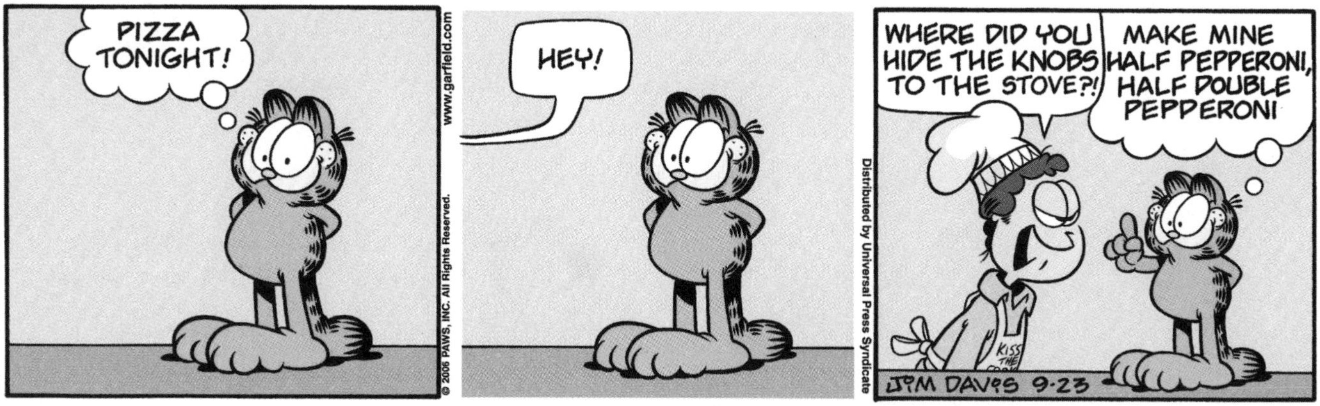
PIZZA TONIGHT!
www.garfield.com
© 2006 PAWS, INC. All Rights Reserved.
HEY!
Distributed by Universal Press Syndicate
WHERE DID YOU HIDE THE KNOBS TO THE STOVE?!
MAKE MINE HALF PEPPERONI, HALF DOUBLE PEPPERONI
JIM DAVIS 9-23

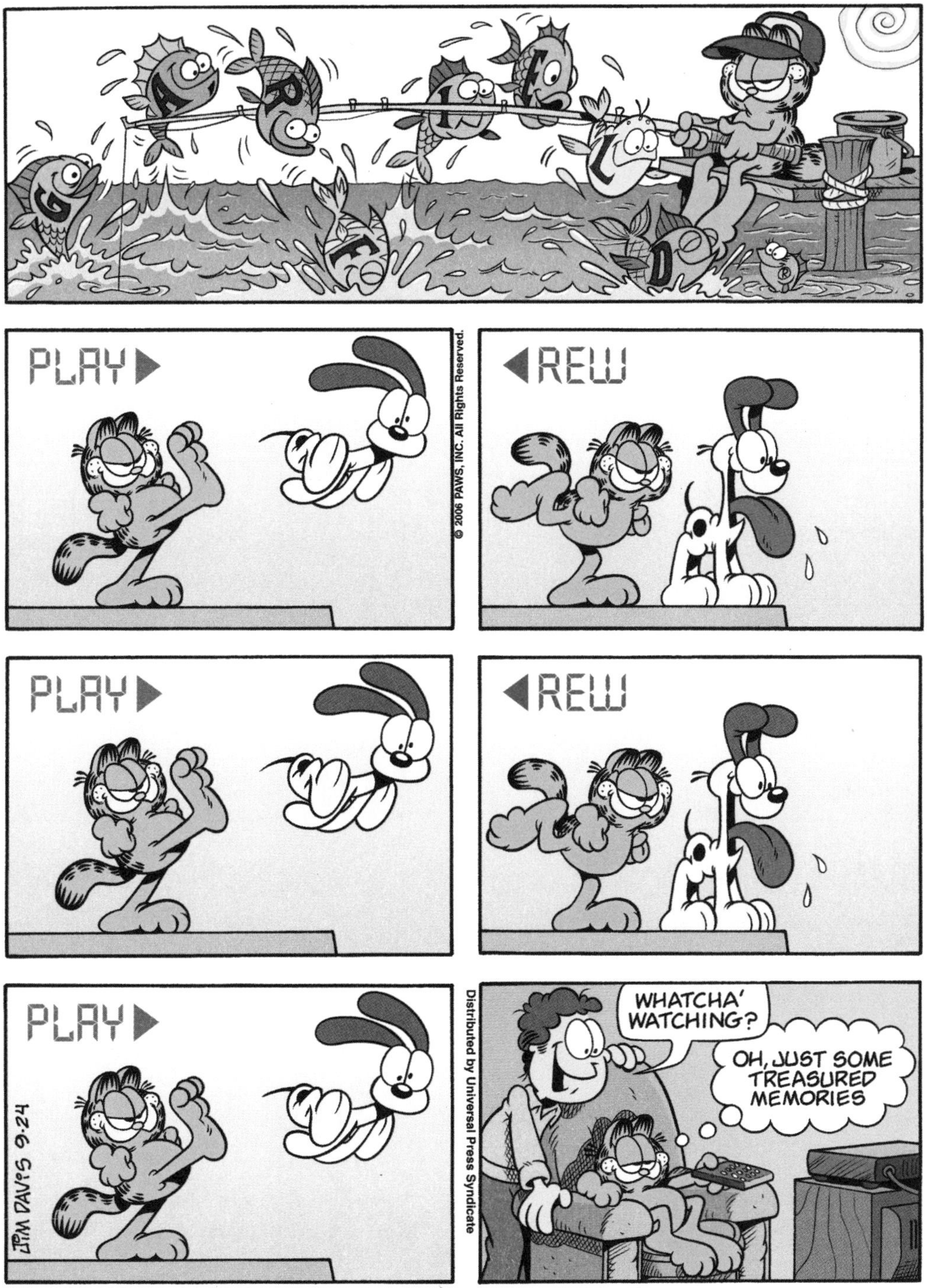
PLAY
REW
PLAY
REW
PLAY
WHATCHA' WATCHING?
OH, JUST SOME TREASURED MEMORIES
JIM DAVIS 9·24
© 2006 PAWS, INC. All Rights Reserved.
Distributed by Universal Press Syndicate

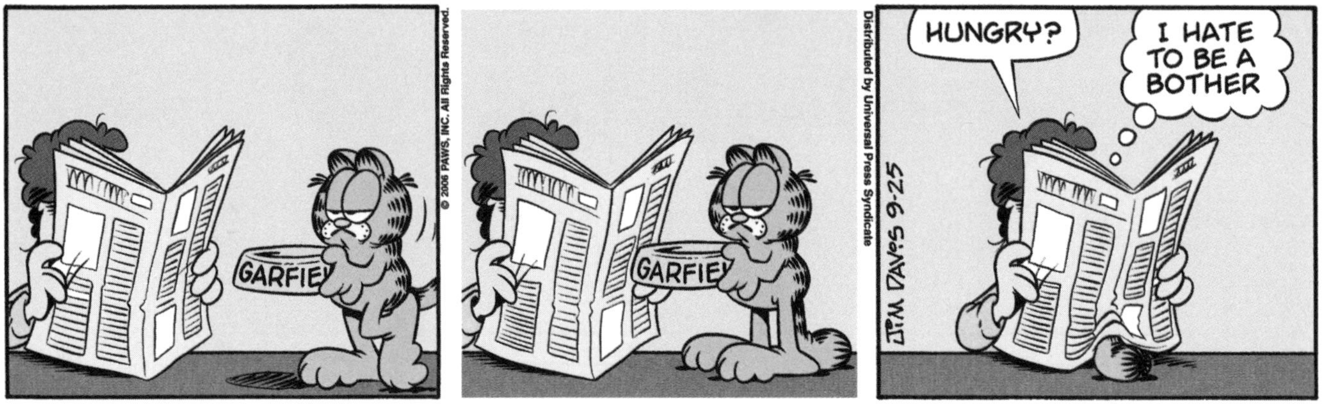

GARFIELD
© 2006 PAWS, INC. All Rights Reserved.
GARFIELD
Distributed by Universal Press Syndicate
JIM DAVIS 9-25
HUNGRY?
I HATE TO BE A BOTHER

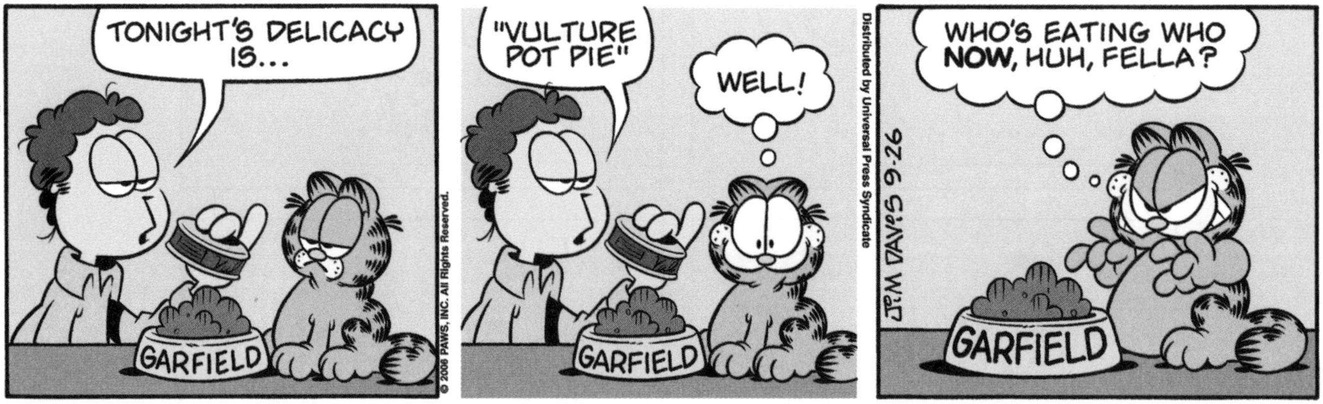

TONIGHT'S DELICACY IS...
GARFIELD
© 2006 PAWS, INC. All Rights Reserved.
"VULTURE POT PIE"
WELL!
GARFIELD
Distributed by Universal Press Syndicate
JIM DAVIS 9-26
WHO'S EATING WHO **NOW**, HUH, FELLA?
GARFIELD

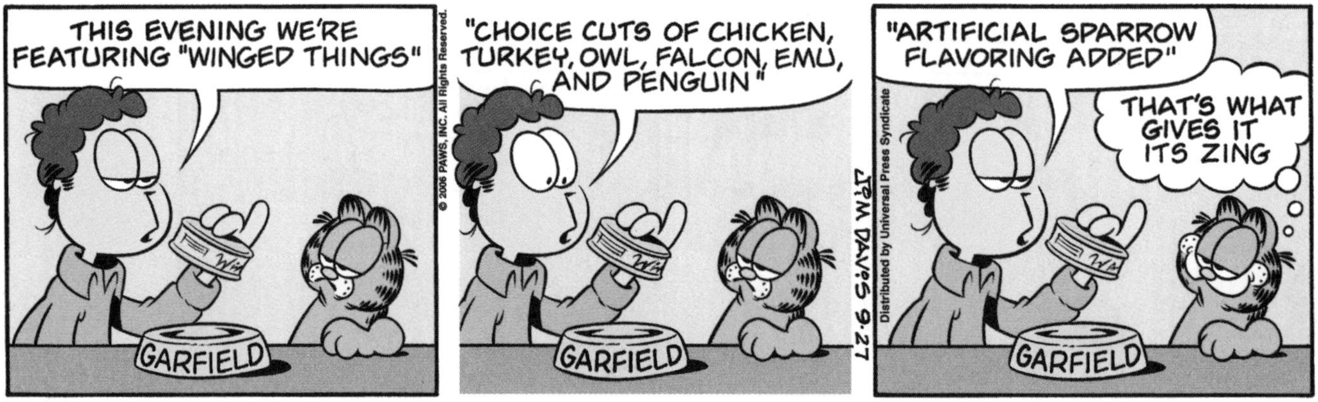

THIS EVENING WE'RE FEATURING "WINGED THINGS"
GARFIELD
© 2006 PAWS, INC. All Rights Reserved.
"CHOICE CUTS OF CHICKEN, TURKEY, OWL, FALCON, EMU, AND PENGUIN"
GARFIELD
JIM DAVIS 9-27
Distributed by Universal Press Syndicate
"ARTIFICIAL SPARROW FLAVORING ADDED"
THAT'S WHAT GIVES IT ITS ZING
GARFIELD

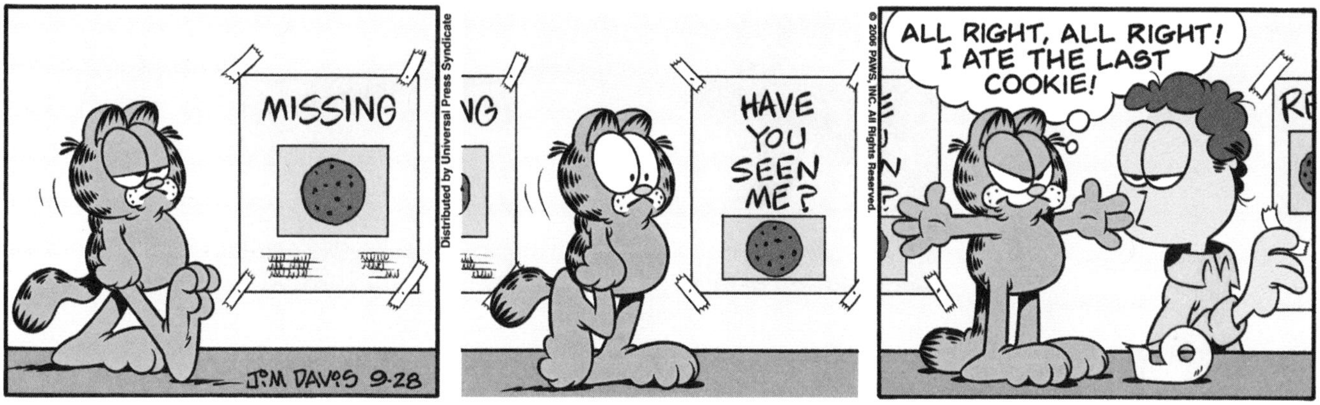
MISSING
HAVE YOU SEEN ME?
ALL RIGHT, ALL RIGHT! I ATE THE LAST COOKIE!
JIM DAVIS 9-28
Distributed by Universal Press Syndicate
© 2006 PAWS, INC. All Rights Reserved.

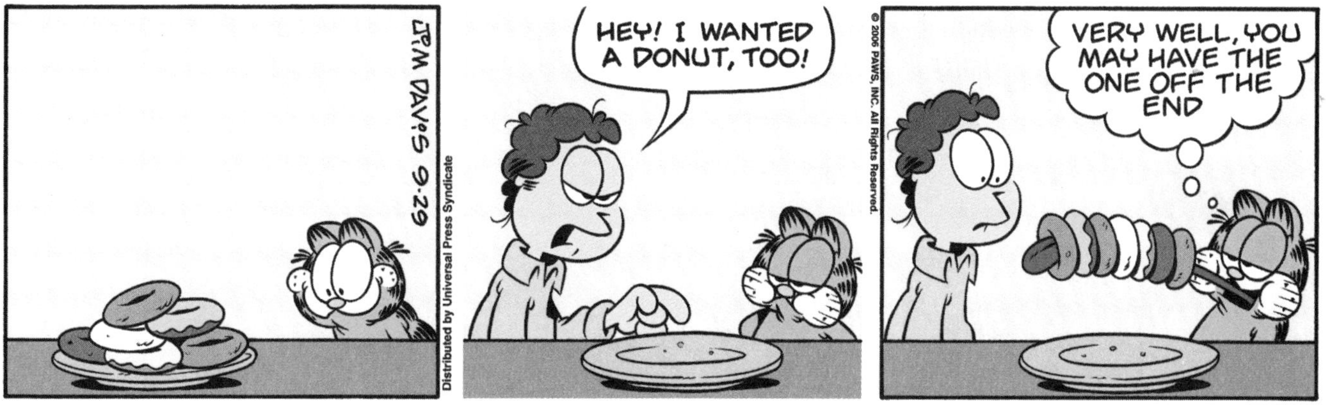
JIM DAVIS 9-29
Distributed by Universal Press Syndicate
HEY! I WANTED A DONUT, TOO!
© 2006 PAWS, INC. All Rights Reserved.
VERY WELL, YOU MAY HAVE THE ONE OFF THE END

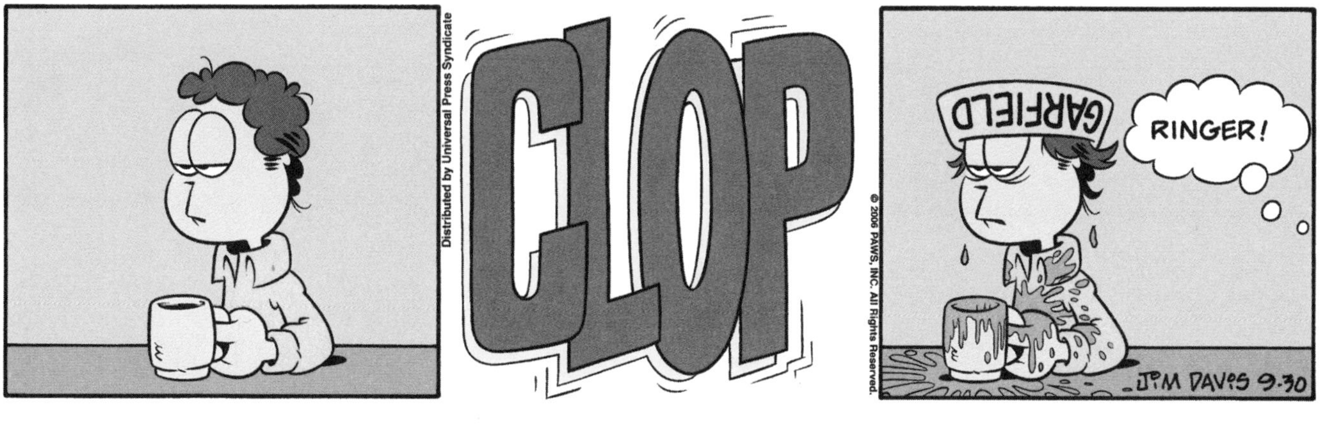
Distributed by Universal Press Syndicate
CLOP
© 2006 PAWS, INC. All Rights Reserved.
GARFIELD
RINGER!
JIM DAVIS 9-30

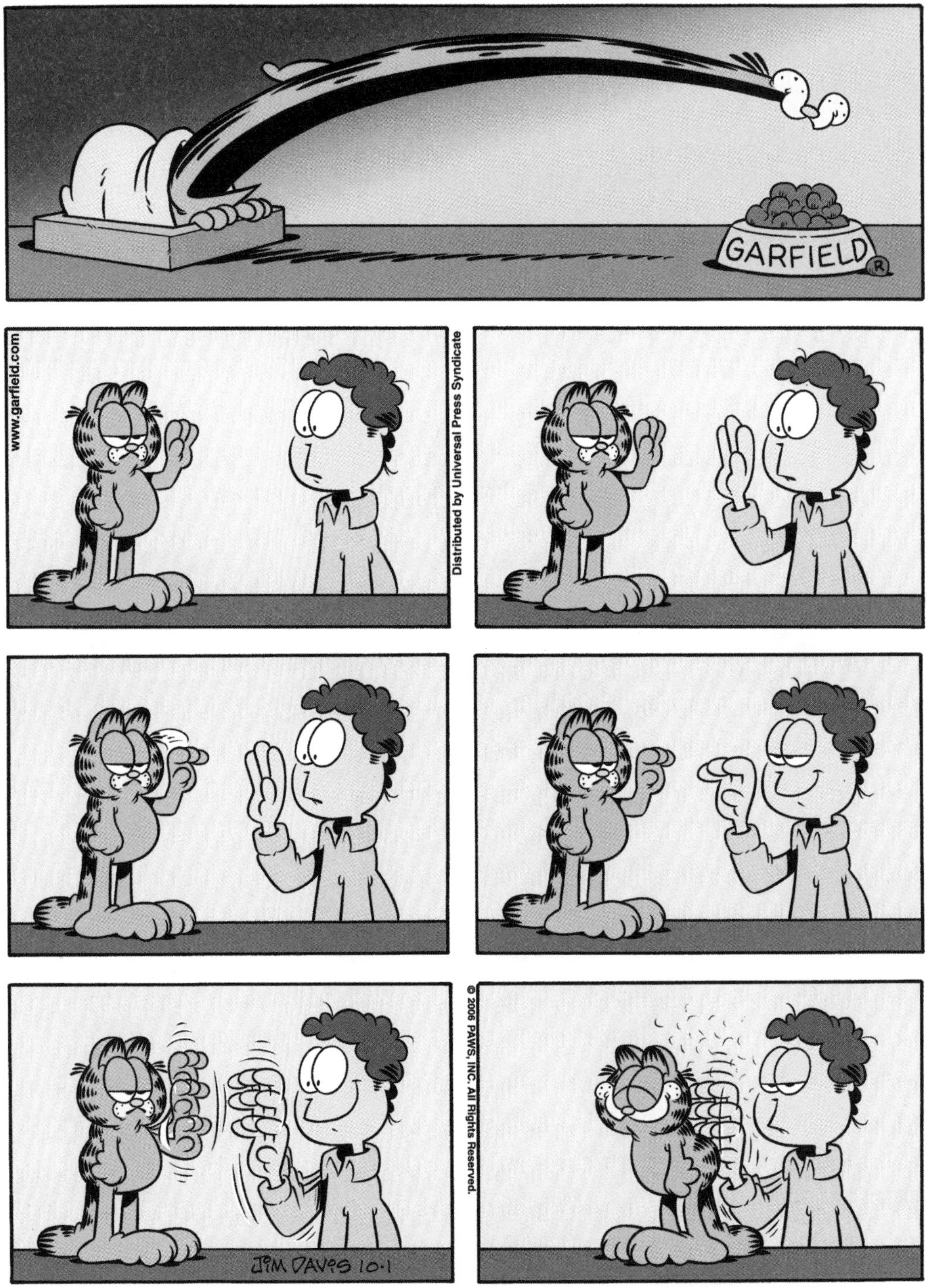
GARFIELD
www.garfield.com
Distributed by Universal Press Syndicate
© 2006 PAWS, INC. All Rights Reserved.
JIM DAVIS 10-1

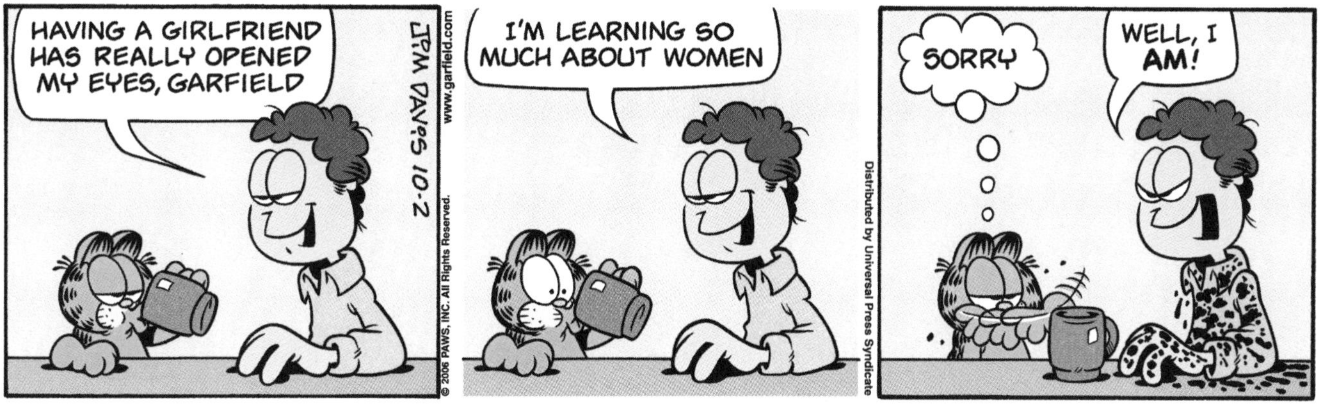
HAVING A GIRLFRIEND HAS REALLY OPENED MY EYES, GARFIELD
JIM DAVIS 10-2
© 2006 PAWS, INC. All Rights Reserved. www.garfield.com
I'M LEARNING SO MUCH ABOUT WOMEN
Distributed by Universal Press Syndicate
SORRY
WELL, I **AM**!

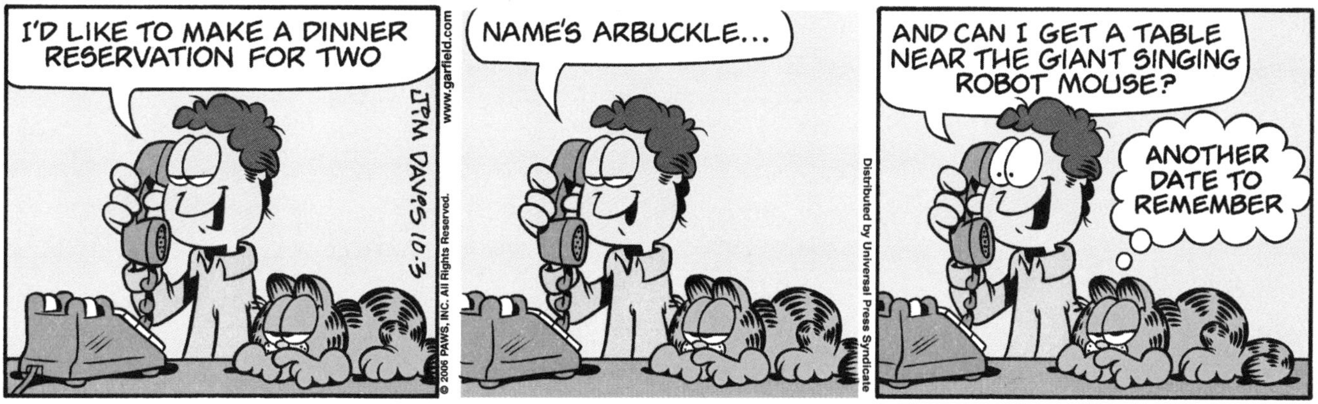
I'D LIKE TO MAKE A DINNER RESERVATION FOR TWO
JIM DAVIS 10-3
© 2006 PAWS, INC. All Rights Reserved. www.garfield.com
NAME'S ARBUCKLE...
Distributed by Universal Press Syndicate
AND CAN I GET A TABLE NEAR THE GIANT SINGING ROBOT MOUSE?
ANOTHER DATE TO REMEMBER

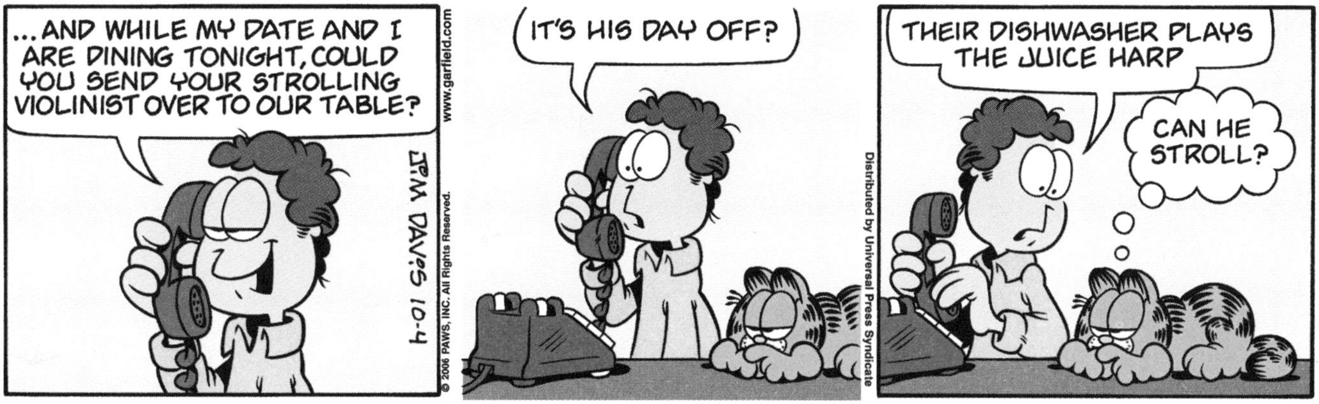
...AND WHILE MY DATE AND I ARE DINING TONIGHT, COULD YOU SEND YOUR STROLLING VIOLINIST OVER TO OUR TABLE?
JIM DAVIS 10-4
© 2006 PAWS, INC. All Rights Reserved. www.garfield.com
IT'S HIS DAY OFF?
Distributed by Universal Press Syndicate
THEIR DISHWASHER PLAYS THE JUICE HARP
CAN HE STROLL?

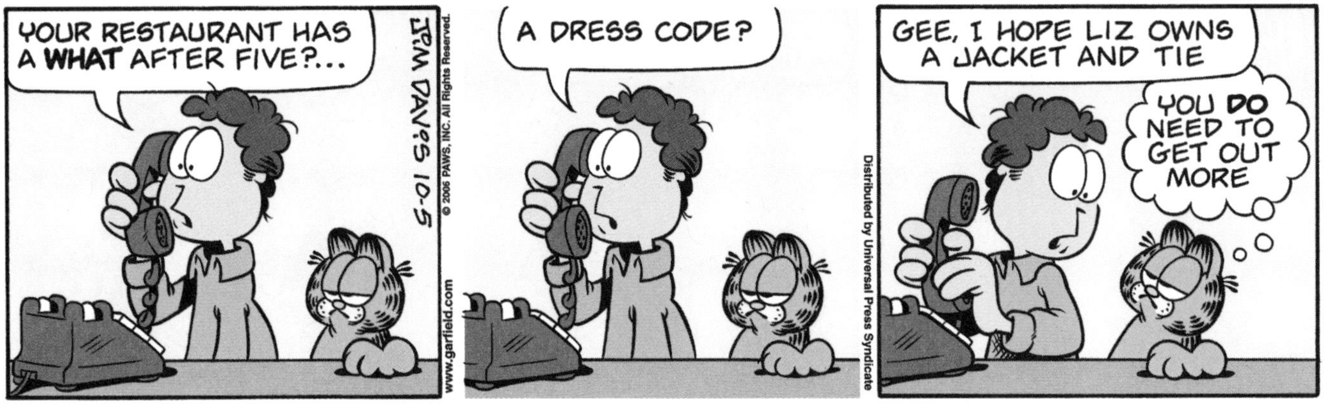
YOUR RESTAURANT HAS A **WHAT** AFTER FIVE?...
JIM DAVIS 10-5
© 2006 PAWS, INC. All Rights Reserved.
www.garfield.com
A DRESS CODE?
Distributed by Universal Press Syndicate
GEE, I HOPE LIZ OWNS A JACKET AND TIE
YOU **DO** NEED TO GET OUT MORE

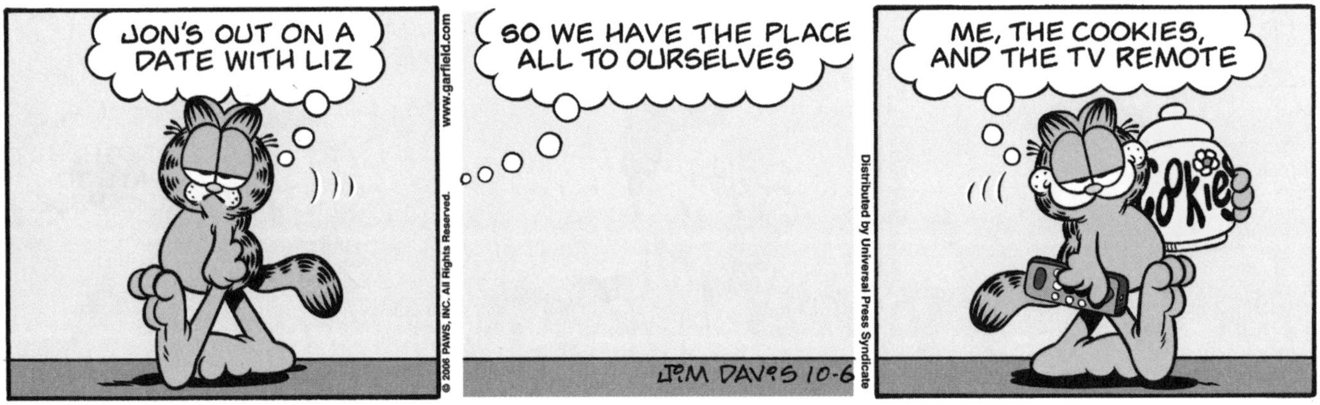
JON'S OUT ON A DATE WITH LIZ
© 2006 PAWS, INC. All Rights Reserved.
www.garfield.com
SO WE HAVE THE PLACE ALL TO OURSELVES
JIM DAVIS 10-6
Distributed by Universal Press Syndicate
ME, THE COOKIES, AND THE TV REMOTE
COOKIES

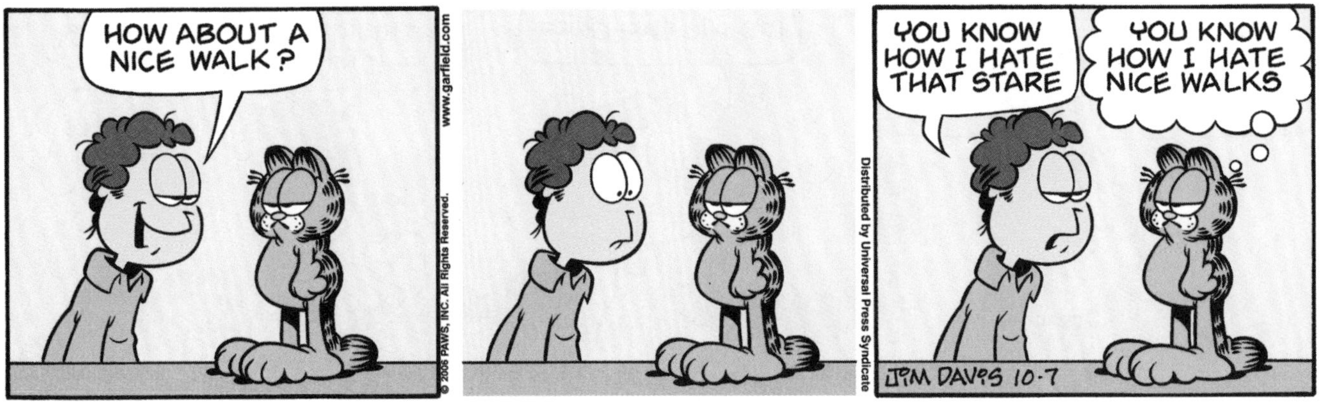
HOW ABOUT A NICE WALK?
© 2006 PAWS, INC. All Rights Reserved.
www.garfield.com
Distributed by Universal Press Syndicate
YOU KNOW HOW I HATE THAT STARE
YOU KNOW HOW I HATE NICE WALKS
JIM DAVIS 10-7

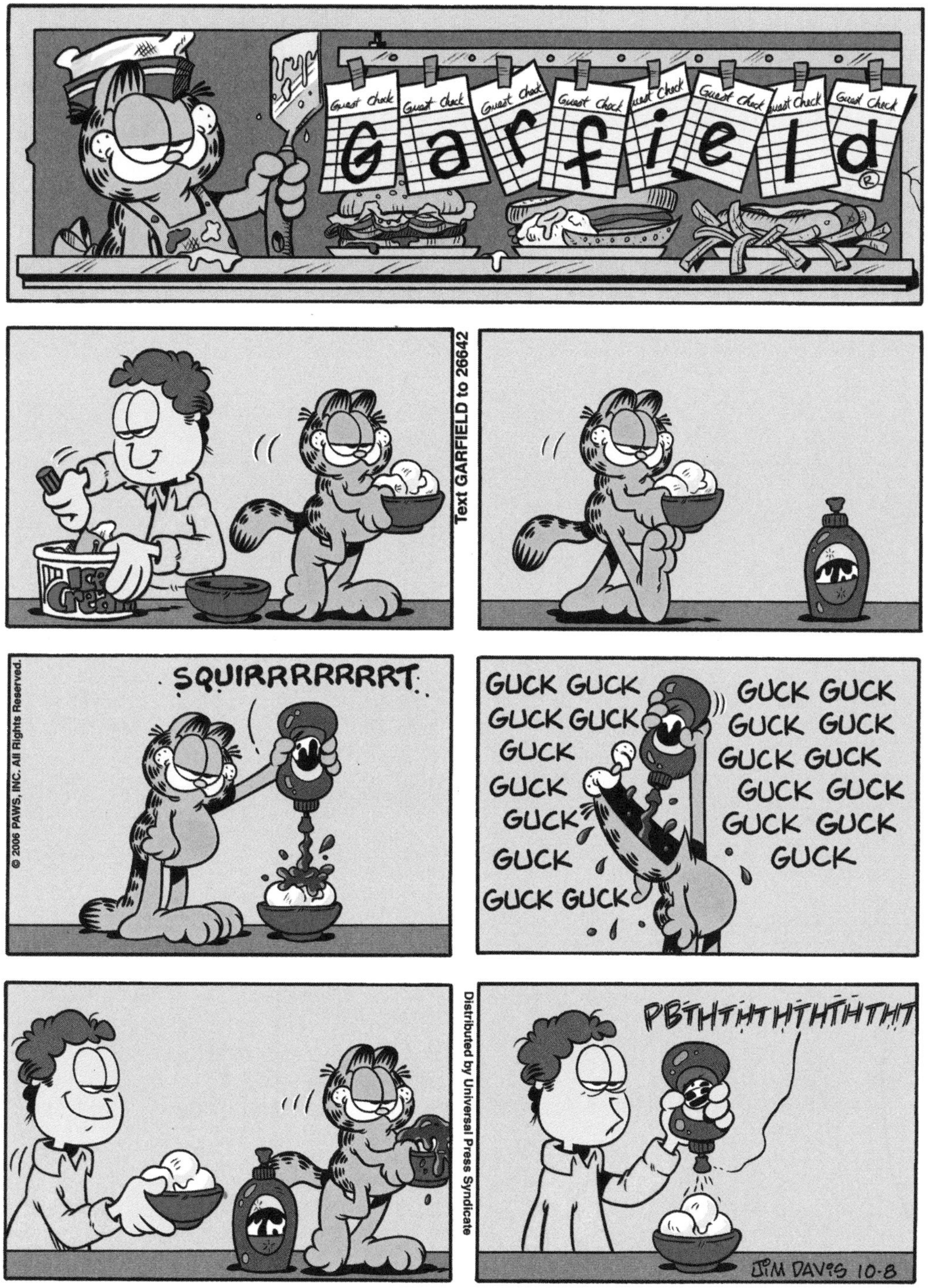
Garfield®
Guest Check
Text GARFIELD to 26642
Ice Cream
© 2006 PAWS, INC. All Rights Reserved.
SQUIRRRRRRRT
GUCK GUCK GUCK GUCK GUCK GUCK GUCK GUCK GUCK GUCK
GUCK GUCK GUCK GUCK GUCK GUCK GUCK GUCK GUCK GUCK GUCK
Distributed by Universal Press Syndicate
PBTHTHTHTHTHTHT
JIM DAVIS 10-8

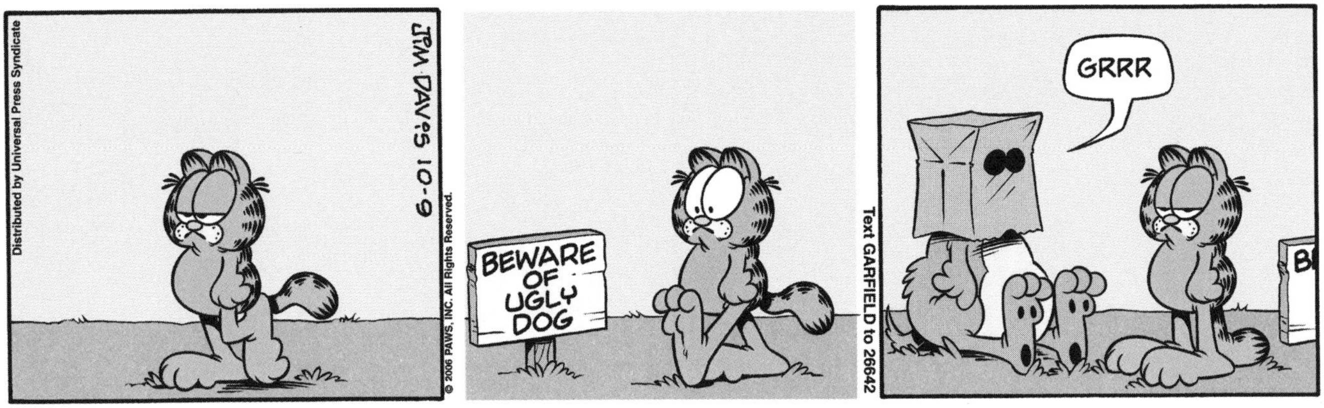
Distributed by Universal Press Syndicate
JIM DAVIS 10-9
© 2006 PAWS, INC. All Rights Reserved.
BEWARE OF UGLY DOG
Text GARFIELD to 26642
GRRR

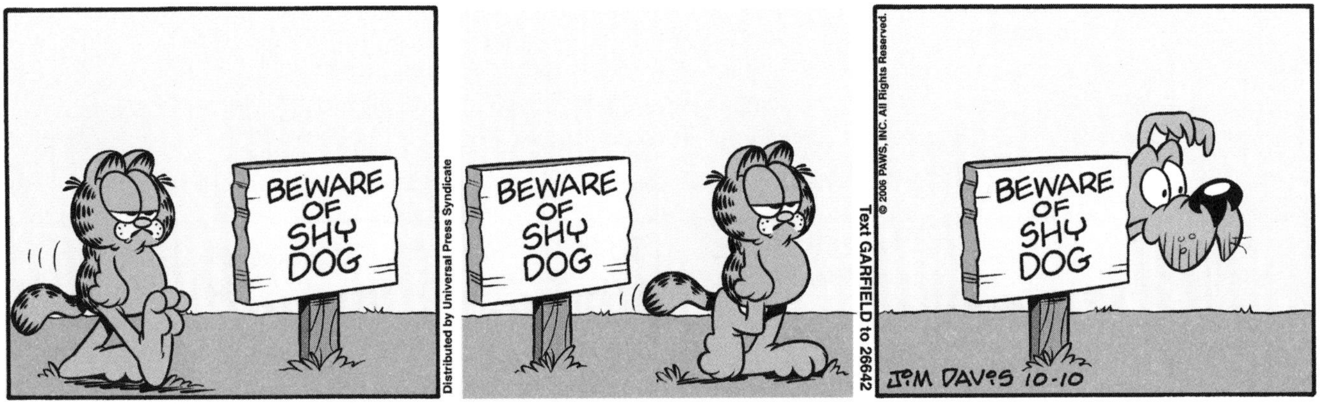
BEWARE OF SHY DOG
Distributed by Universal Press Syndicate
BEWARE OF SHY DOG
Text GARFIELD to 26642
© 2006 PAWS, INC. All Rights Reserved.
BEWARE OF SHY DOG
JIM DAVIS 10-10

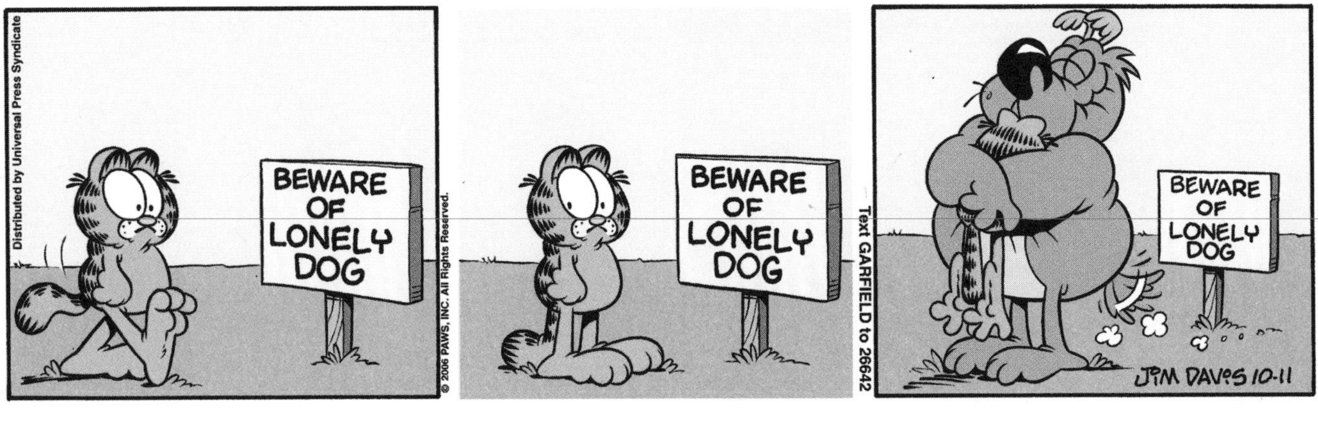
Distributed by Universal Press Syndicate
BEWARE OF LONELY DOG
© 2006 PAWS, INC. All Rights Reserved.
BEWARE OF LONELY DOG
Text GARFIELD to 26642
BEWARE OF LONELY DOG
JIM DAVIS 10-11

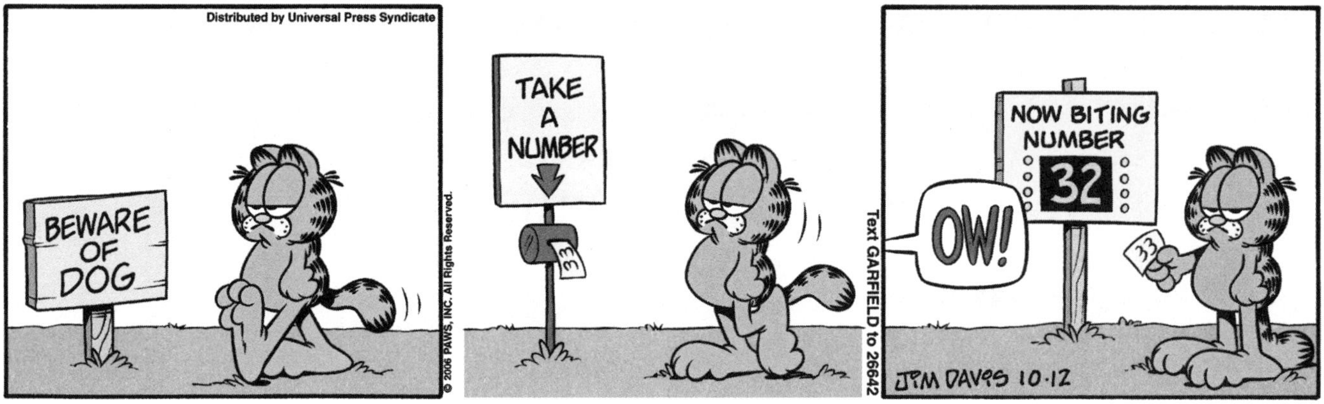
Distributed by Universal Press Syndicate
BEWARE OF DOG
© 2006 PAWS, INC. All Rights Reserved.
TAKE A NUMBER
33
Text GARFIELD to 26642
NOW BITING NUMBER
32
OW!
33
JIM DAVIS 10-12

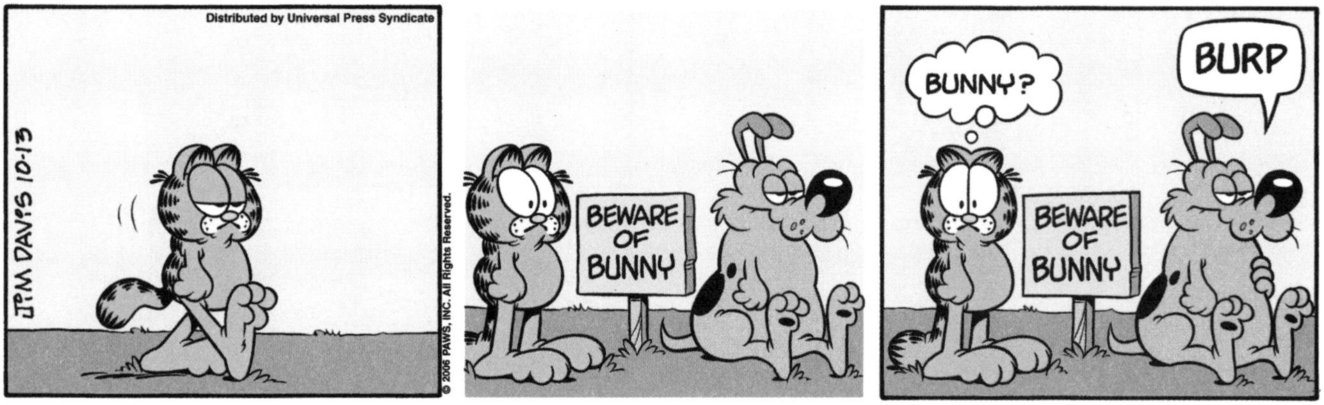
Distributed by Universal Press Syndicate
JIM DAVIS 10-13
© 2006 PAWS, INC. All Rights Reserved.
BEWARE OF BUNNY
BUNNY?
BURP
BEWARE OF BUNNY

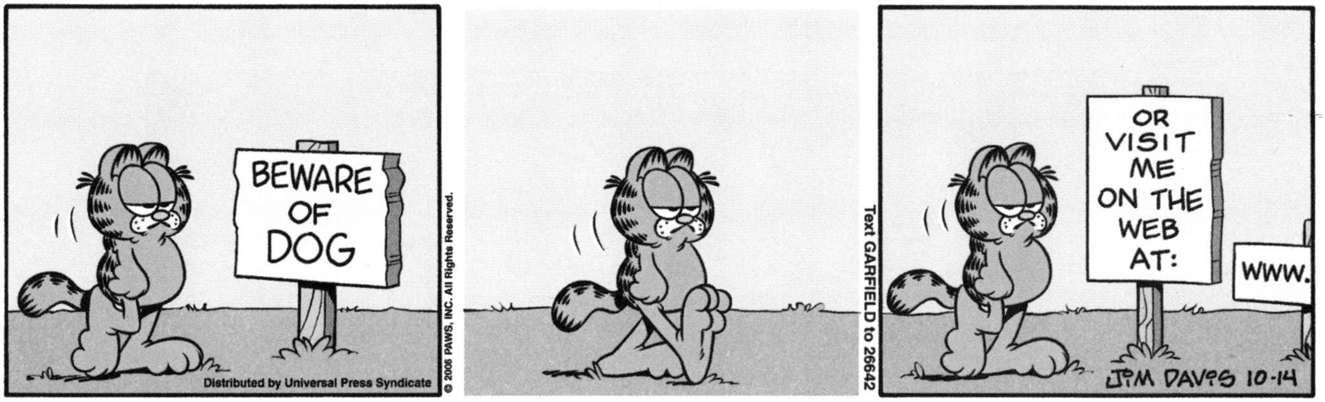
BEWARE OF DOG
Distributed by Universal Press Syndicate
© 2006 PAWS, INC. All Rights Reserved.
Text GARFIELD to 26642
OR VISIT ME ON THE WEB AT:
WWW.
JIM DAVIS 10-14

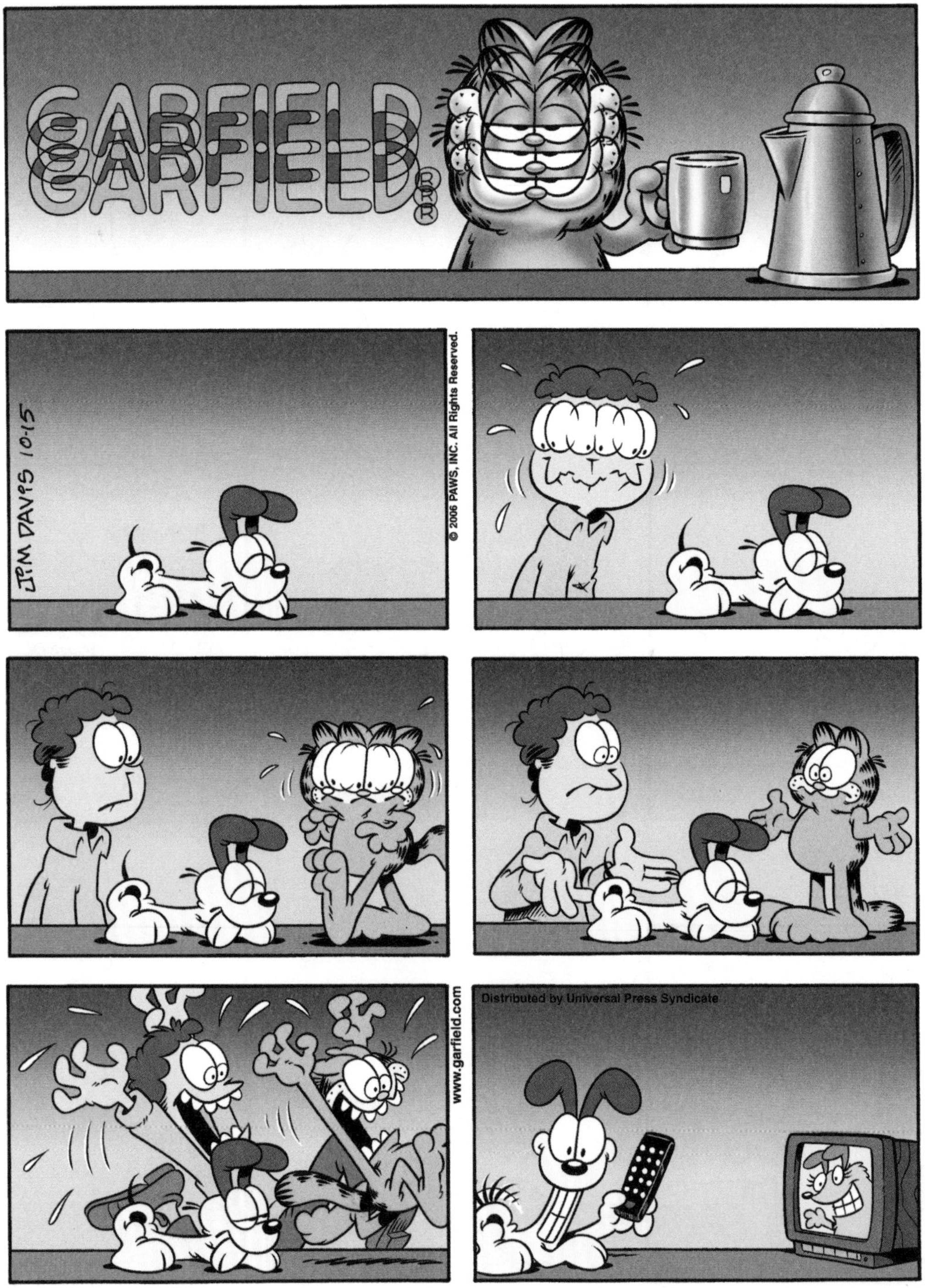
GARFIELD
JPM DAVPS 10-15
© 2006 PAWS, INC. All Rights Reserved.
www.garfield.com
Distributed by Universal Press Syndicate

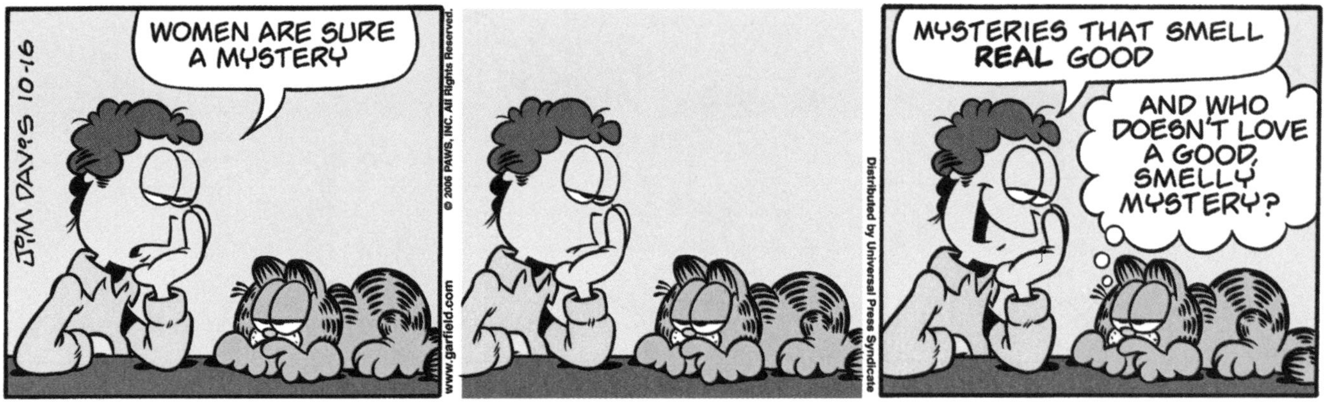
JIM DAVIS 10-16
WOMEN ARE SURE A MYSTERY
© 2006 PAWS, INC. All Rights Reserved.
www.garfield.com
Distributed by Universal Press Syndicate
MYSTERIES THAT SMELL **REAL** GOOD
AND WHO DOESN'T LOVE A GOOD, SMELLY MYSTERY?

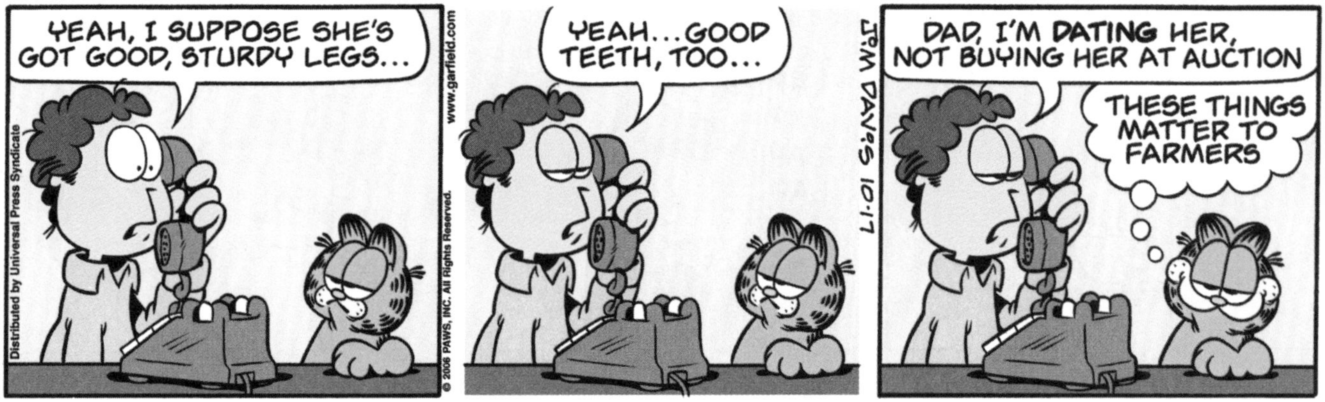
Distributed by Universal Press Syndicate
YEAH, I SUPPOSE SHE'S GOT GOOD, STURDY LEGS...
© 2006 PAWS, INC. All Rights Reserved.
www.garfield.com
YEAH...GOOD TEETH, TOO...
JIM DAVIS 10-17
DAD, I'M **DATING** HER, NOT BUYING HER AT AUCTION
THESE THINGS MATTER TO FARMERS

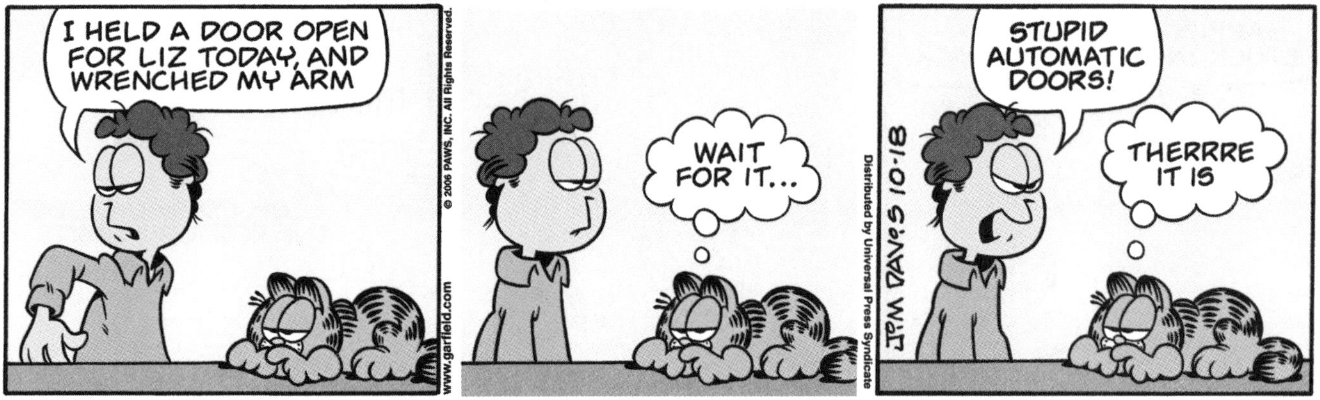
I HELD A DOOR OPEN FOR LIZ TODAY, AND WRENCHED MY ARM
© 2006 PAWS, INC. All Rights Reserved.
www.garfield.com
WAIT FOR IT...
JIM DAVIS 10-18
Distributed by Universal Press Syndicate
STUPID AUTOMATIC DOORS!
THERRRE IT IS

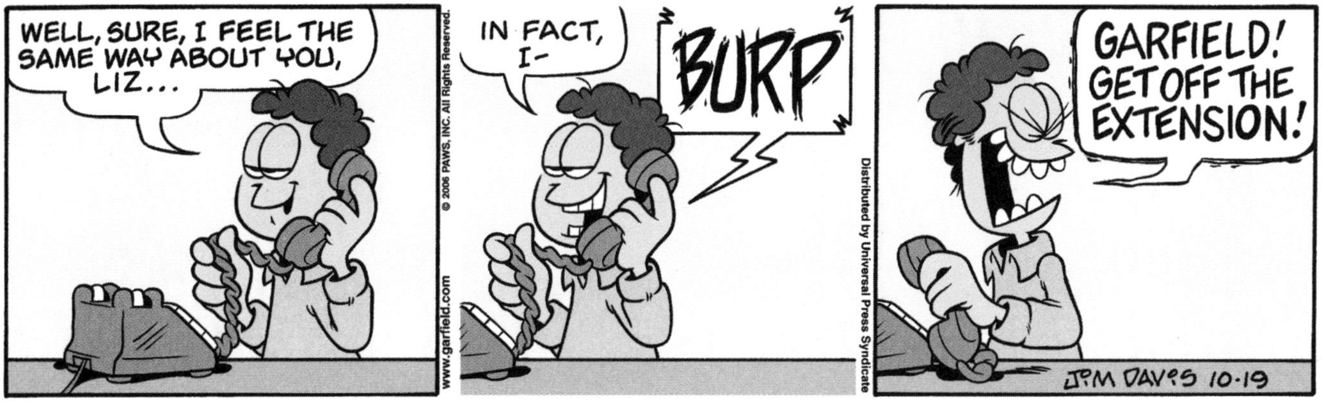
WELL, SURE, I FEEL THE SAME WAY ABOUT YOU, LIZ...
IN FACT, I-
BURP
GARFIELD! GET OFF THE EXTENSION!
JIM DAVIS 10-19
© 2006 PAWS, INC. All Rights Reserved.
www.garfield.com
Distributed by Universal Press Syndicate

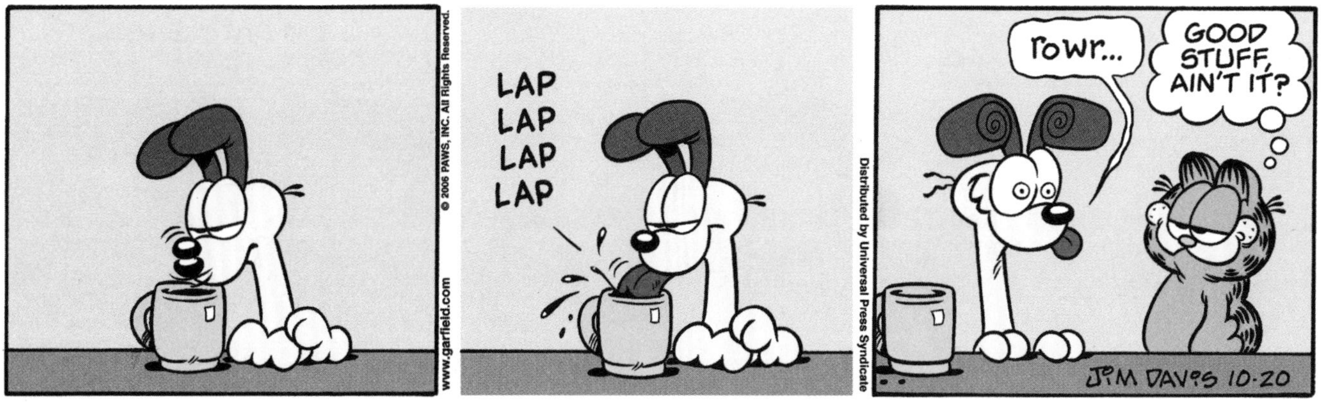
LAP LAP LAP LAP
rowr...
GOOD STUFF, AIN'T IT?
JIM DAVIS 10-20
© 2006 PAWS, INC. All Rights Reserved.
www.garfield.com
Distributed by Universal Press Syndicate

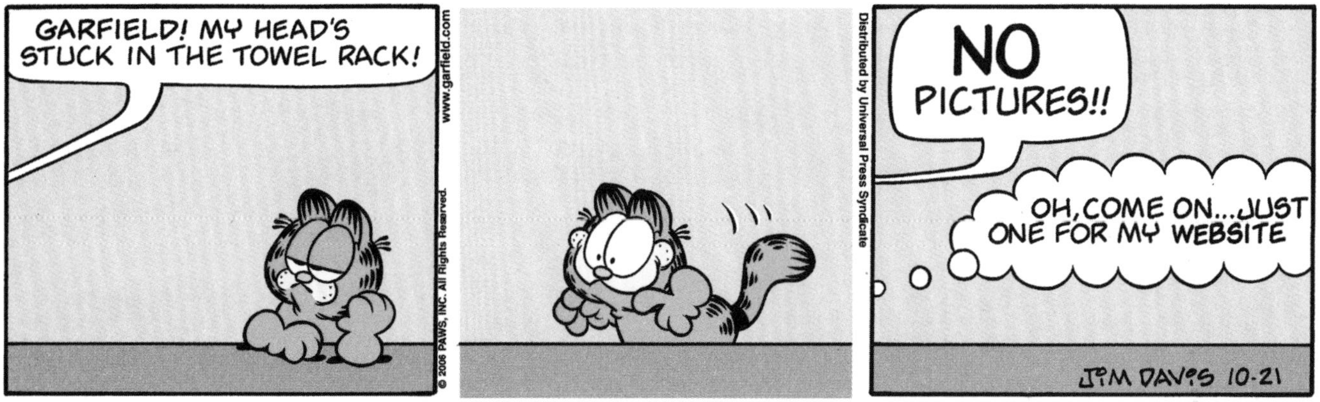
GARFIELD! MY HEAD'S STUCK IN THE TOWEL RACK!
NO PICTURES!!
OH, COME ON...JUST ONE FOR MY WEBSITE
JIM DAVIS 10-21
© 2006 PAWS, INC. All Rights Reserved.
www.garfield.com
Distributed by Universal Press Syndicate

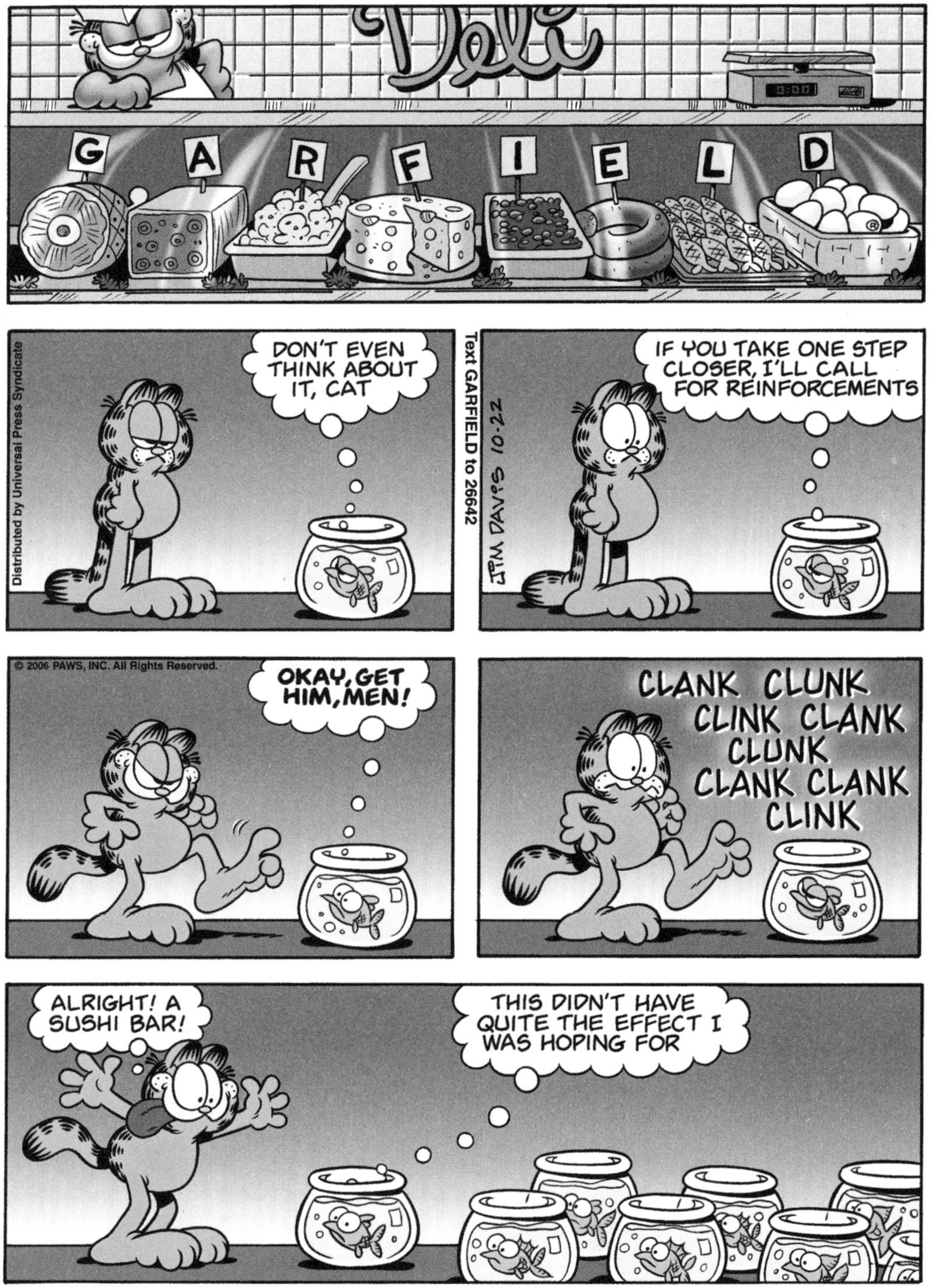
Deli
G A R F I E L D
DON'T EVEN THINK ABOUT IT, CAT
Distributed by Universal Press Syndicate
Text GARFIELD to 26642
JIM DAVIS 10-22
IF YOU TAKE ONE STEP CLOSER, I'LL CALL FOR REINFORCEMENTS
© 2006 PAWS, INC. All Rights Reserved.
OKAY, GET HIM, MEN!
CLANK CLUNK CLINK CLANK CLUNK CLANK CLANK CLINK
ALRIGHT! A SUSHI BAR!
THIS DIDN'T HAVE QUITE THE EFFECT I WAS HOPING FOR

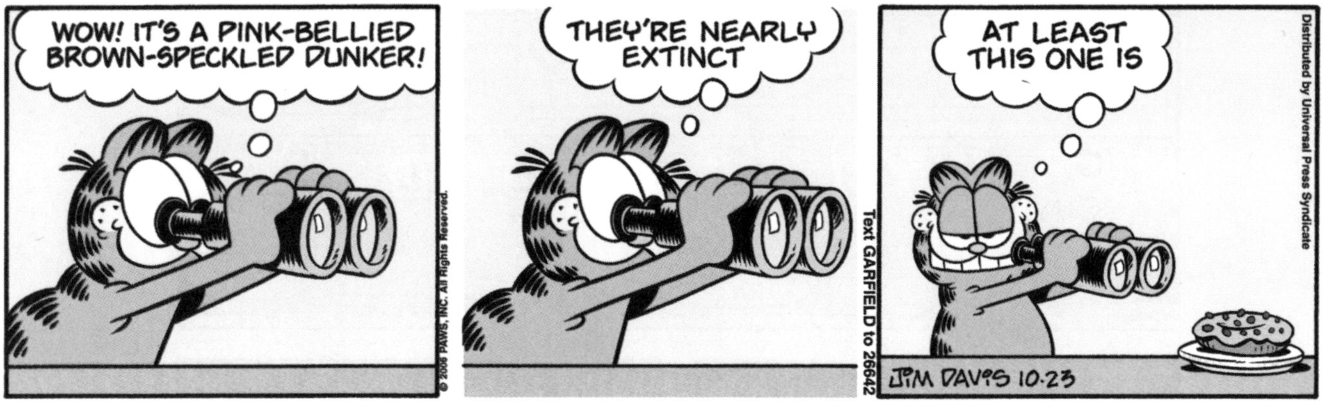
WOW! IT'S A PINK-BELLIED BROWN-SPECKLED DUNKER!
© 2006 PAWS, INC. All Rights Reserved.
THEY'RE NEARLY EXTINCT
Text GARFIELD to 26642
AT LEAST THIS ONE IS
JIM DAVIS 10.23
Distributed by Universal Press Syndicate

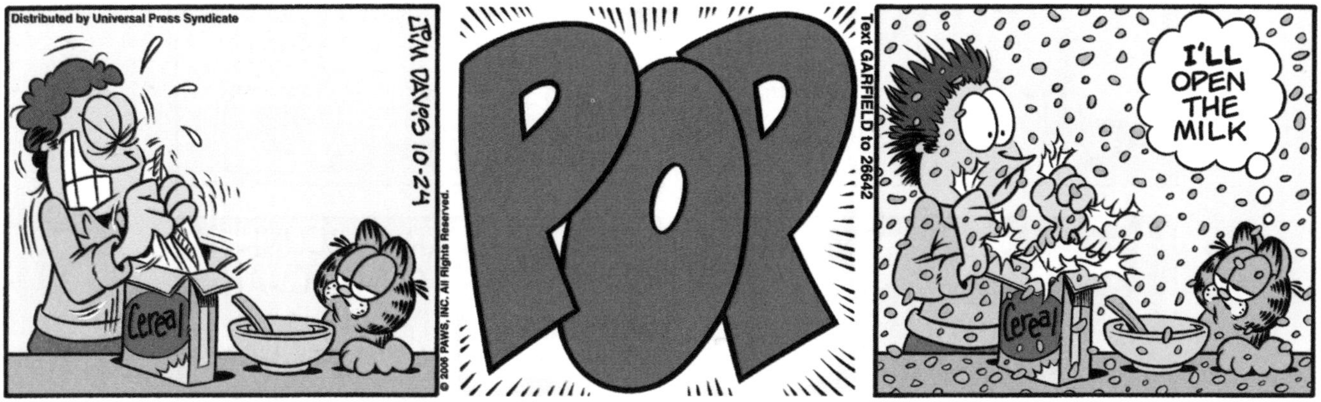
Distributed by Universal Press Syndicate
Cereal
JIM DAVIS 10-24
© 2006 PAWS, INC. All Rights Reserved.
POP
Text GARFIELD to 26642
I'LL OPEN THE MILK
Cereal

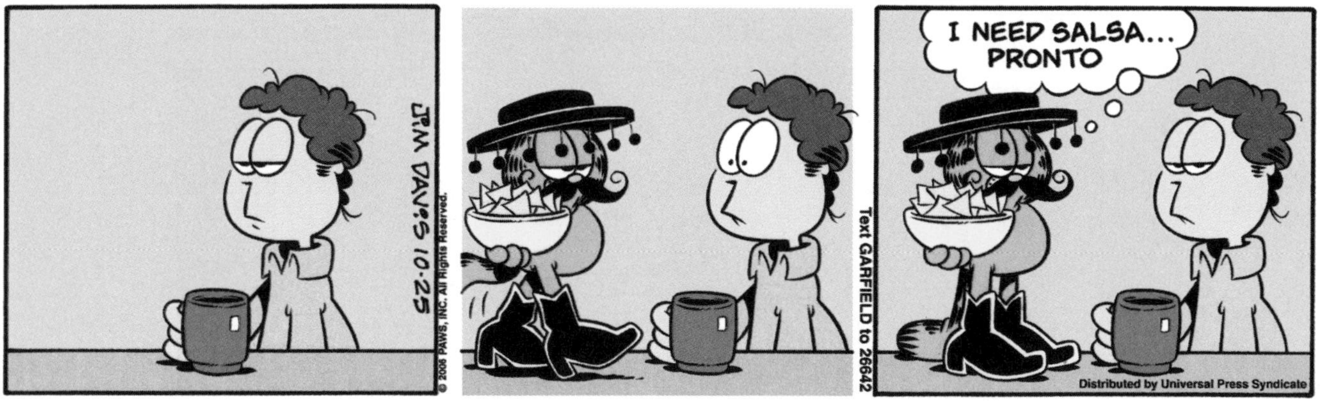
JIM DAVIS 10-25
© 2006 PAWS, INC. All Rights Reserved.
Text GARFIELD to 26642
I NEED SALSA... PRONTO
Distributed by Universal Press Syndicate

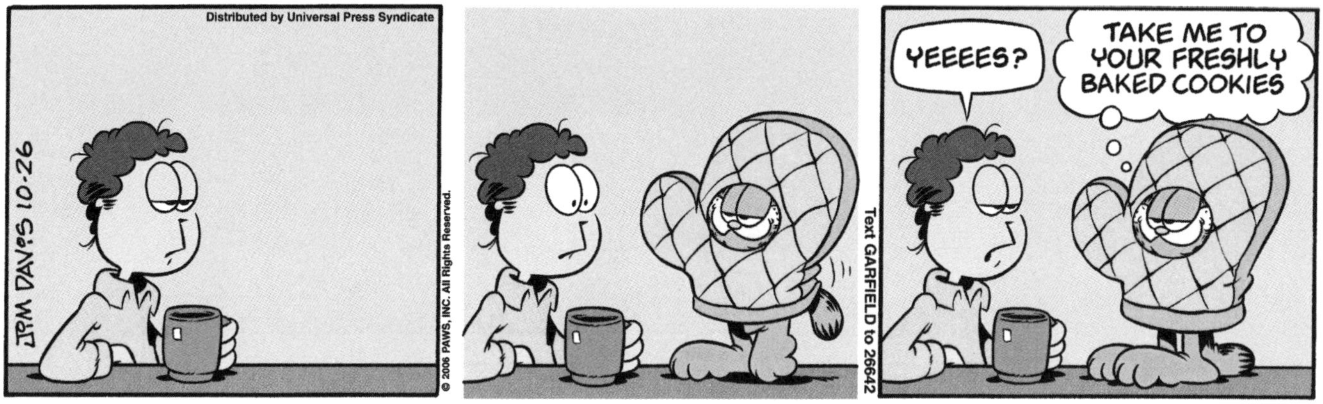
Distributed by Universal Press Syndicate
JIM DAVIS 10-26
© 2006 PAWS, INC. All Rights Reserved.
Text GARFIELD to 26642
YEEEES?
TAKE ME TO YOUR FRESHLY BAKED COOKIES

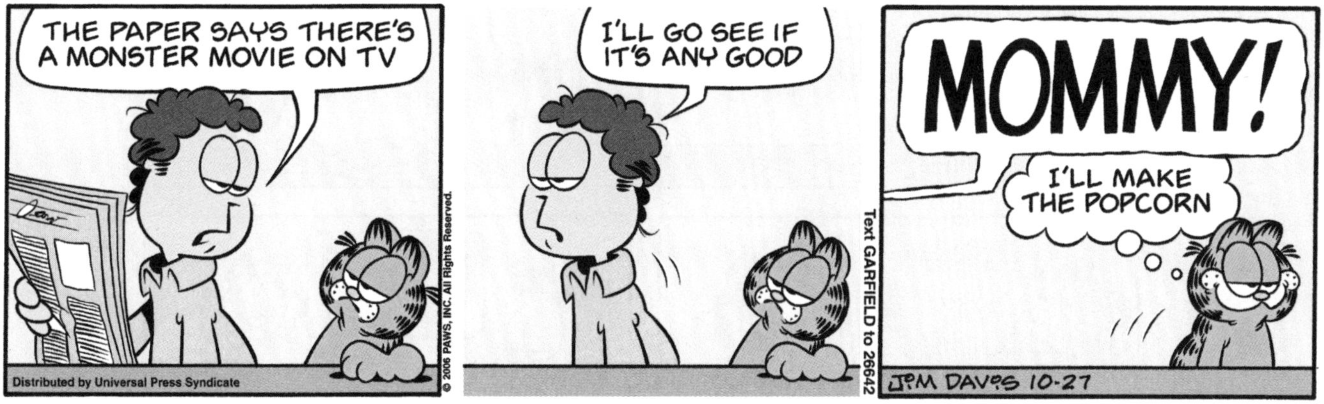
THE PAPER SAYS THERE'S A MONSTER MOVIE ON TV
Distributed by Universal Press Syndicate
© 2006 PAWS, INC. All Rights Reserved.
I'LL GO SEE IF IT'S ANY GOOD
Text GARFIELD to 26642
MOMMY!
I'LL MAKE THE POPCORN
JIM DAVIS 10-27

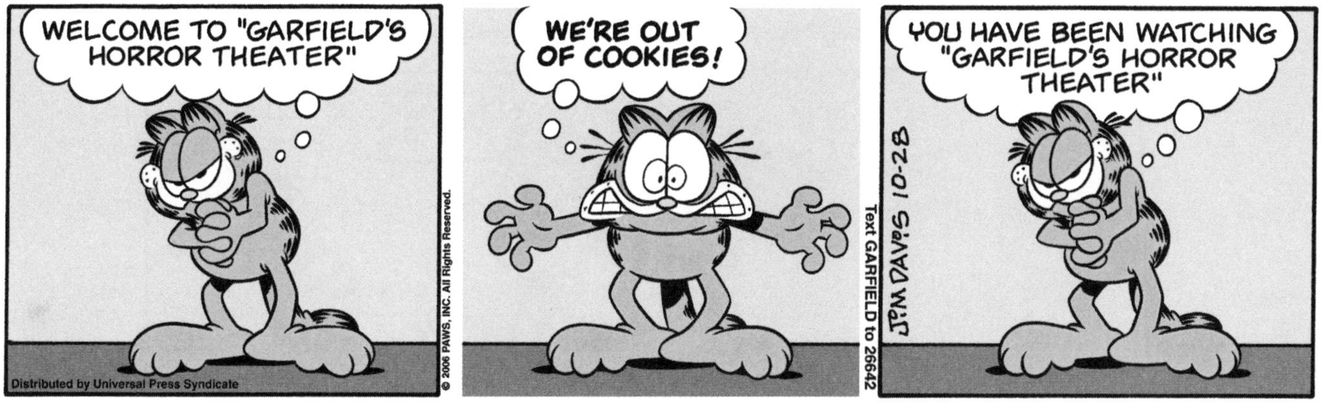
WELCOME TO "GARFIELD'S HORROR THEATER"
Distributed by Universal Press Syndicate
© 2006 PAWS, INC. All Rights Reserved.
WE'RE OUT OF COOKIES!
Text GARFIELD to 26642
JIM DAVIS 10-28
YOU HAVE BEEN WATCHING "GARFIELD'S HORROR THEATER"

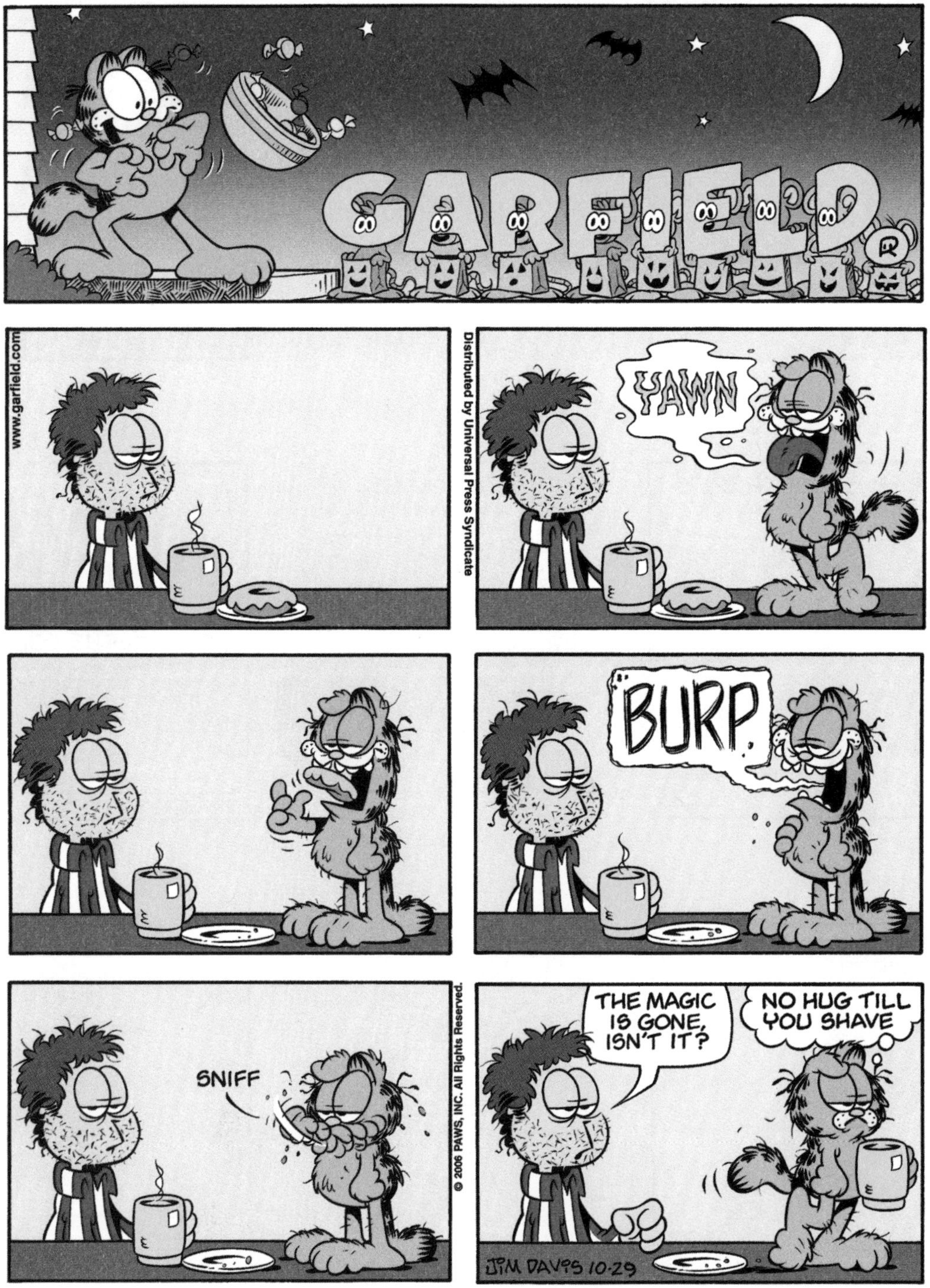
GARFIELD
www.garfield.com
Distributed by Universal Press Syndicate
YAWN
BURP
© 2006 PAWS, INC. All Rights Reserved.
SNIFF
THE MAGIC IS GONE, ISN'T IT?
NO HUG TILL YOU SHAVE
JIM DAVIS 10-29

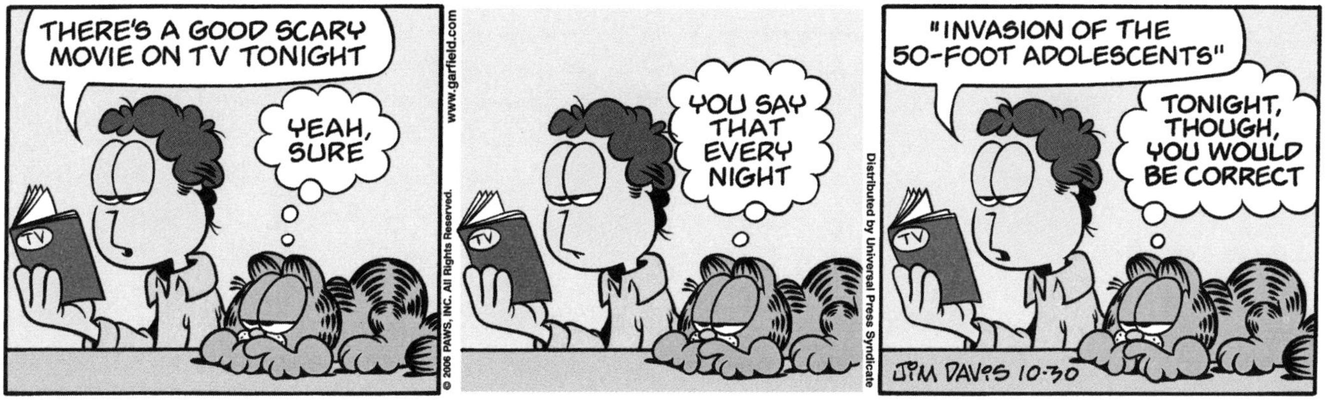
THERE'S A GOOD SCARY MOVIE ON TV TONIGHT
YEAH, SURE
TV
© 2006 PAWS, INC. All Rights Reserved. www.garfield.com
YOU SAY THAT EVERY NIGHT
Distributed by Universal Press Syndicate
"INVASION OF THE 50-FOOT ADOLESCENTS"
TONIGHT, THOUGH, YOU WOULD BE CORRECT
JIM DAVIS 10-30

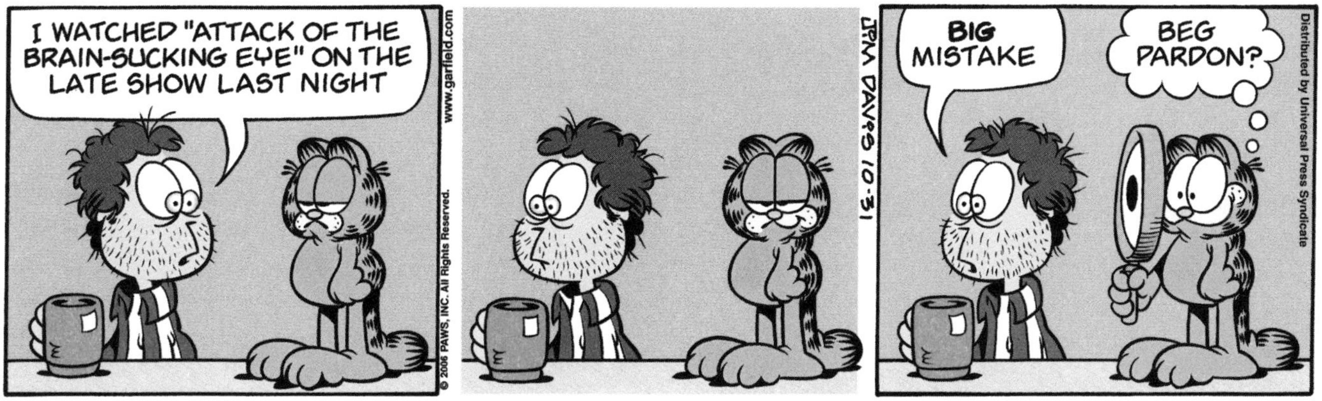
I WATCHED "ATTACK OF THE BRAIN-SUCKING EYE" ON THE LATE SHOW LAST NIGHT
© 2006 PAWS, INC. All Rights Reserved. www.garfield.com
JIM DAVIS 10-31
BIG MISTAKE
BEG PARDON?
Distributed by Universal Press Syndicate

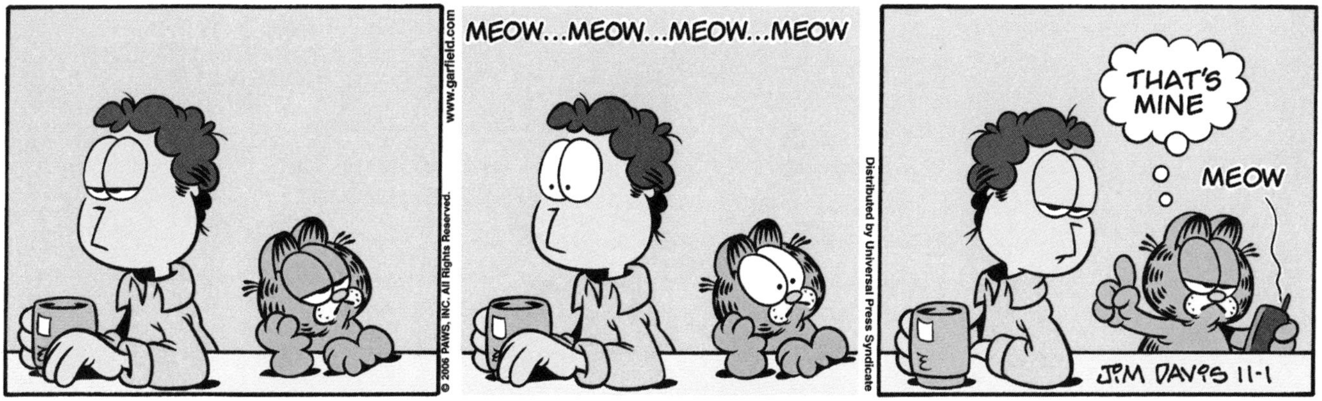
© 2006 PAWS, INC. All Rights Reserved. www.garfield.com
MEOW...MEOW...MEOW...MEOW
Distributed by Universal Press Syndicate
THAT'S MINE
MEOW
JIM DAVIS 11-1

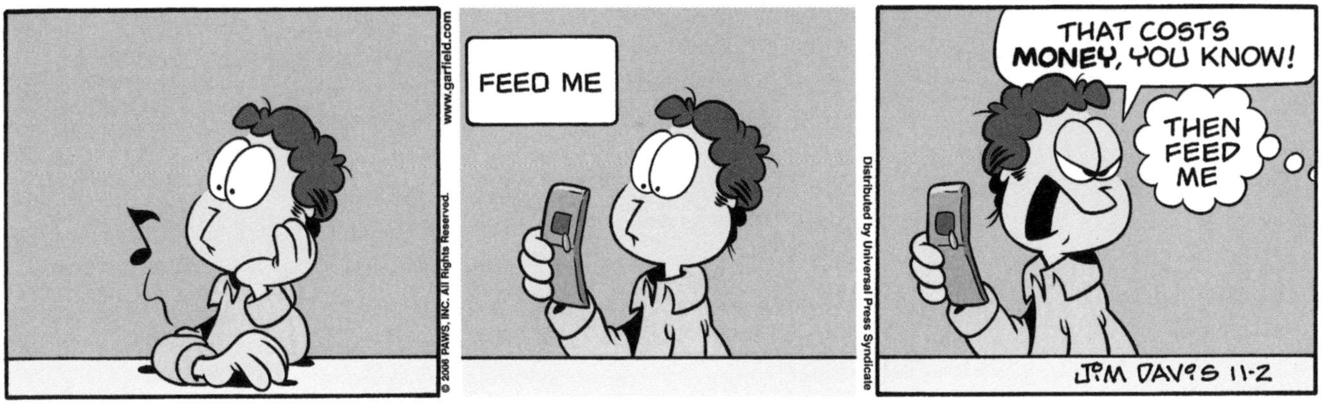

© 2006 PAWS, INC. All Rights Reserved.
www.garfield.com
FEED ME
Distributed by Universal Press Syndicate
THAT COSTS **MONEY**, YOU KNOW!
THEN FEED ME
JIM DAVIS 11-2

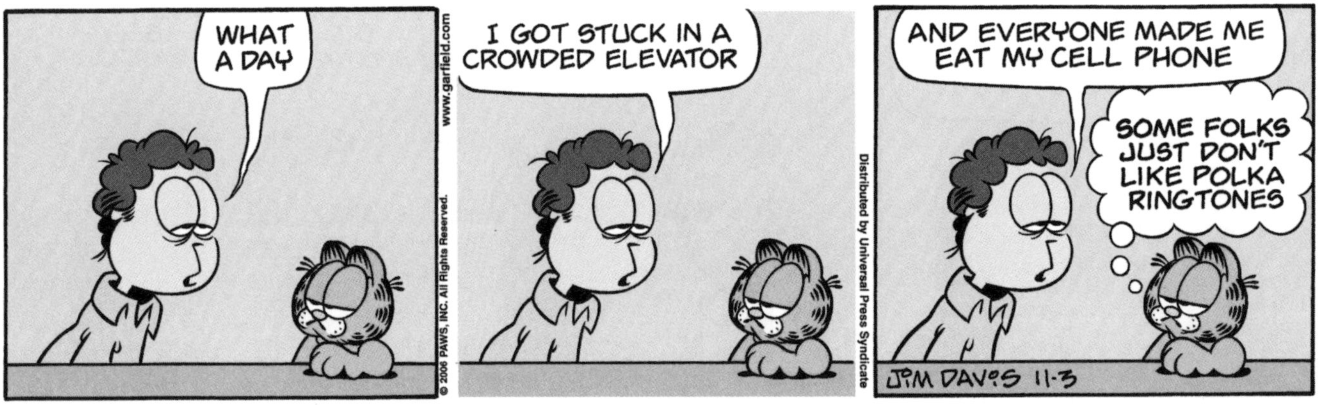

WHAT A DAY
© 2006 PAWS, INC. All Rights Reserved.
www.garfield.com
I GOT STUCK IN A CROWDED ELEVATOR
Distributed by Universal Press Syndicate
AND EVERYONE MADE ME EAT MY CELL PHONE
SOME FOLKS JUST DON'T LIKE POLKA RINGTONES
JIM DAVIS 11-3

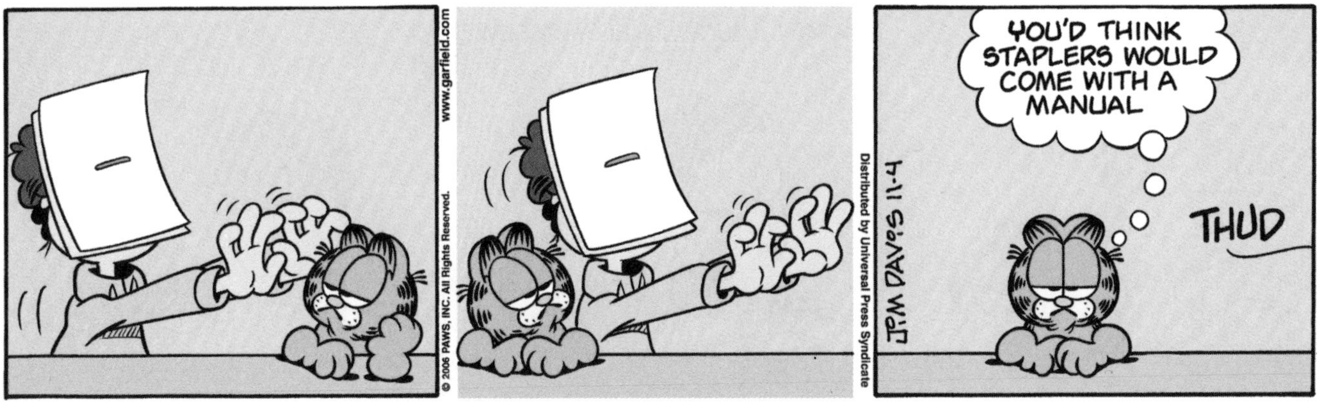

© 2006 PAWS, INC. All Rights Reserved.
www.garfield.com
Distributed by Universal Press Syndicate
JIM DAVIS 11-4
YOU'D THINK STAPLERS WOULD COME WITH A MANUAL
THUD

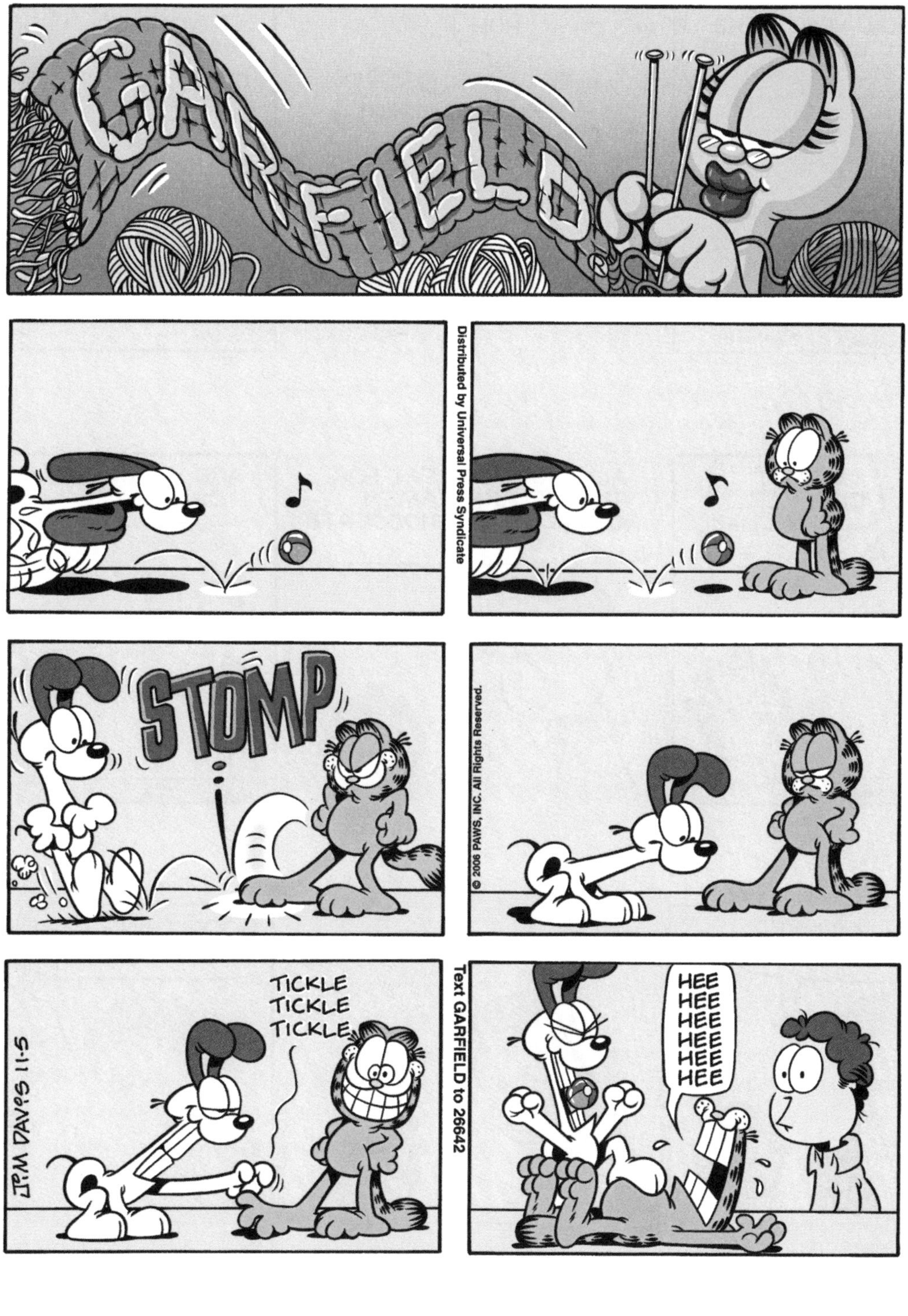
GARFIELD
Distributed by Universal Press Syndicate
STOMP
© 2006 PAWS, INC. All Rights Reserved.
JPM DAVIS 11-5
TICKLE
TICKLE
TICKLE
Text GARFIELD to 26642
HEE
HEE
HEE
HEE
HEE
HEE

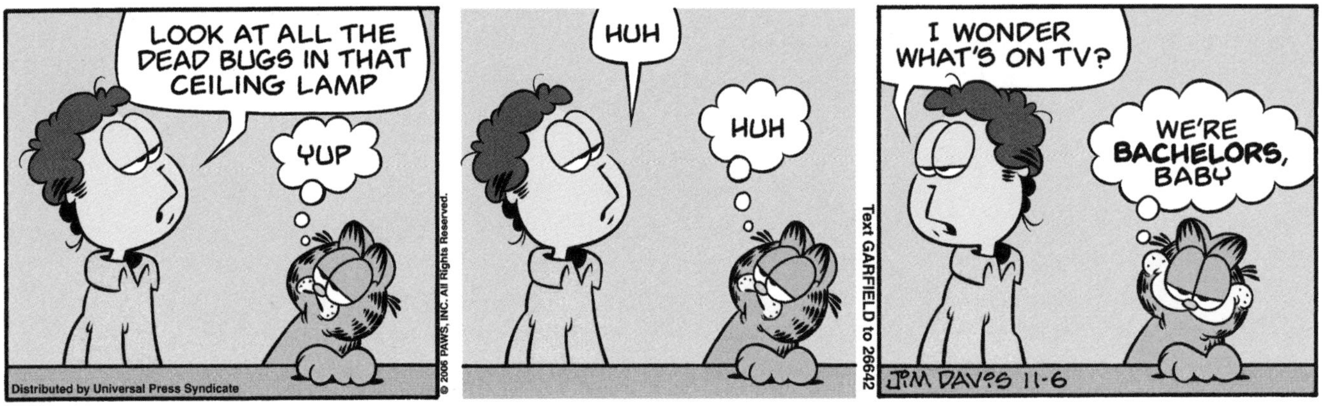
LOOK AT ALL THE DEAD BUGS IN THAT CEILING LAMP
YUP
HUH
HUH
I WONDER WHAT'S ON TV?
WE'RE **BACHELORS,** BABY
Distributed by Universal Press Syndicate
© 2006 PAWS, INC. All Rights Reserved.
Text GARFIELD to 26642
JIM DAVIS 11-6

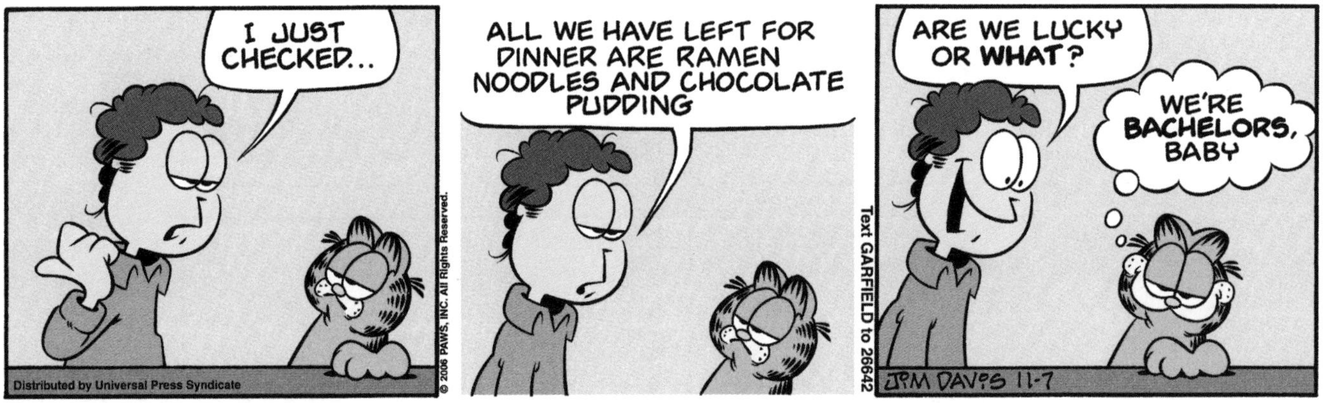
I JUST CHECKED...
ALL WE HAVE LEFT FOR DINNER ARE RAMEN NOODLES AND CHOCOLATE PUDDING
ARE WE LUCKY OR **WHAT**?
WE'RE **BACHELORS,** BABY
Distributed by Universal Press Syndicate
© 2006 PAWS, INC. All Rights Reserved.
Text GARFIELD to 26642
JIM DAVIS 11-7

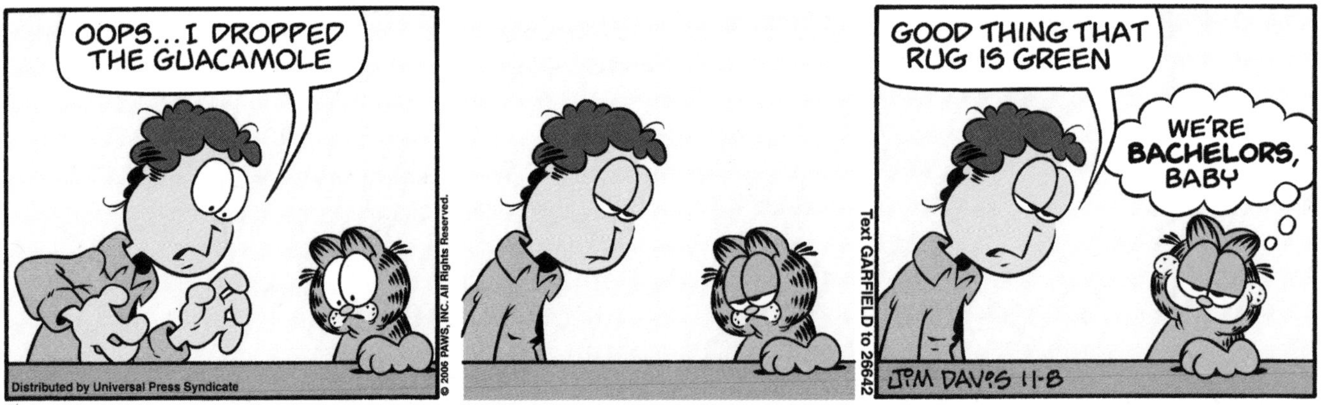
OOPS...I DROPPED THE GUACAMOLE
GOOD THING THAT RUG IS GREEN
WE'RE **BACHELORS,** BABY
Distributed by Universal Press Syndicate
© 2006 PAWS, INC. All Rights Reserved.
Text GARFIELD to 26642
JIM DAVIS 11-8

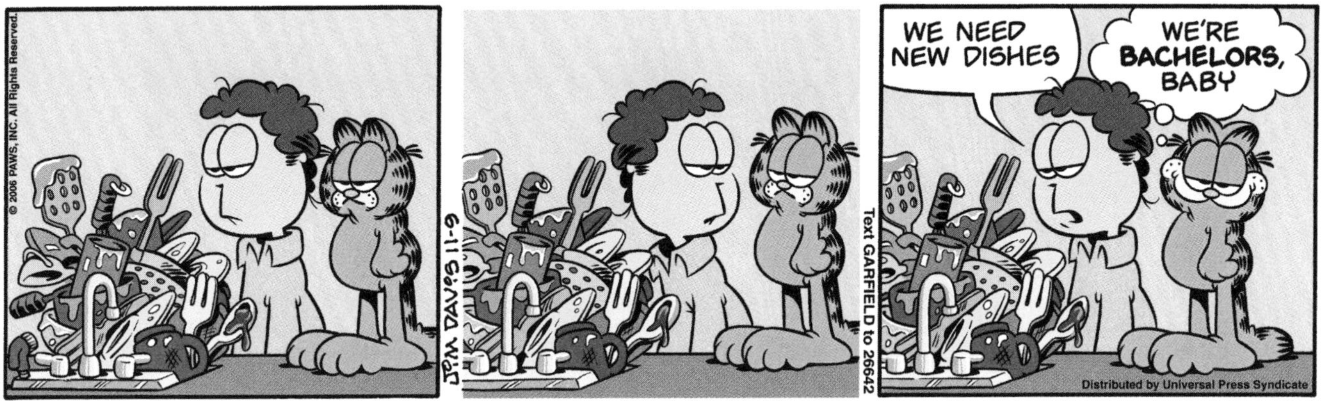
© 2006 PAWS, INC. All Rights Reserved.
JIM DAVIS 11-9
Text GARFIELD to 26642
WE NEED NEW DISHES
WE'RE **BACHELORS,** BABY
Distributed by Universal Press Syndicate

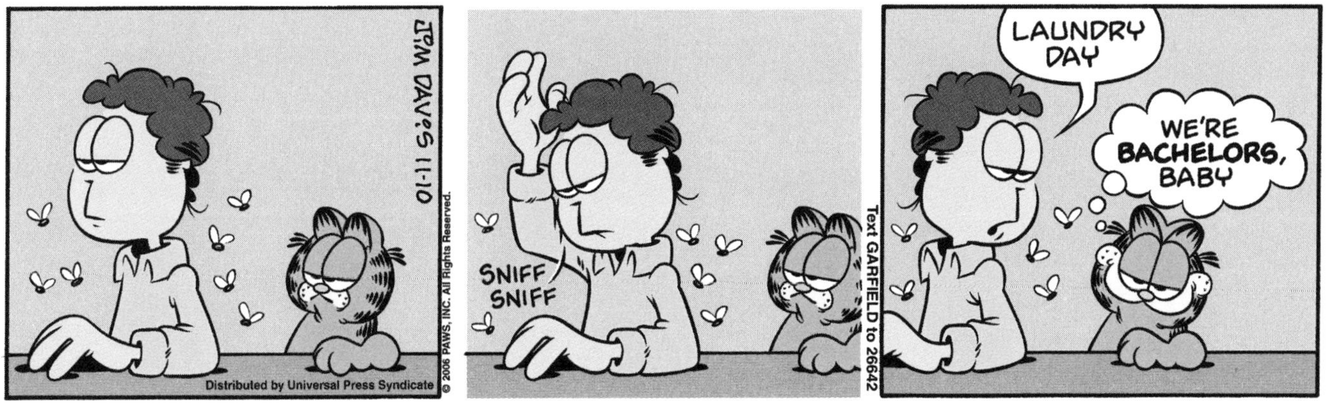
JIM DAVIS 11-10
Distributed by Universal Press Syndicate
© 2006 PAWS, INC. All Rights Reserved.
SNIFF SNIFF
Text GARFIELD to 26642
LAUNDRY DAY
WE'RE **BACHELORS,** BABY

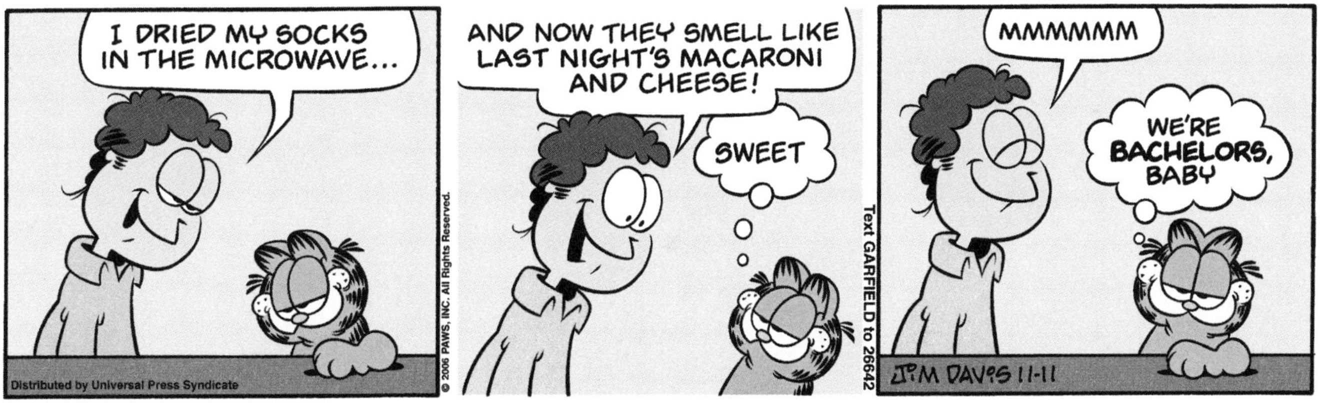
I DRIED MY SOCKS IN THE MICROWAVE...
Distributed by Universal Press Syndicate
© 2006 PAWS, INC. All Rights Reserved.
AND NOW THEY SMELL LIKE LAST NIGHT'S MACARONI AND CHEESE!
SWEET
Text GARFIELD to 26642
MMMMMM
WE'RE **BACHELORS,** BABY
JIM DAVIS 11-11

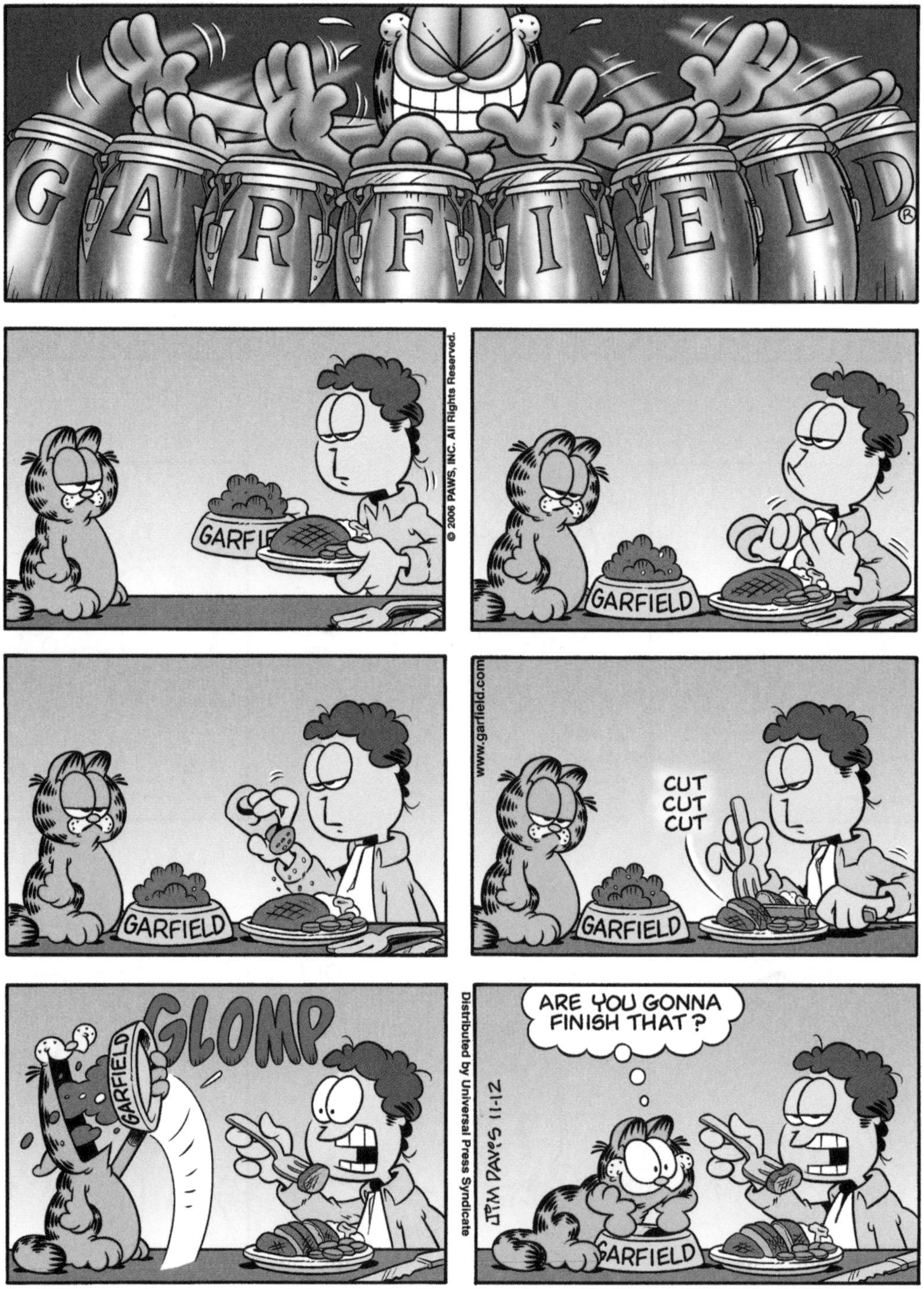
GARFIELD®
© 2006 PAWS, INC. All Rights Reserved.
GARFIELD
www.garfield.com
CUT
CUT
CUT
GLOMP
Distributed by Universal Press Syndicate
JIM DAVIS 11-12
ARE YOU GONNA FINISH THAT?

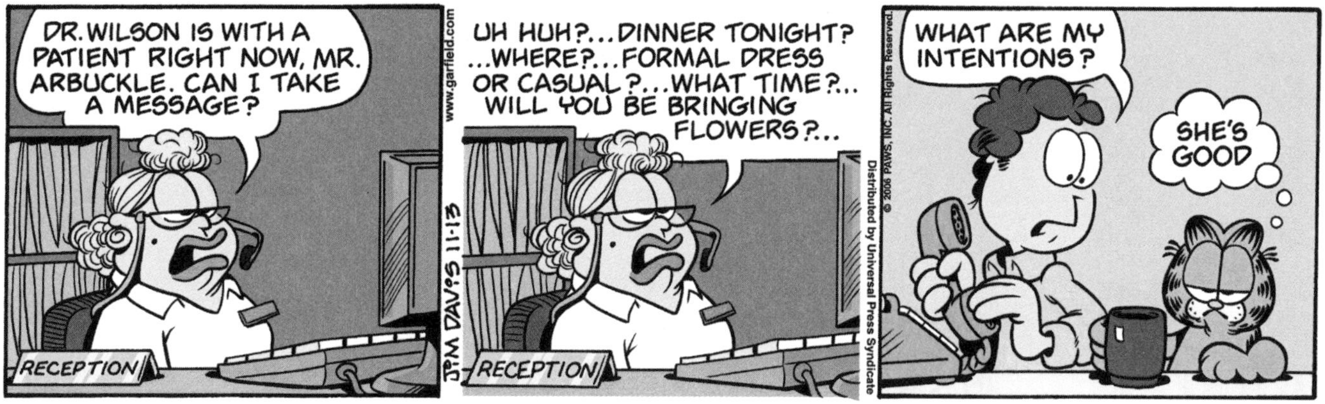
DR. WILSON IS WITH A PATIENT RIGHT NOW, MR. ARBUCKLE. CAN I TAKE A MESSAGE?
RECEPTION
UH HUH?... DINNER TONIGHT? ...WHERE?... FORMAL DRESS OR CASUAL?... WHAT TIME?... WILL YOU BE BRINGING FLOWERS?...
WHAT ARE MY INTENTIONS?
SHE'S GOOD
JPM DAVPS 11-13
www.garfield.com
Distributed by Universal Press Syndicate
© 2006 PAWS, INC. All Rights Reserved.

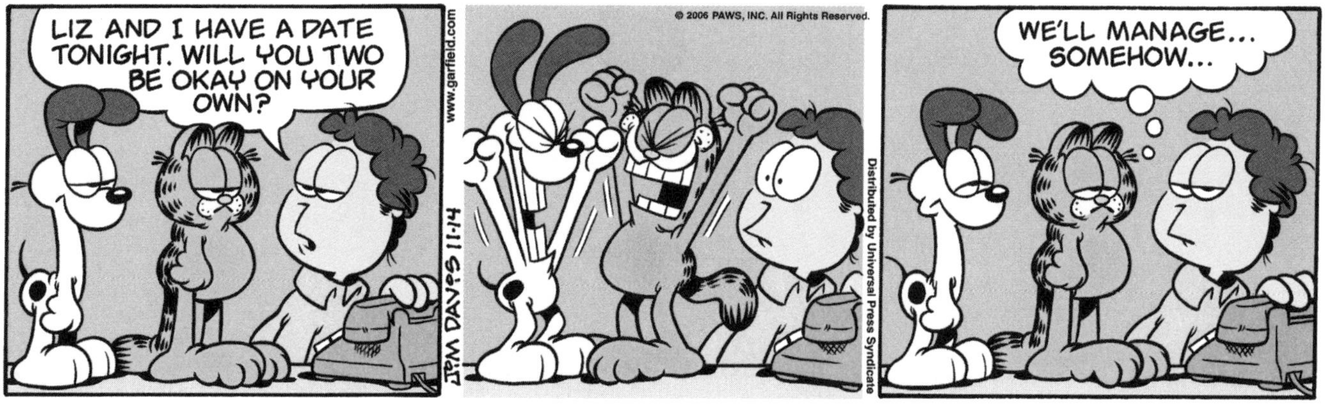
LIZ AND I HAVE A DATE TONIGHT. WILL YOU TWO BE OKAY ON YOUR OWN?
WE'LL MANAGE... SOMEHOW...
JPM DAVPS 11-14
www.garfield.com
Distributed by Universal Press Syndicate
© 2006 PAWS, INC. All Rights Reserved.

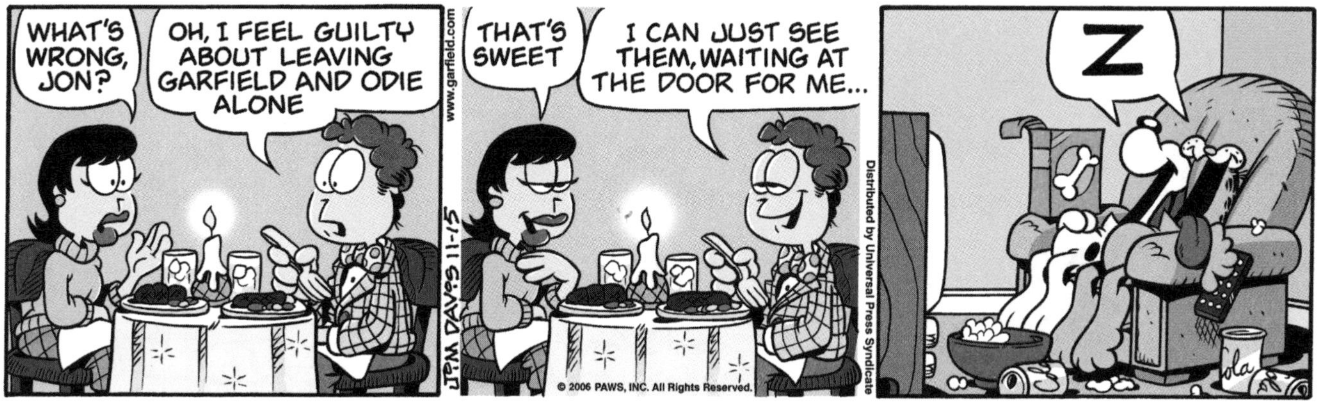
WHAT'S WRONG, JON?
OH, I FEEL GUILTY ABOUT LEAVING GARFIELD AND ODIE ALONE
THAT'S SWEET
I CAN JUST SEE THEM, WAITING AT THE DOOR FOR ME...
Z
JPM DAVPS 11-15
www.garfield.com
Distributed by Universal Press Syndicate
© 2006 PAWS, INC. All Rights Reserved.

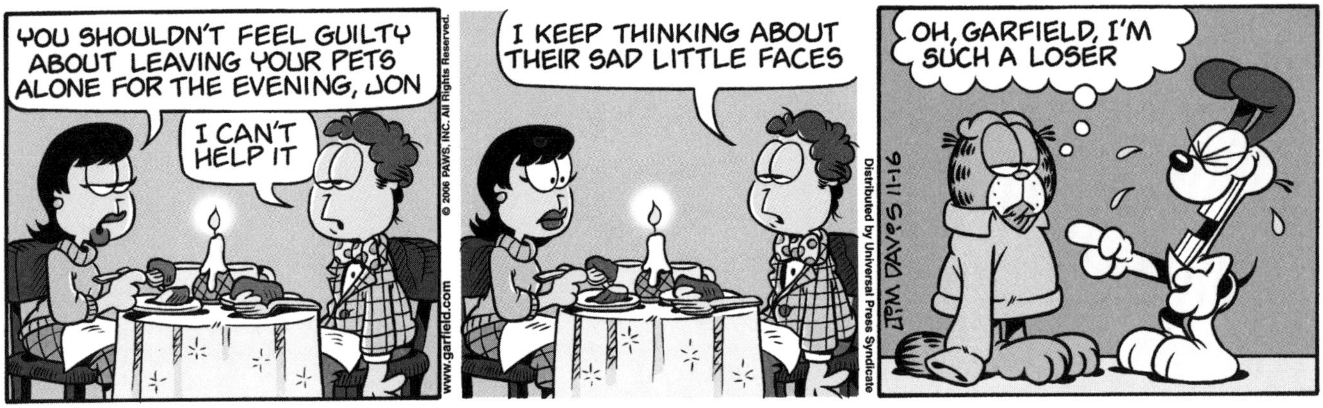
YOU SHOULDN'T FEEL GUILTY ABOUT LEAVING YOUR PETS ALONE FOR THE EVENING, JON
I CAN'T HELP IT
© 2006 PAWS, INC. All Rights Reserved.
www.garfield.com
I KEEP THINKING ABOUT THEIR SAD LITTLE FACES
Distributed by Universal Press Syndicate
OH, GARFIELD, I'M SUCH A LOSER
JIM DAVIS 11-16

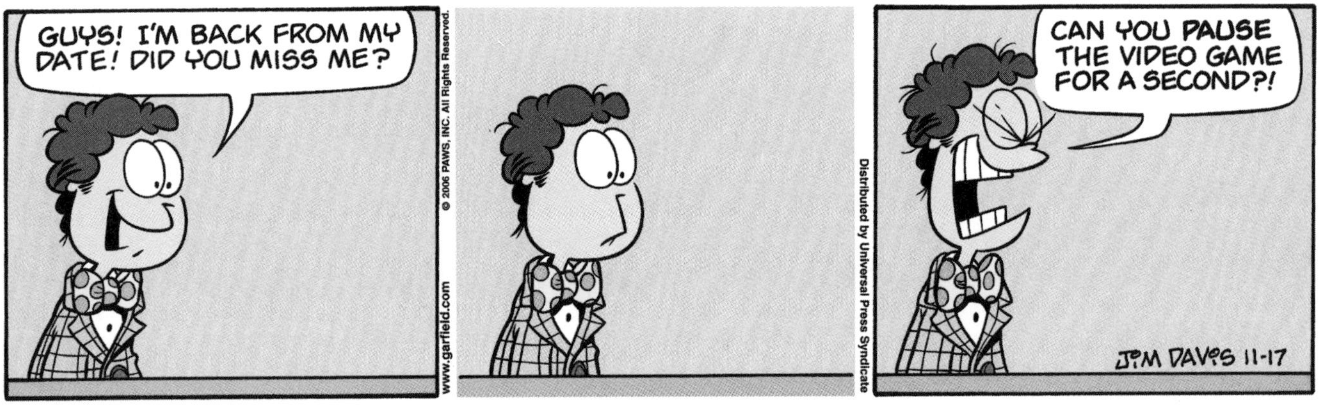
GUYS! I'M BACK FROM MY DATE! DID YOU MISS ME?
© 2006 PAWS, INC. All Rights Reserved.
www.garfield.com
Distributed by Universal Press Syndicate
CAN YOU PAUSE THE VIDEO GAME FOR A SECOND?!
JIM DAVIS 11-17

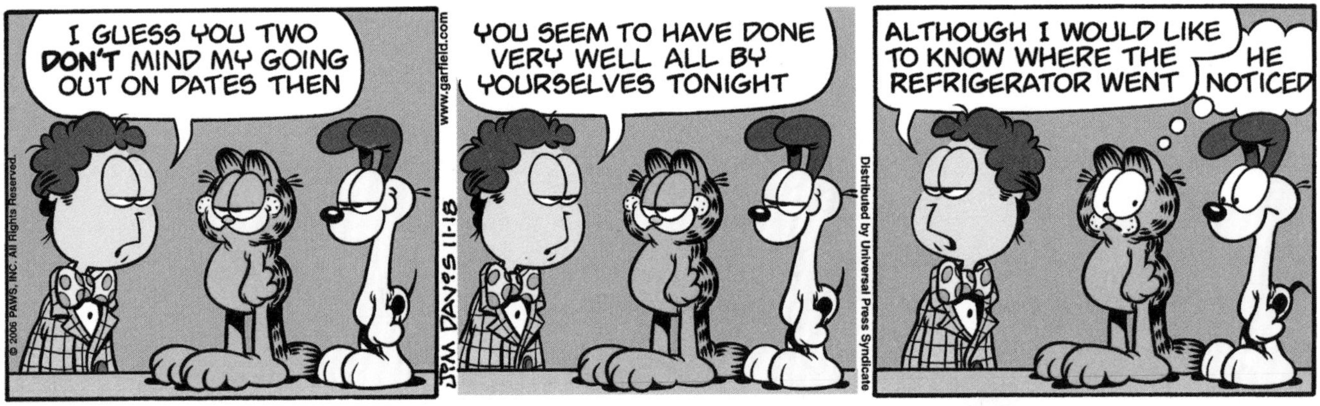
I GUESS YOU TWO DON'T MIND MY GOING OUT ON DATES THEN
© 2006 PAWS, INC. All Rights Reserved.
www.garfield.com
JIM DAVIS 11-18
YOU SEEM TO HAVE DONE VERY WELL ALL BY YOURSELVES TONIGHT
Distributed by Universal Press Syndicate
ALTHOUGH I WOULD LIKE TO KNOW WHERE THE REFRIGERATOR WENT
HE NOTICED

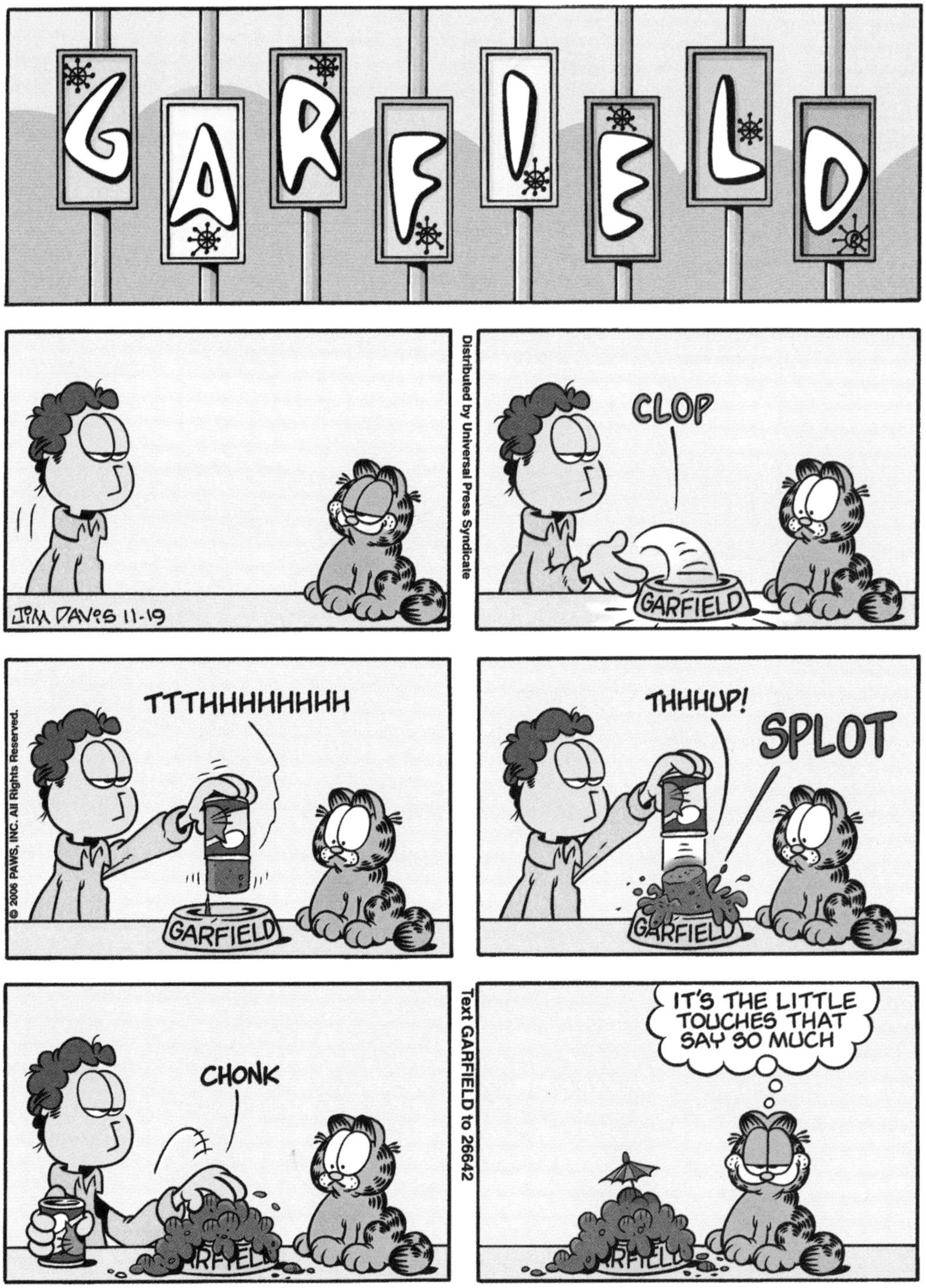
GARFIELD
JIM DAVIS 11-19
Distributed by Universal Press Syndicate
CLOP
GARFIELD
© 2006 PAWS, INC. All Rights Reserved.
TTTHHHHHHHH
GARFIELD
THHHUP!
SPLOT
GARFIELD
Text GARFIELD to 26642
CHONK
IT'S THE LITTLE TOUCHES THAT SAY SO MUCH

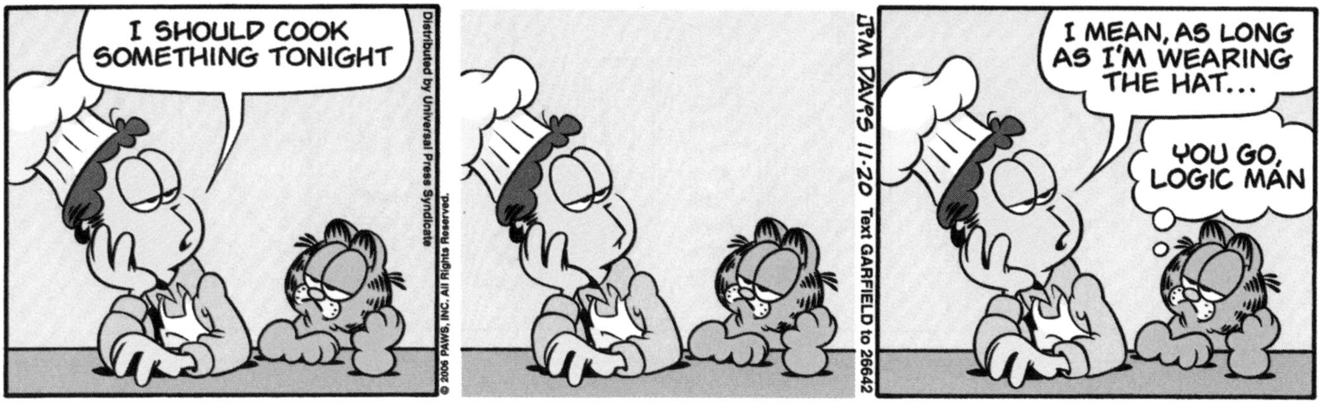
I SHOULD COOK SOMETHING TONIGHT
Distributed by Universal Press Syndicate
© 2006 PAWS, INC. All Rights Reserved.
JIM DAVIS 11-20 Text GARFIELD to 26642
I MEAN, AS LONG AS I'M WEARING THE HAT...
YOU GO, LOGIC MAN

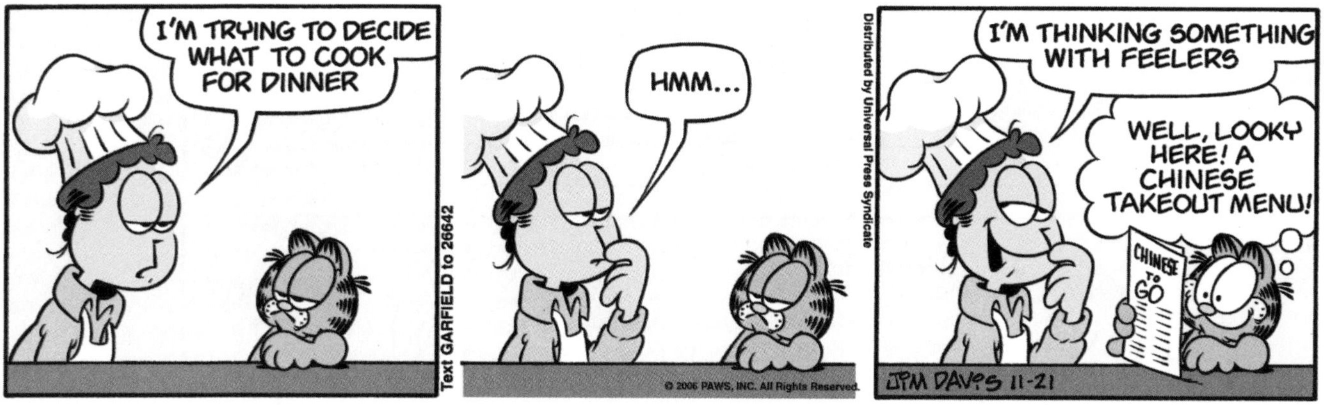
I'M TRYING TO DECIDE WHAT TO COOK FOR DINNER
Text GARFIELD to 26642
HMM...
© 2006 PAWS, INC. All Rights Reserved.
Distributed by Universal Press Syndicate
I'M THINKING SOMETHING WITH FEELERS
WELL, LOOKY HERE! A CHINESE TAKEOUT MENU!
CHINESE TO GO
JIM DAVIS 11-21

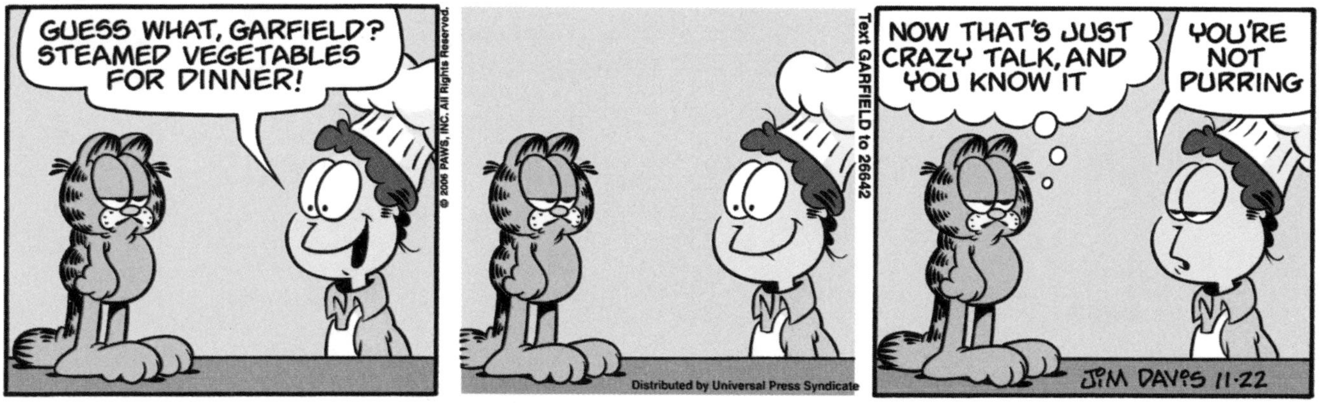
GUESS WHAT, GARFIELD? STEAMED VEGETABLES FOR DINNER!
© 2006 PAWS, INC. All Rights Reserved.
Distributed by Universal Press Syndicate
Text GARFIELD to 26642
NOW THAT'S JUST CRAZY TALK, AND YOU KNOW IT
YOU'RE NOT PURRING
JIM DAVIS 11-22

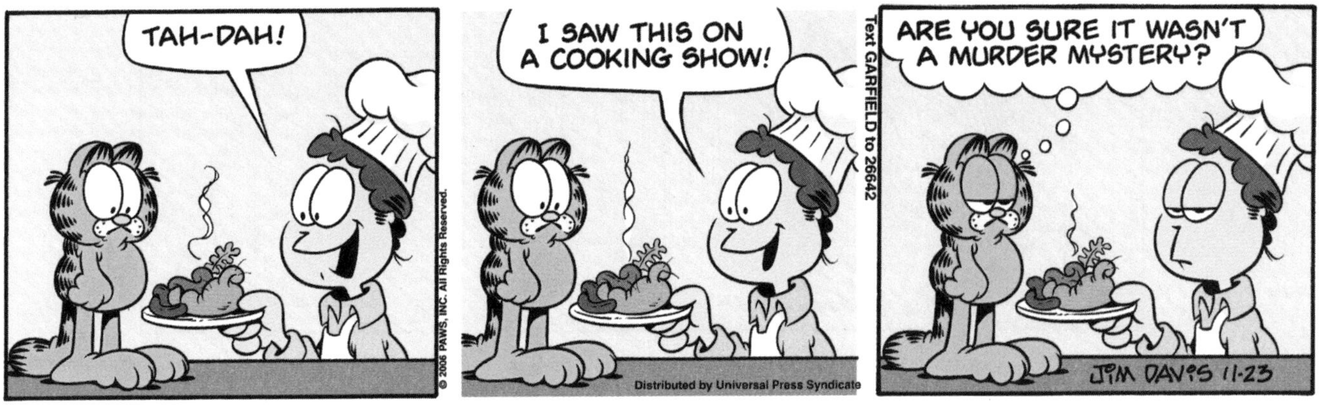
TAH-DAH!
© 2006 PAWS, INC. All Rights Reserved.
I SAW THIS ON A COOKING SHOW!
Distributed by Universal Press Syndicate
Text GARFIELD to 26642
ARE YOU SURE IT WASN'T A MURDER MYSTERY?
JIM DAVIS 11-23

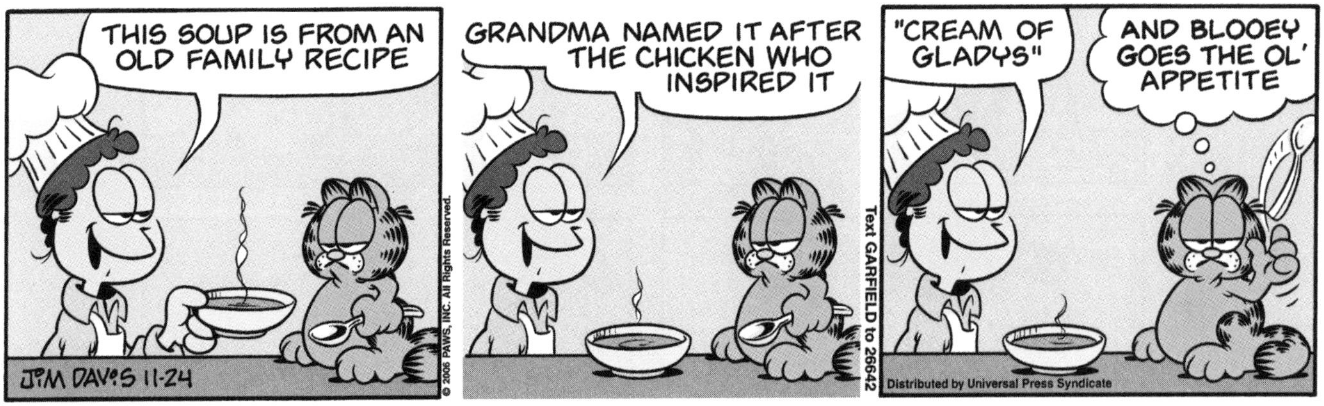
THIS SOUP IS FROM AN OLD FAMILY RECIPE
JIM DAVIS 11-24
© 2006 PAWS, INC. All Rights Reserved.
GRANDMA NAMED IT AFTER THE CHICKEN WHO INSPIRED IT
Text GARFIELD to 26642
"CREAM OF GLADYS"
AND BLOOEY GOES THE OL' APPETITE
Distributed by Universal Press Syndicate

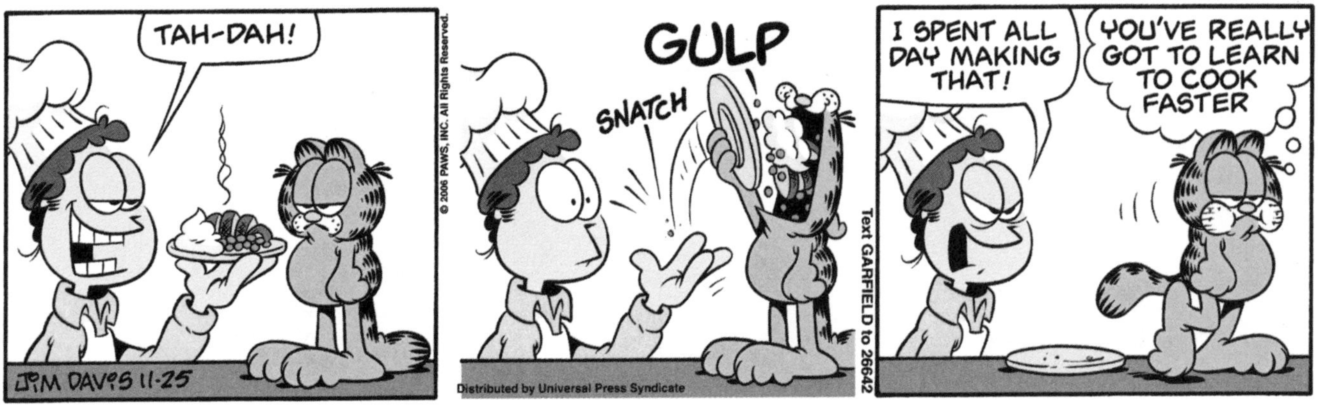
TAH-DAH!
JIM DAVIS 11-25
© 2006 PAWS, INC. All Rights Reserved.
GULP
SNATCH
Distributed by Universal Press Syndicate
Text GARFIELD to 26642
I SPENT ALL DAY MAKING THAT!
YOU'VE REALLY GOT TO LEARN TO COOK FASTER

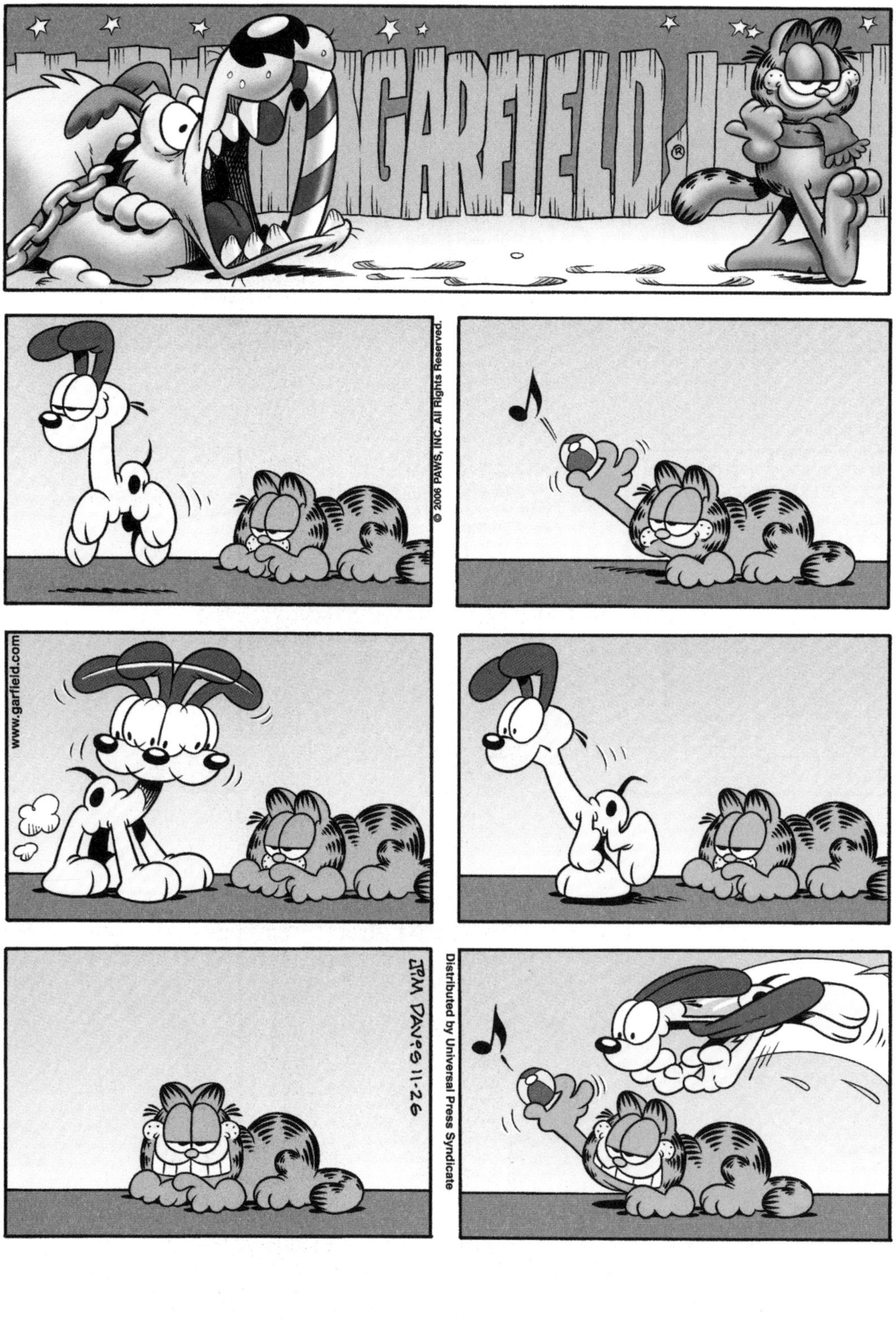
GARFIELD®
© 2006 PAWS, INC. All Rights Reserved.
www.garfield.com
JIM DAVIS 11-26
Distributed by Universal Press Syndicate

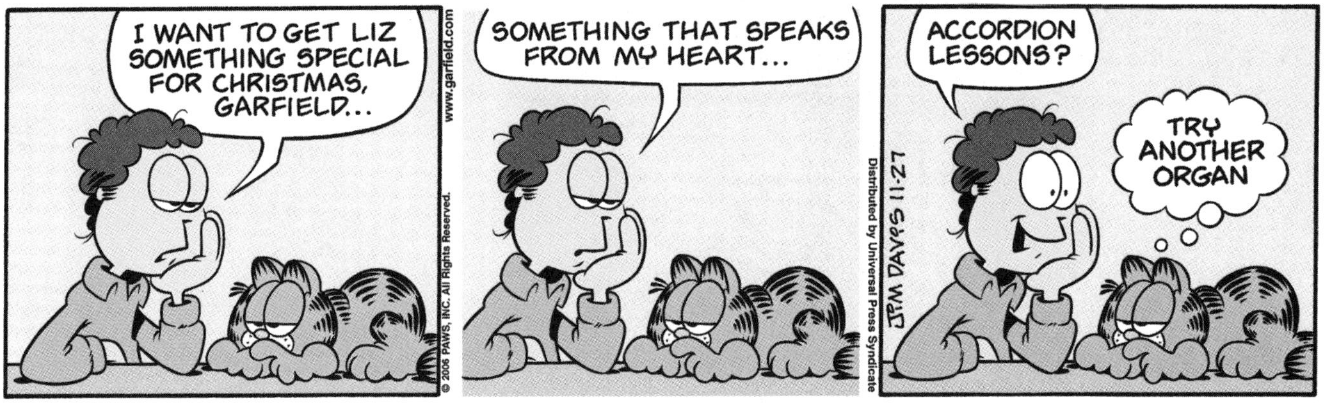
I WANT TO GET LIZ SOMETHING SPECIAL FOR CHRISTMAS, GARFIELD...
SOMETHING THAT SPEAKS FROM MY HEART...
ACCORDION LESSONS?
TRY ANOTHER ORGAN
© 2006 PAWS, INC. All Rights Reserved. www.garfield.com
Distributed by Universal Press Syndicate

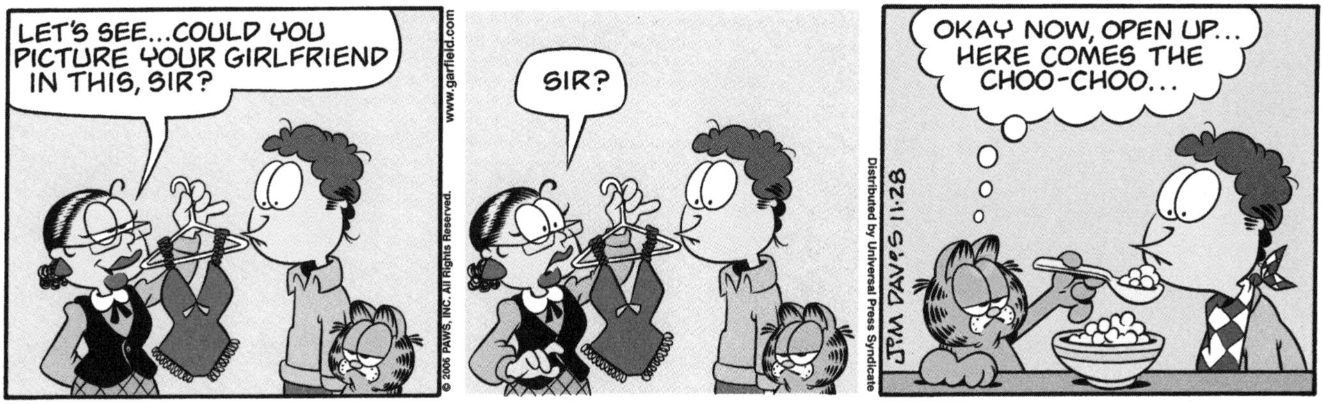
LET'S SEE...COULD YOU PICTURE YOUR GIRLFRIEND IN THIS, SIR?
SIR?
OKAY NOW, OPEN UP... HERE COMES THE CHOO-CHOO...
© 2006 PAWS, INC. All Rights Reserved. www.garfield.com
Distributed by Universal Press Syndicate

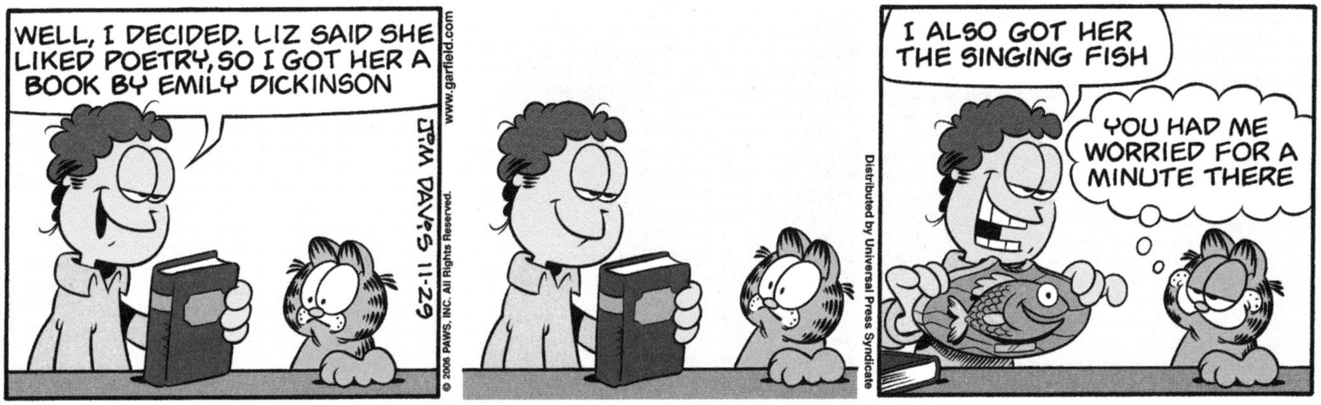
WELL, I DECIDED. LIZ SAID SHE LIKED POETRY, SO I GOT HER A BOOK BY EMILY DICKINSON
I ALSO GOT HER THE SINGING FISH
YOU HAD ME WORRIED FOR A MINUTE THERE
© 2006 PAWS, INC. All Rights Reserved. www.garfield.com
Distributed by Universal Press Syndicate

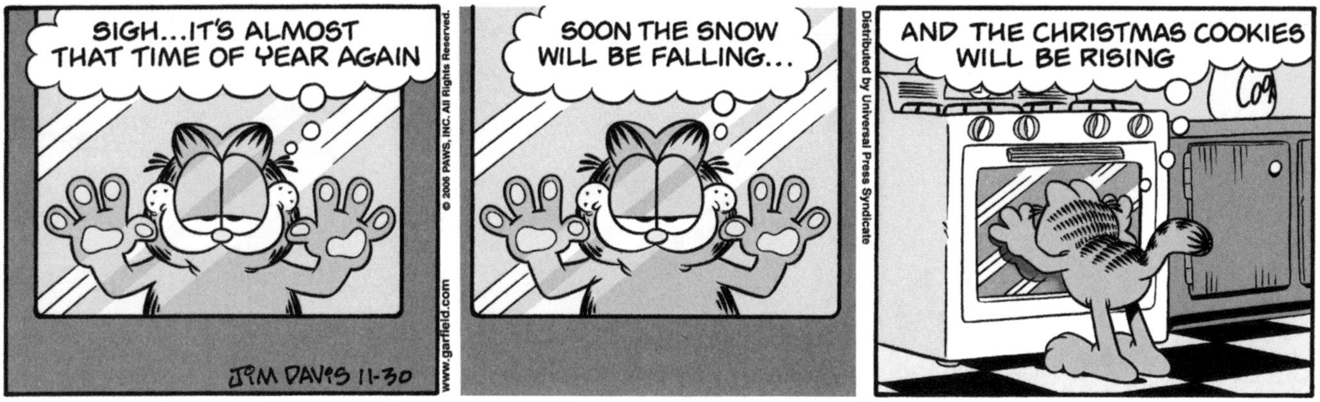
SIGH...IT'S ALMOST THAT TIME OF YEAR AGAIN
JIM DAVIS 11-30
© 2006 PAWS, INC. All Rights Reserved.
www.garfield.com
SOON THE SNOW WILL BE FALLING...
Distributed by Universal Press Syndicate
AND THE CHRISTMAS COOKIES WILL BE RISING

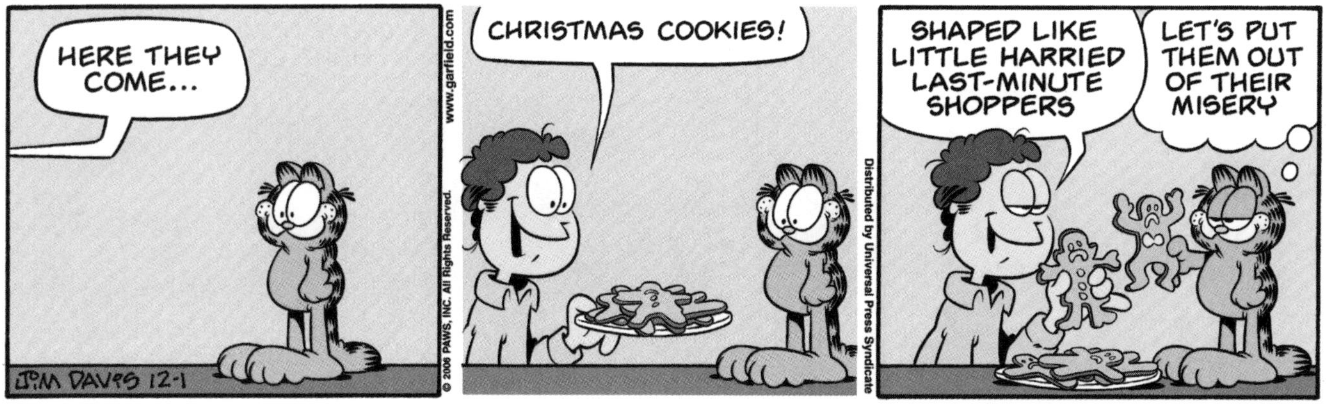
HERE THEY COME...
JIM DAVIS 12-1
© 2006 PAWS, INC. All Rights Reserved.
www.garfield.com
CHRISTMAS COOKIES!
Distributed by Universal Press Syndicate
SHAPED LIKE LITTLE HARRIED LAST-MINUTE SHOPPERS
LET'S PUT THEM OUT OF THEIR MISERY

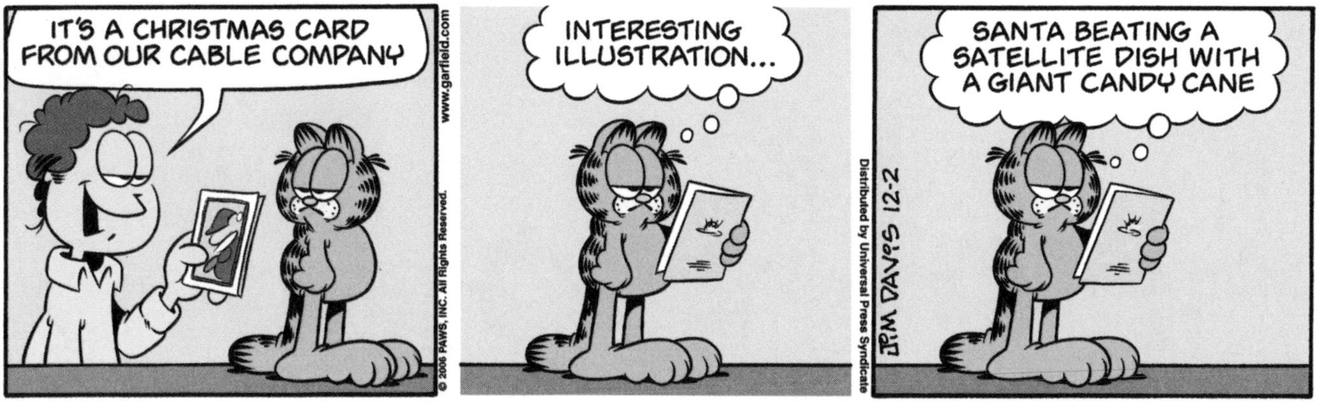
IT'S A CHRISTMAS CARD FROM OUR CABLE COMPANY
© 2006 PAWS, INC. All Rights Reserved.
www.garfield.com
INTERESTING ILLUSTRATION...
JIM DAVIS 12-2
Distributed by Universal Press Syndicate
SANTA BEATING A SATELLITE DISH WITH A GIANT CANDY CANE

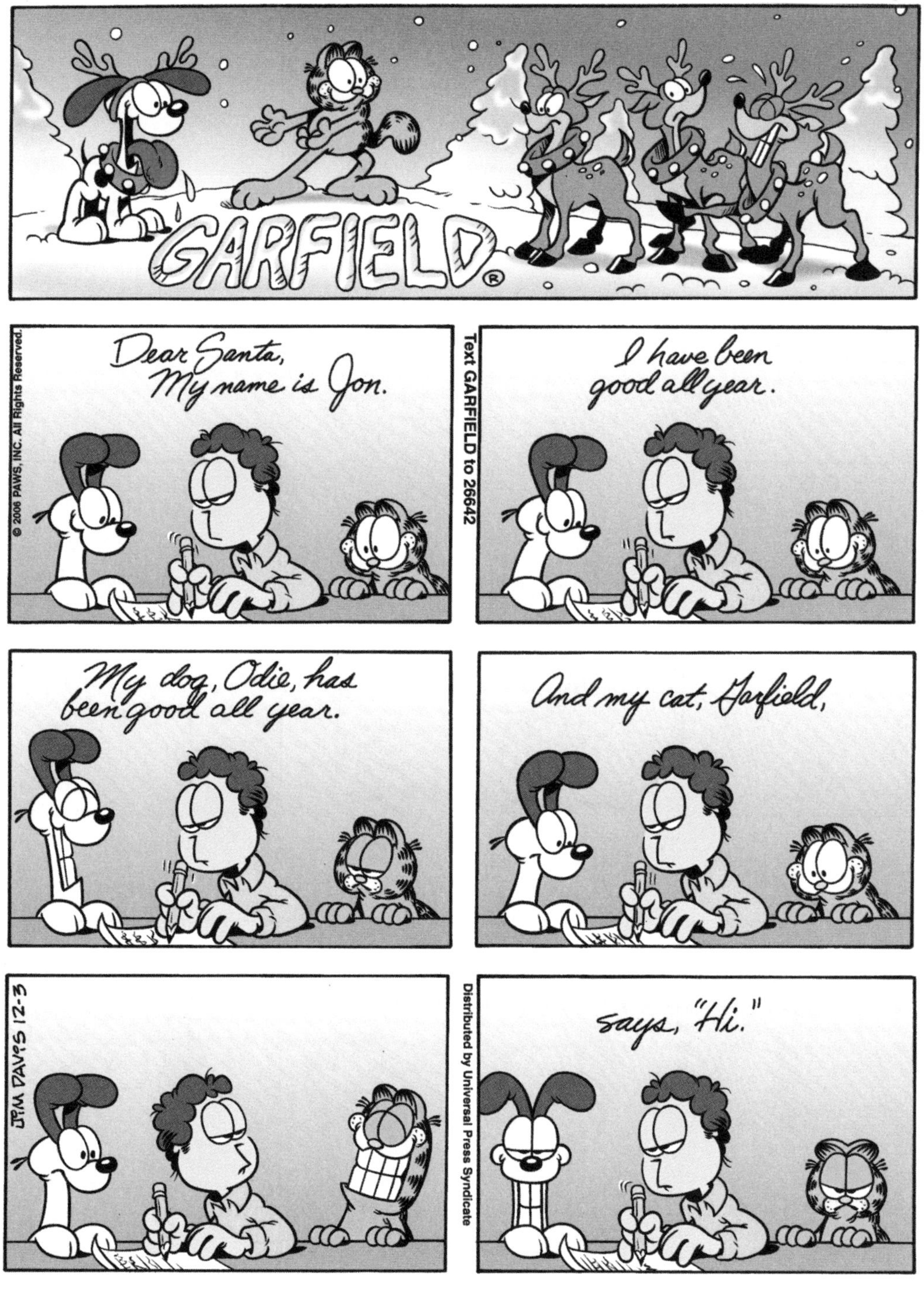
GARFIELD®
© 2006 PAWS, INC. All Rights Reserved.
Dear Santa,
My name is Jon.
Text GARFIELD to 26642
I have been
good all year.
My dog, Odie, has
been good all year.
And my cat, Garfield,
JPM DAVIS 12-3
Distributed by Universal Press Syndicate
says, "Hi."

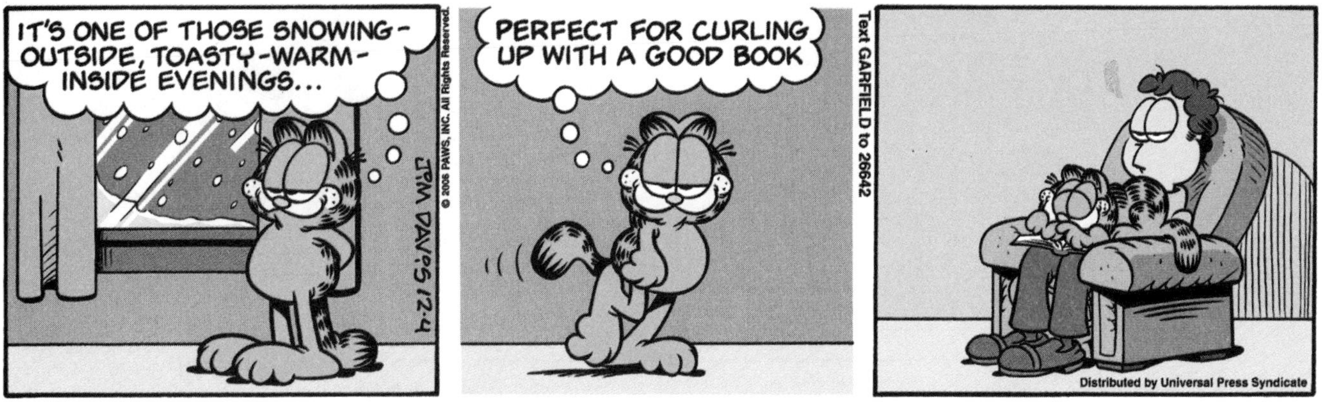
IT'S ONE OF THOSE SNOWING-OUTSIDE, TOASTY-WARM-INSIDE EVENINGS...
PERFECT FOR CURLING UP WITH A GOOD BOOK
© 2006 PAWS, INC. All Rights Reserved.
Text GARFIELD to 26642
Distributed by Universal Press Syndicate

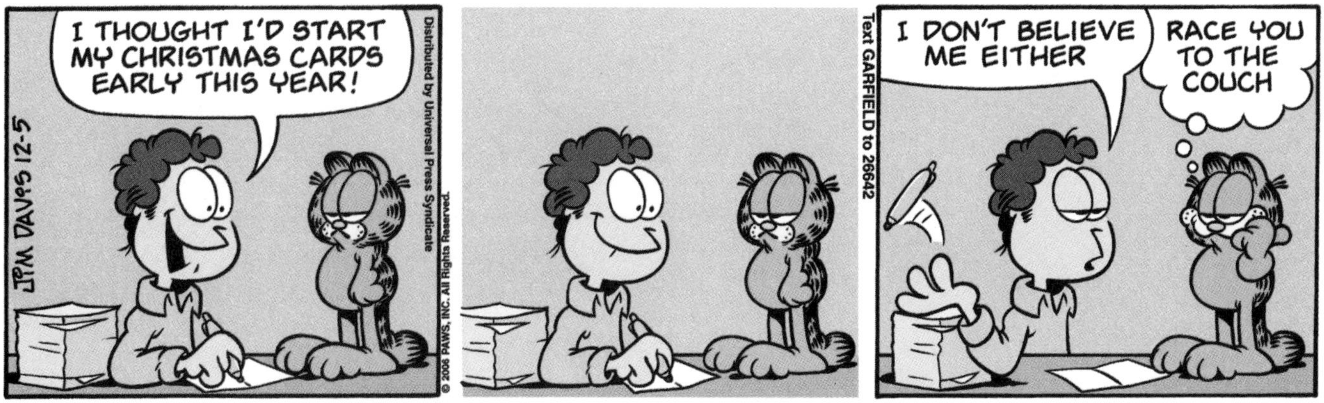
I THOUGHT I'D START MY CHRISTMAS CARDS EARLY THIS YEAR!
I DON'T BELIEVE ME EITHER
RACE YOU TO THE COUCH
Distributed by Universal Press Syndicate
© 2006 PAWS, INC. All Rights Reserved.
Text GARFIELD to 26642

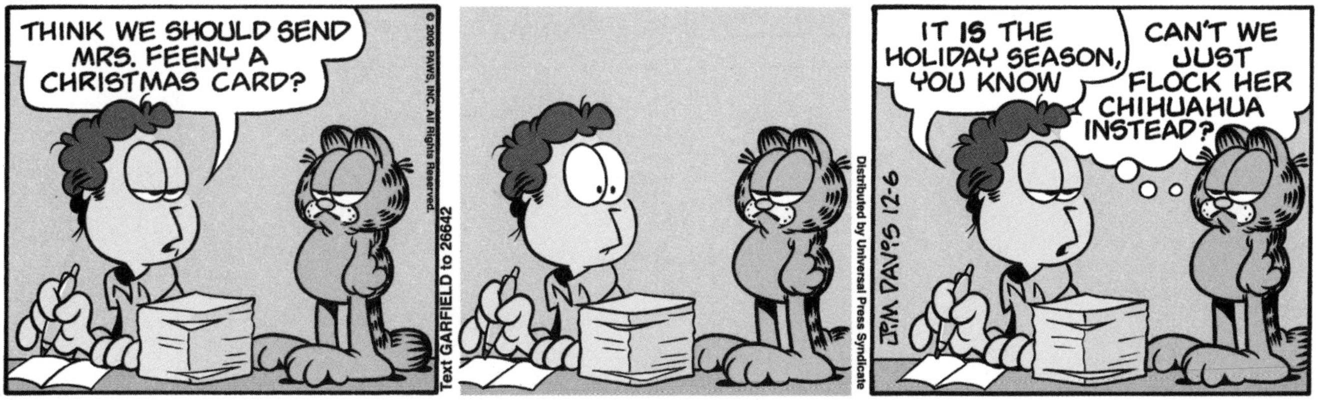
THINK WE SHOULD SEND MRS. FEENY A CHRISTMAS CARD?
IT IS THE HOLIDAY SEASON, YOU KNOW
CAN'T WE JUST FLOCK HER CHIHUAHUA INSTEAD?
© 2006 PAWS, INC. All Rights Reserved.
Text GARFIELD to 26642
Distributed by Universal Press Syndicate

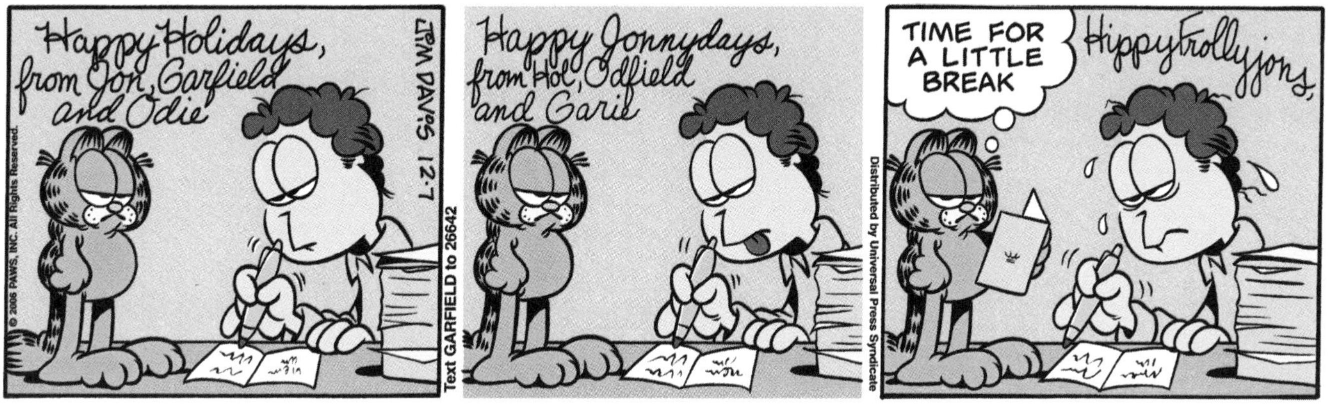
Happy Holidays, from Jon, Garfield and Odie
JIM DAVIS 12-7
© 2006 PAWS, INC. All Rights Reserved.
Happy Jonnydays, from Hol, Odfield and Garie
Text GARFIELD to 26642
TIME FOR A LITTLE BREAK
Hippy Frollyjons,
Distributed by Universal Press Syndicate

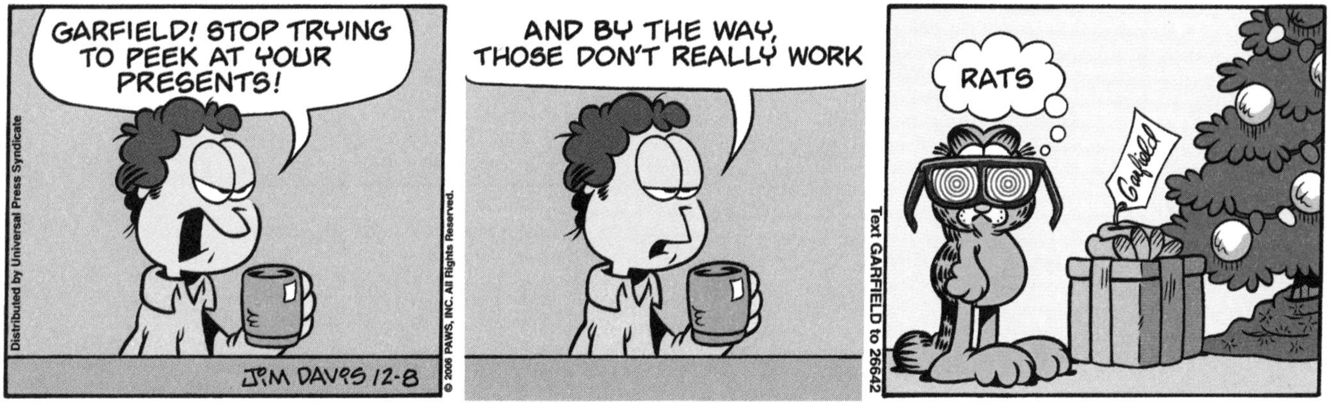
GARFIELD! STOP TRYING TO PEEK AT YOUR PRESENTS!
JIM DAVIS 12-8
Distributed by Universal Press Syndicate
© 2006 PAWS, INC. All Rights Reserved.
AND BY THE WAY, THOSE DON'T REALLY WORK
Text GARFIELD to 26642
RATS
Garfield

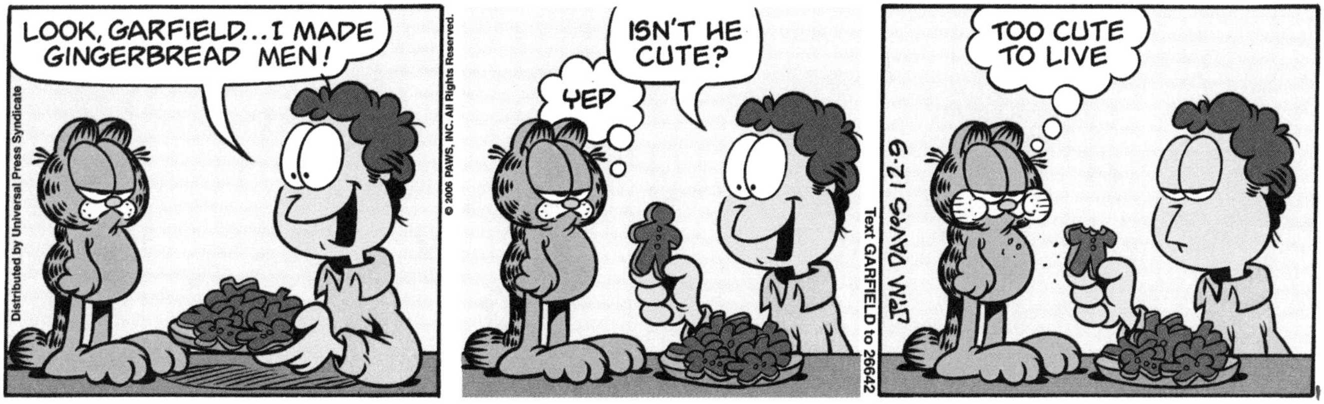
LOOK, GARFIELD...I MADE GINGERBREAD MEN!
Distributed by Universal Press Syndicate
© 2006 PAWS, INC. All Rights Reserved.
ISN'T HE CUTE?
YEP
JIM DAVIS 12-9
Text GARFIELD to 26642
TOO CUTE TO LIVE

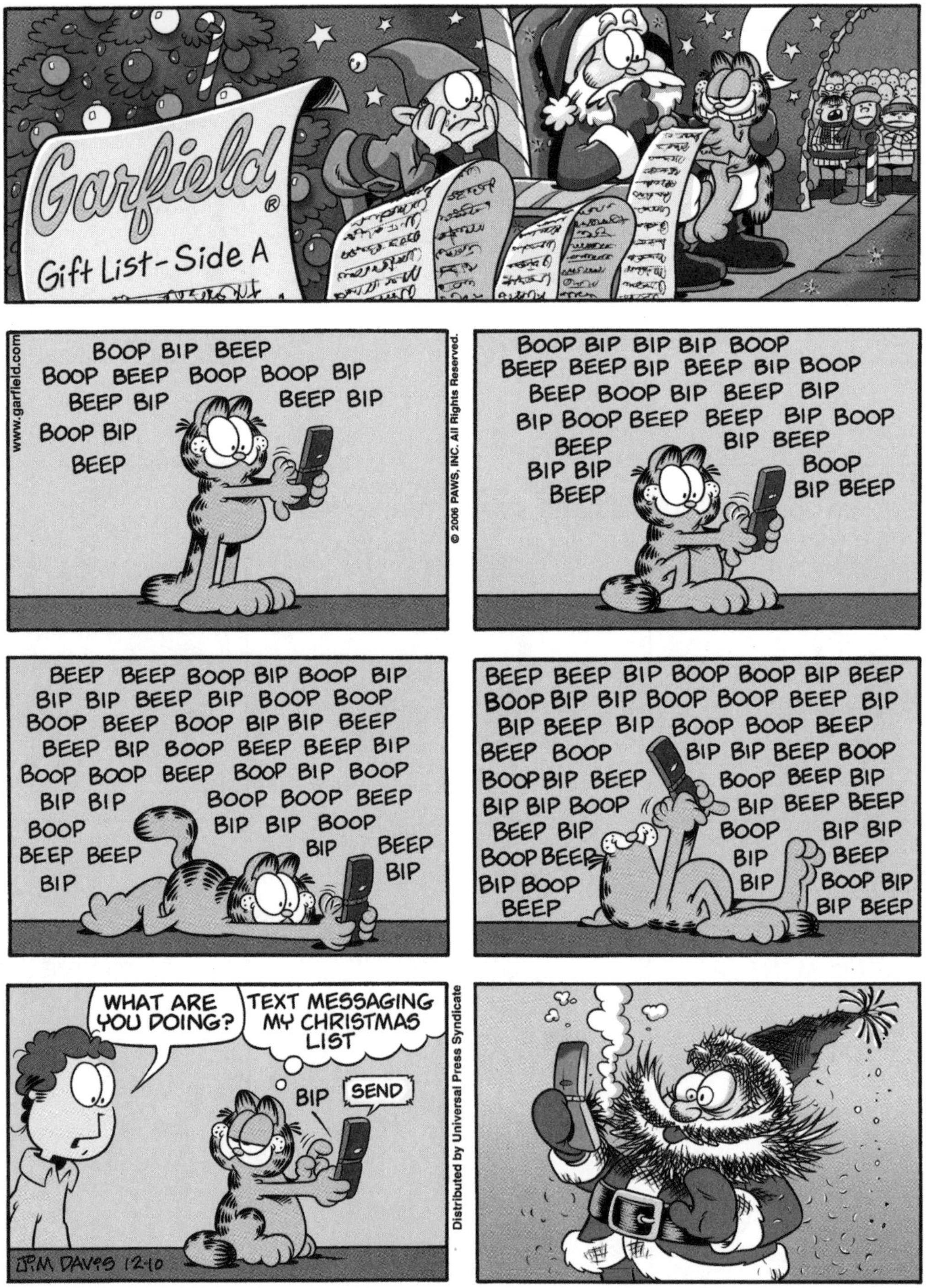
Garfield®
Gift List-Side A
www.garfield.com
BOOP BIP BEEP
BOOP BEEP BOOP BOOP BIP
BEEP BIP BEEP BIP
BOOP BIP
BEEP
© 2006 PAWS, INC. All Rights Reserved.
BOOP BIP BIP BIP BOOP
BEEP BEEP BIP BEEP BIP BOOP
BEEP BOOP BIP BEEP BIP
BIP BOOP BEEP BEEP BIP BOOP
BEEP BIP BEEP
BIP BIP BOOP
BEEP BIP BEEP
BEEP BEEP BOOP BIP BOOP BIP
BIP BIP BEEP BIP BOOP BOOP
BOOP BEEP BOOP BIP BIP BEEP
BEEP BIP BOOP BEEP BEEP BIP
BOOP BOOP BEEP BOOP BIP BOOP
BIP BIP BOOP BOOP BEEP
BOOP BIP BIP BOOP
BEEP BEEP BIP BEEP
BIP BIP
BEEP BEEP BIP BOOP BOOP BIP BEEP
BOOP BIP BIP BOOP BOOP BEEP BIP
BIP BEEP BIP BOOP BOOP BEEP
BEEP BOOP BIP BIP BEEP BOOP
BOOP BIP BEEP BOOP BEEP BIP
BIP BIP BOOP BIP BEEP BEEP
BEEP BIP BOOP BIP BIP
BOOP BEEP BIP BEEP
BIP BOOP BIP BOOP BIP
BEEP BIP BEEP
WHAT ARE YOU DOING?
TEXT MESSAGING MY CHRISTMAS LIST
BIP
SEND
JIM DAVIS 12-10
Distributed by Universal Press Syndicate

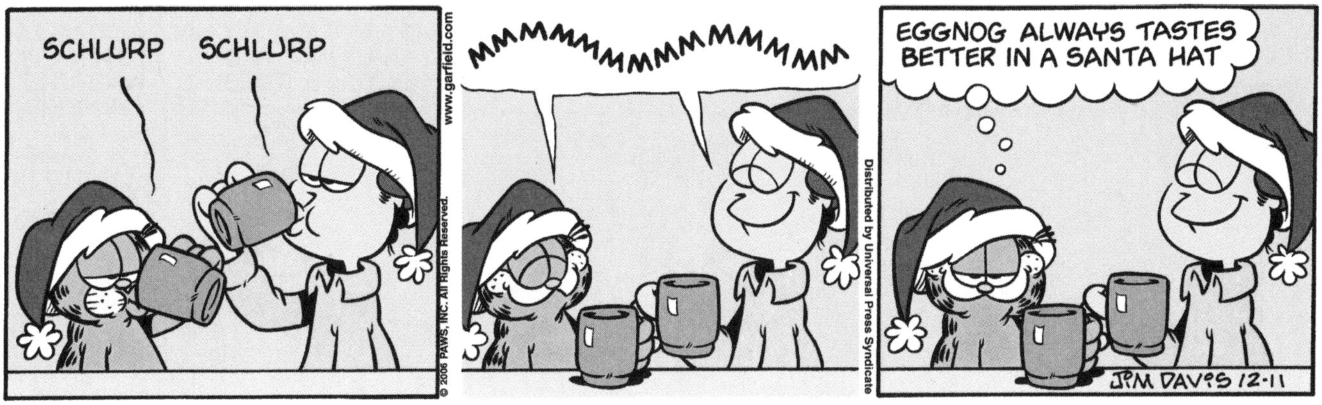
SCHLURP SCHLURP
MMMMMMMMMMMMMMMMMM
EGGNOG ALWAYS TASTES BETTER IN A SANTA HAT
JIM DAVIS 12-11
© 2006 PAWS, INC. All Rights Reserved. www.garfield.com
Distributed by Universal Press Syndicate

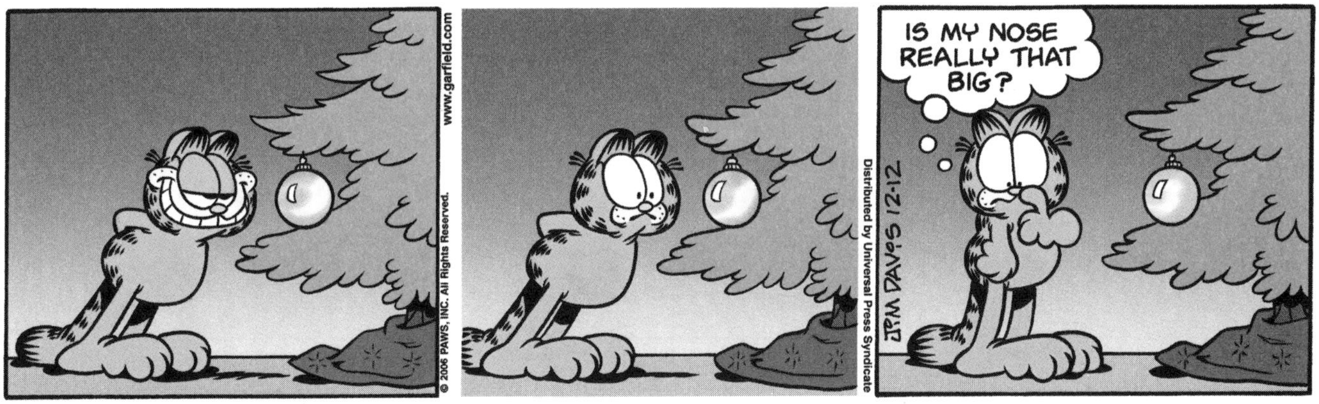
IS MY NOSE REALLY THAT BIG?
JIM DAVIS 12-12
© 2006 PAWS, INC. All Rights Reserved. www.garfield.com
Distributed by Universal Press Syndicate

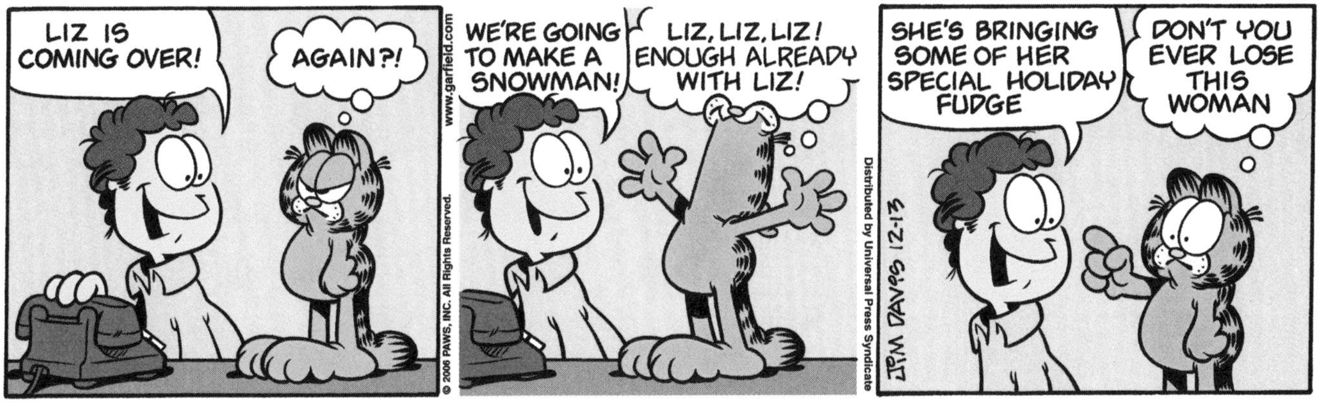
LIZ IS COMING OVER!
AGAIN?!
WE'RE GOING TO MAKE A SNOWMAN!
LIZ, LIZ, LIZ! ENOUGH ALREADY WITH LIZ!
SHE'S BRINGING SOME OF HER SPECIAL HOLIDAY FUDGE
DON'T YOU EVER LOSE THIS WOMAN
JIM DAVIS 12-13
© 2006 PAWS, INC. All Rights Reserved. www.garfield.com
Distributed by Universal Press Syndicate

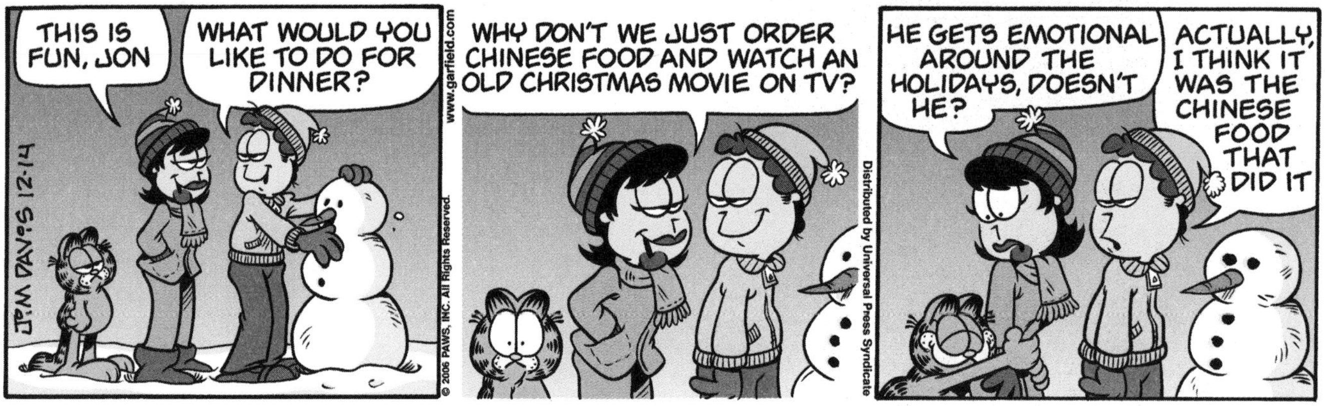
THIS IS FUN, JON
WHAT WOULD YOU LIKE TO DO FOR DINNER?
JIM DAVIS 12-14
www.garfield.com
© 2006 PAWS, INC. All Rights Reserved.
WHY DON'T WE JUST ORDER CHINESE FOOD AND WATCH AN OLD CHRISTMAS MOVIE ON TV?
Distributed by Universal Press Syndicate
HE GETS EMOTIONAL AROUND THE HOLIDAYS, DOESN'T HE?
ACTUALLY, I THINK IT WAS THE CHINESE FOOD THAT DID IT

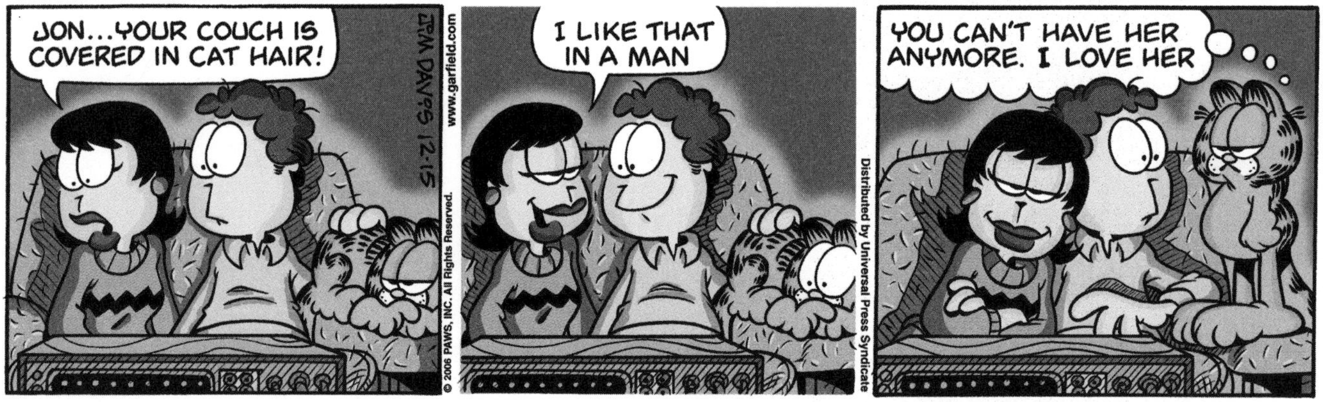
JON...YOUR COUCH IS COVERED IN CAT HAIR!
JIM DAVIS 12-15
www.garfield.com
© 2006 PAWS, INC. All Rights Reserved.
I LIKE THAT IN A MAN
Distributed by Universal Press Syndicate
YOU CAN'T HAVE HER ANYMORE. I LOVE HER

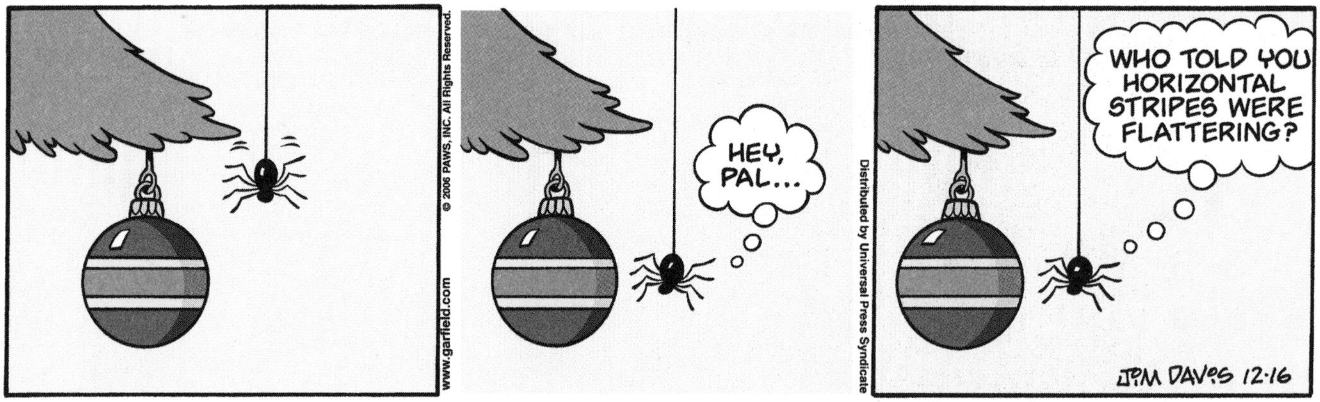
© 2006 PAWS, INC. All Rights Reserved.
www.garfield.com
HEY, PAL...
Distributed by Universal Press Syndicate
WHO TOLD YOU HORIZONTAL STRIPES WERE FLATTERING?
JIM DAVIS 12-16

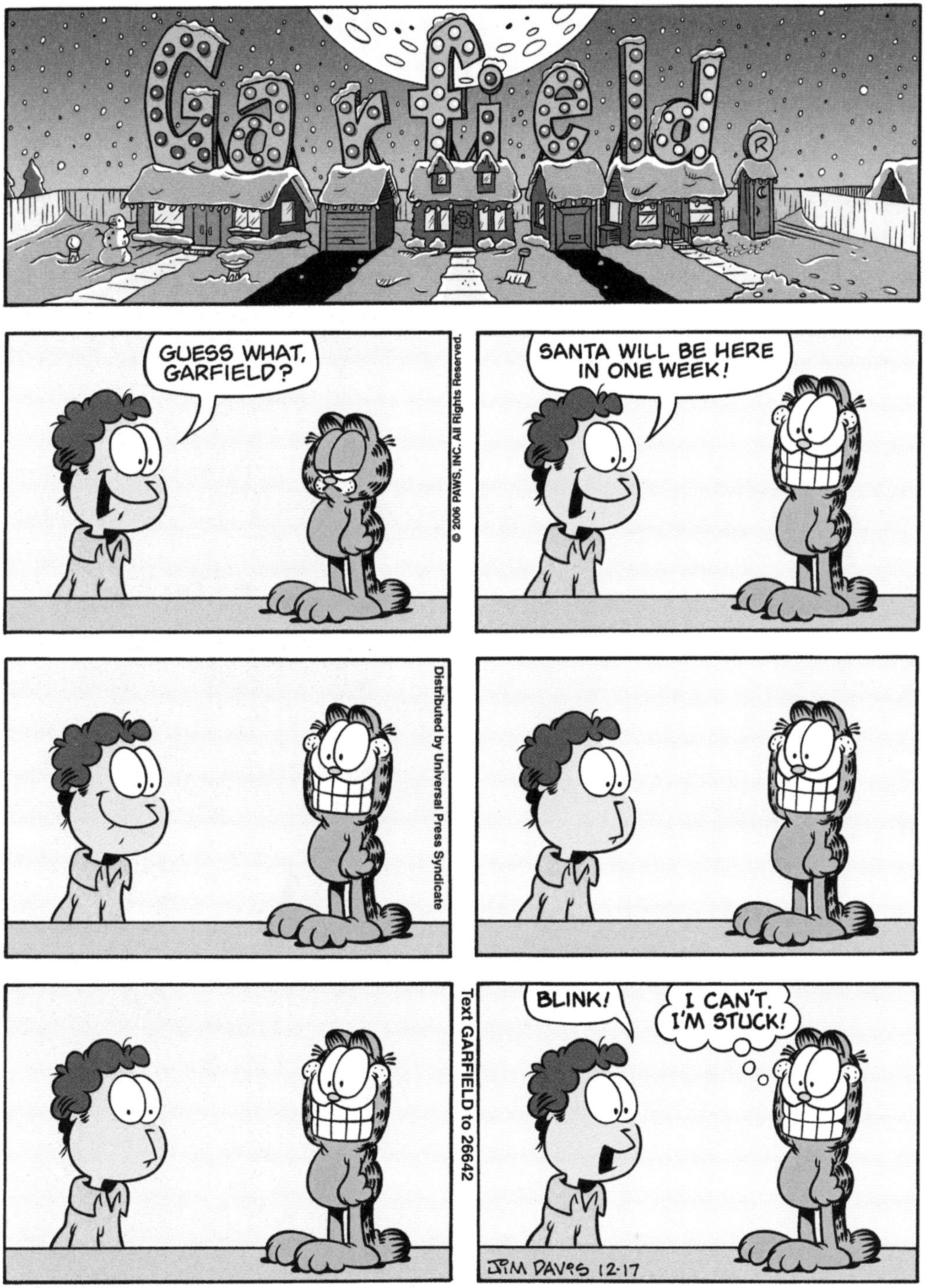
Garfield®
GUESS WHAT, GARFIELD?
© 2006 PAWS, INC. All Rights Reserved.
SANTA WILL BE HERE IN ONE WEEK!
Distributed by Universal Press Syndicate
Text GARFIELD to 26642
BLINK!
I CAN'T. I'M STUCK!
JIM DAVIS 12-17

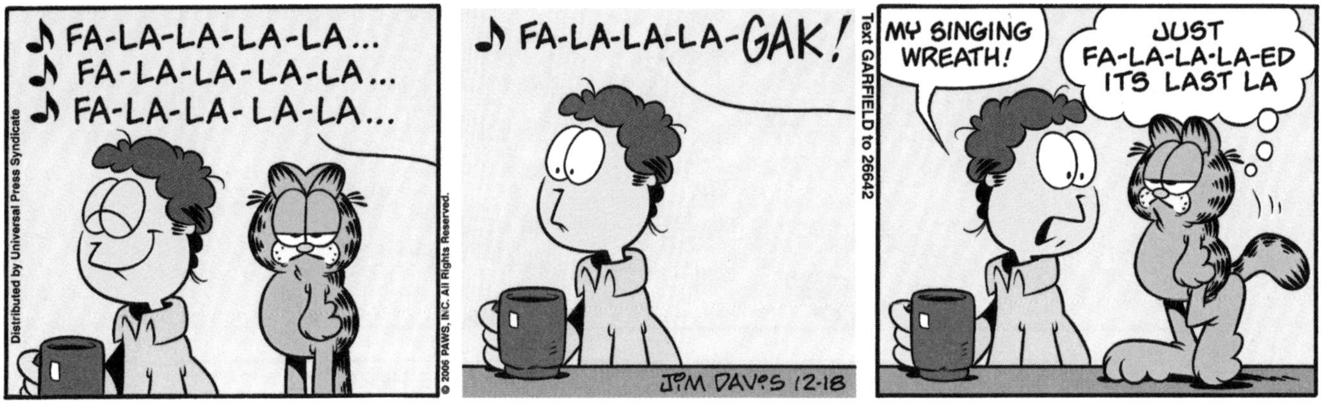
♪ FA-LA-LA-LA-LA...
♪ FA-LA-LA-LA-LA...
♪ FA-LA-LA-LA-LA...
♪ FA-LA-LA-LA-GAK!
MY SINGING WREATH!
JUST FA-LA-LA-LA-ED ITS LAST LA
JIM DAVIS 12-18
Distributed by Universal Press Syndicate
© 2006 PAWS, INC. All Rights Reserved.
Text GARFIELD to 26642

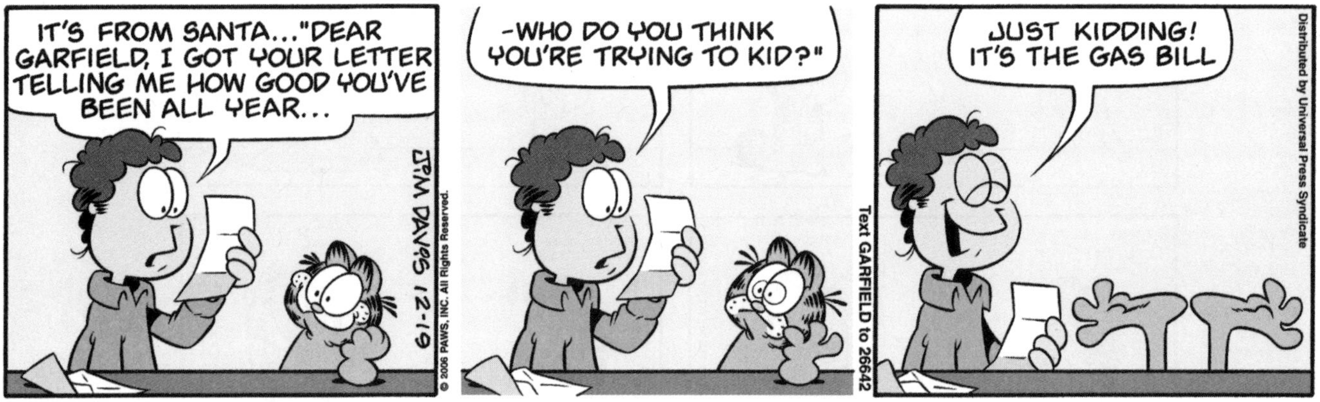
IT'S FROM SANTA..."DEAR GARFIELD, I GOT YOUR LETTER TELLING ME HOW GOOD YOU'VE BEEN ALL YEAR...
-WHO DO YOU THINK YOU'RE TRYING TO KID?"
JUST KIDDING! IT'S THE GAS BILL
JIM DAVIS 12-19
© 2006 PAWS, INC. All Rights Reserved.
Text GARFIELD to 26642
Distributed by Universal Press Syndicate

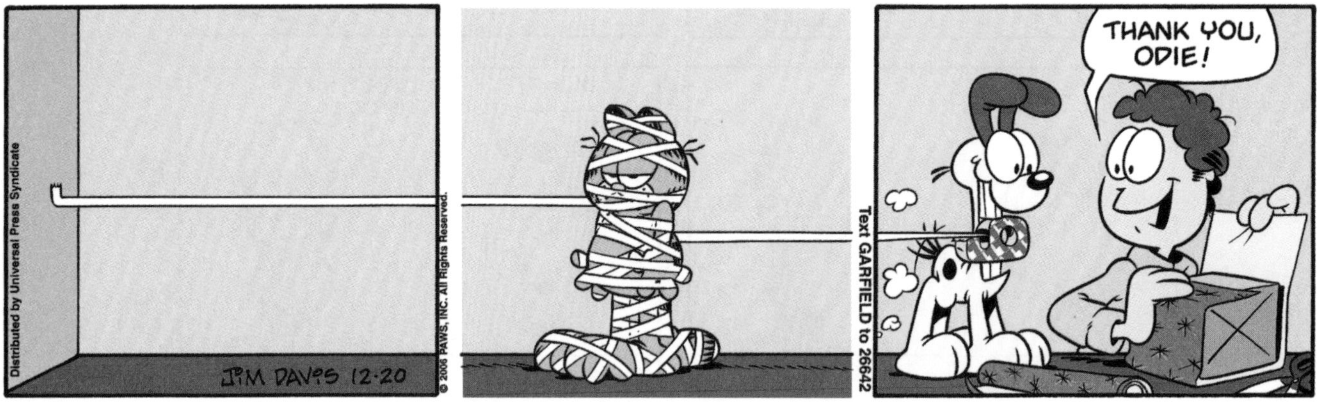
THANK YOU, ODIE!
JIM DAVIS 12-20
Distributed by Universal Press Syndicate
© 2006 PAWS, INC. All Rights Reserved.
Text GARFIELD to 26642

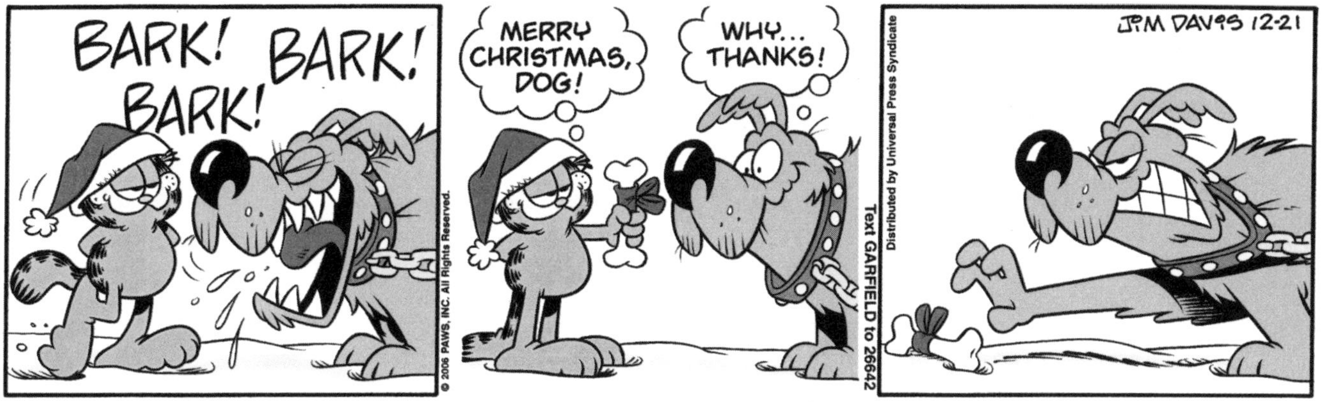
BARK! BARK! BARK!
MERRY CHRISTMAS, DOG!
WHY... THANKS!
© 2006 PAWS, INC. All Rights Reserved.
Text GARFIELD to 26642
Distributed by Universal Press Syndicate
JIM DAVIS 12-21

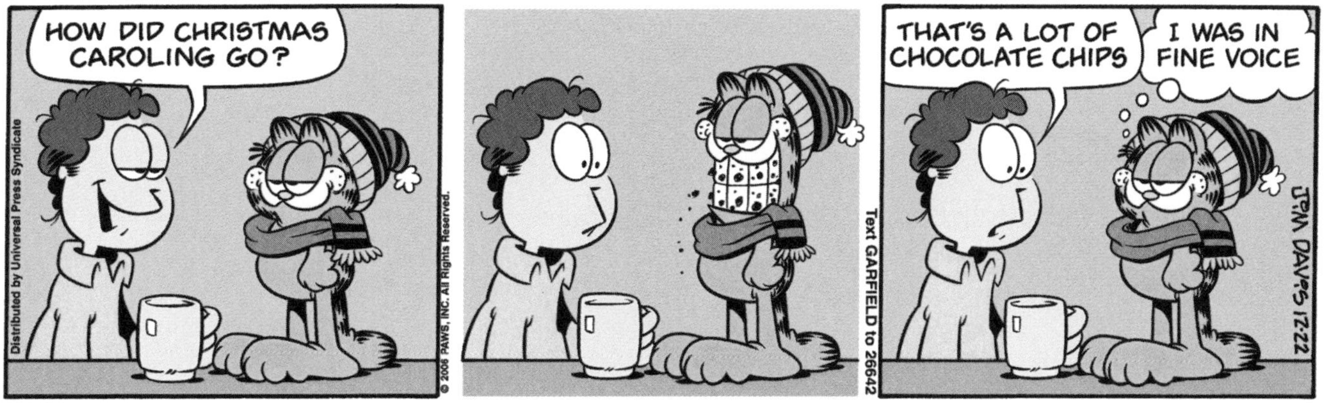
HOW DID CHRISTMAS CAROLING GO?
THAT'S A LOT OF CHOCOLATE CHIPS
I WAS IN FINE VOICE
Distributed by Universal Press Syndicate
© 2006 PAWS, INC. All Rights Reserved.
Text GARFIELD to 26642
JIM DAVIS 12-22

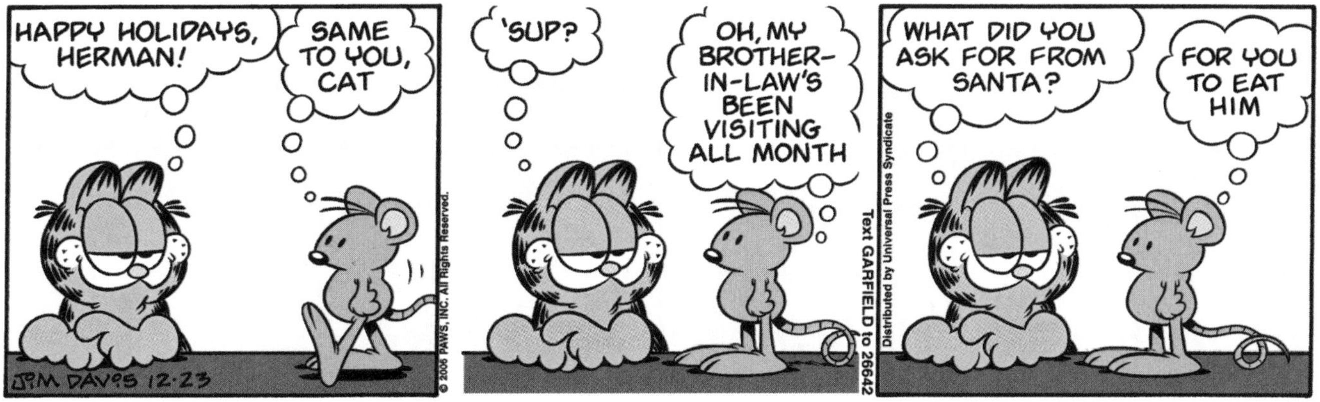
HAPPY HOLIDAYS, HERMAN!
SAME TO YOU, CAT
'SUP?
OH, MY BROTHER-IN-LAW'S BEEN VISITING ALL MONTH
WHAT DID YOU ASK FOR FROM SANTA?
FOR YOU TO EAT HIM
JIM DAVIS 12-23
© 2006 PAWS, INC. All Rights Reserved.
Text GARFIELD to 26642
Distributed by Universal Press Syndicate

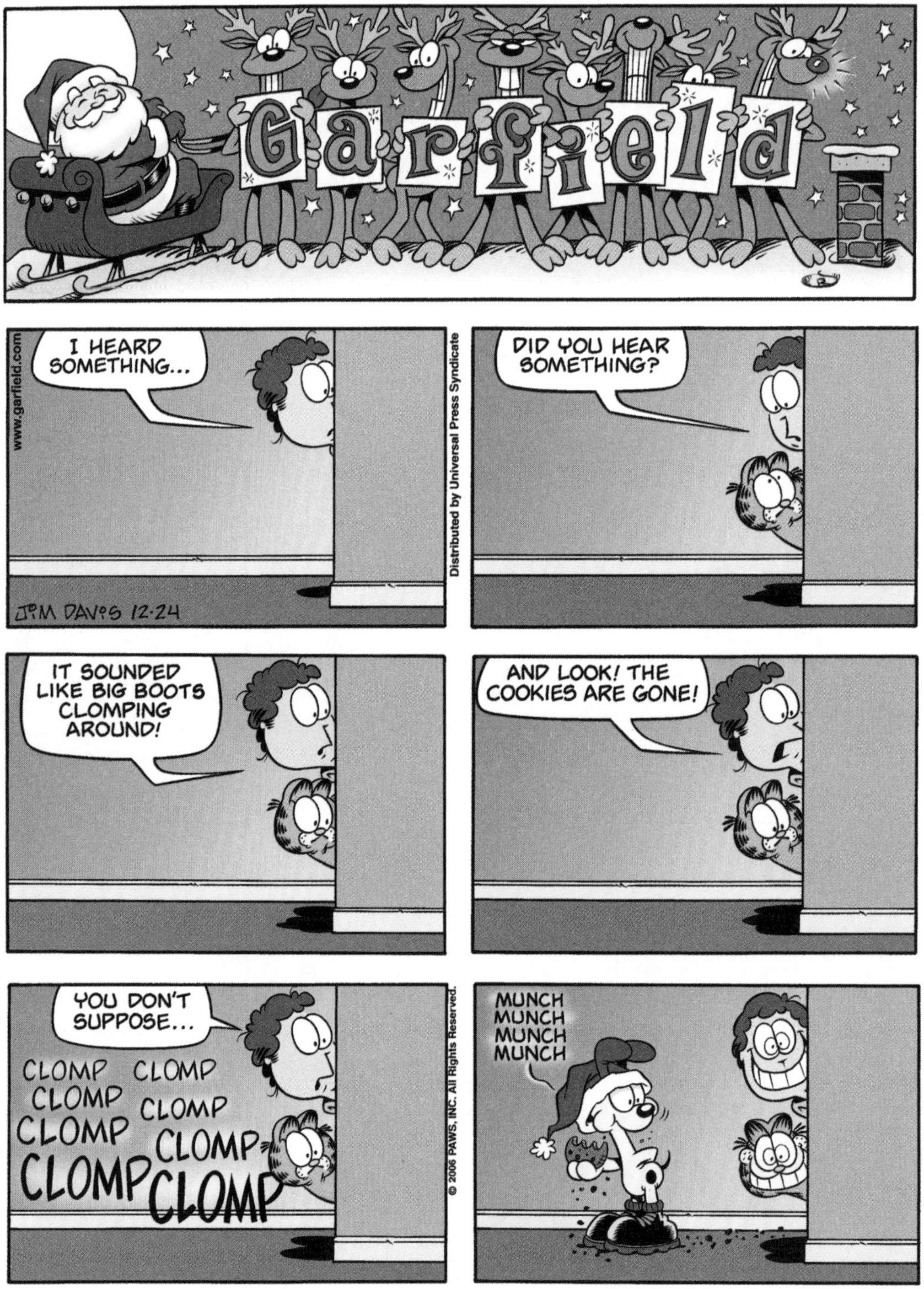
Garfield
www.garfield.com
I HEARD SOMETHING...
JIM DAVIS 12·24
Distributed by Universal Press Syndicate
DID YOU HEAR SOMETHING?
IT SOUNDED LIKE BIG BOOTS CLOMPING AROUND!
AND LOOK! THE COOKIES ARE GONE!
YOU DON'T SUPPOSE...
CLOMP CLOMP CLOMP CLOMP CLOMP CLOMP CLOMP CLOMP
© 2006 PAWS, INC. All Rights Reserved.
MUNCH MUNCH MUNCH MUNCH

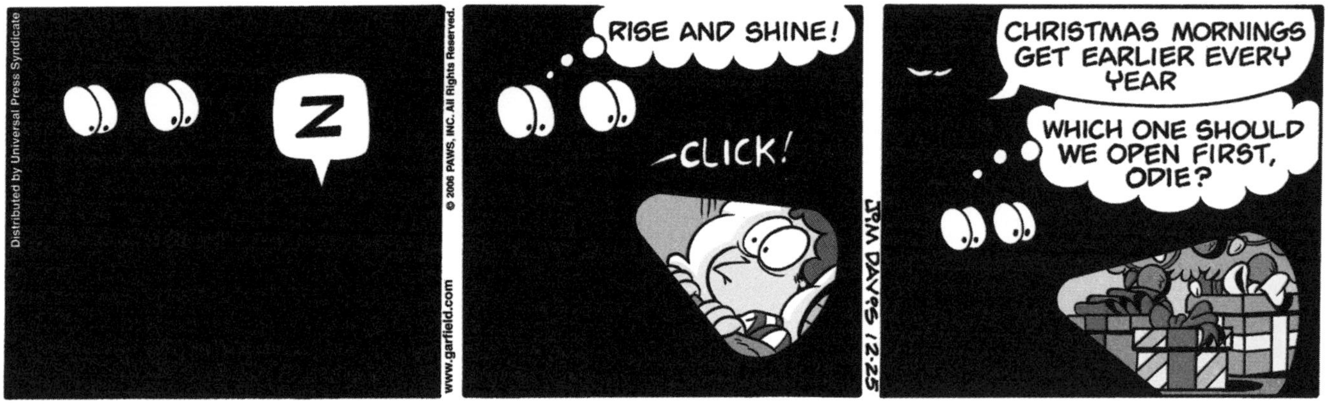
Z
RISE AND SHINE!
-CLICK!
CHRISTMAS MORNINGS GET EARLIER EVERY YEAR
WHICH ONE SHOULD WE OPEN FIRST, ODIE?
JIM DAVIS 12-25

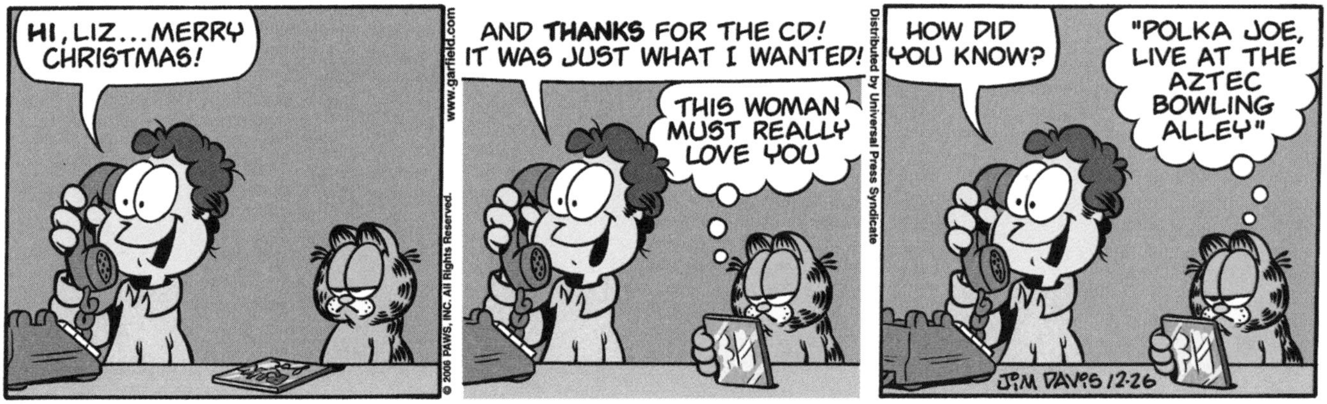
HI, LIZ... MERRY CHRISTMAS!
AND THANKS FOR THE CD! IT WAS JUST WHAT I WANTED!
THIS WOMAN MUST REALLY LOVE YOU
HOW DID YOU KNOW?
"POLKA JOE, LIVE AT THE AZTEC BOWLING ALLEY"
JIM DAVIS 12-26

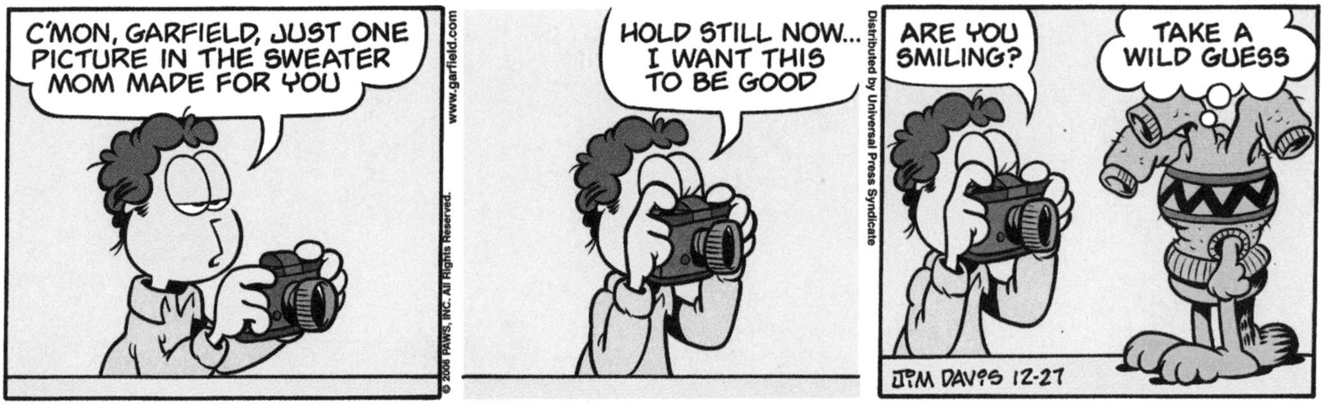
C'MON, GARFIELD, JUST ONE PICTURE IN THE SWEATER MOM MADE FOR YOU
HOLD STILL NOW... I WANT THIS TO BE GOOD
ARE YOU SMILING?
TAKE A WILD GUESS
JIM DAVIS 12-27

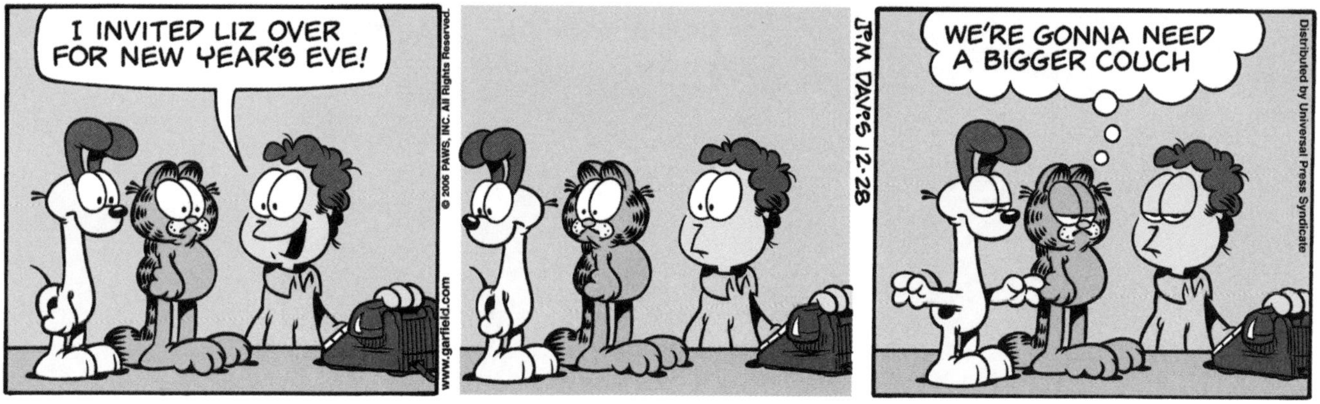
I INVITED LIZ OVER FOR NEW YEAR'S EVE!
© 2006 PAWS, INC. All Rights Reserved.
www.garfield.com
JPM DAVPS 12-28
WE'RE GONNA NEED A BIGGER COUCH
Distributed by Universal Press Syndicate

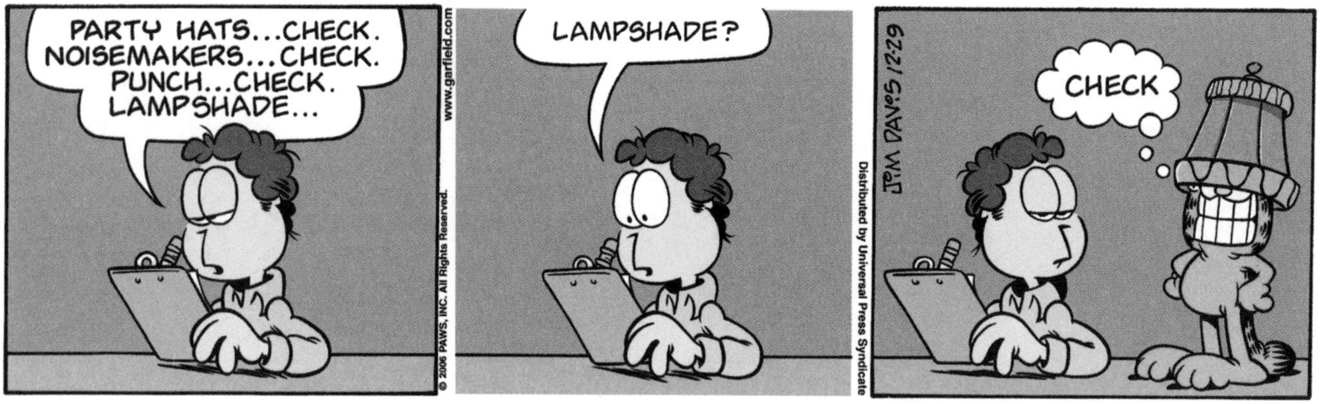
PARTY HATS...CHECK. NOISEMAKERS...CHECK. PUNCH...CHECK. LAMPSHADE...
www.garfield.com
© 2006 PAWS, INC. All Rights Reserved.
LAMPSHADE?
Distributed by Universal Press Syndicate
JPM DAVPS 12-29
CHECK

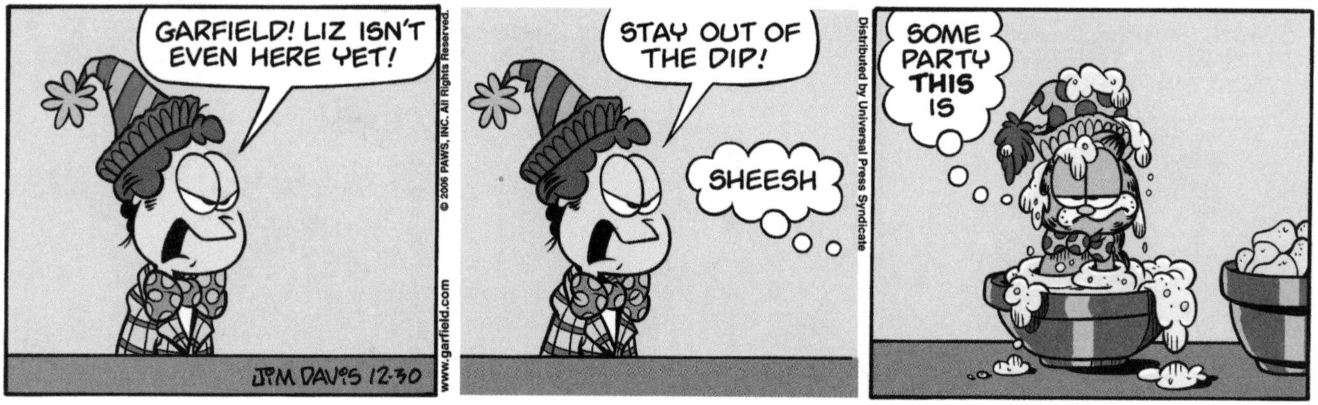
GARFIELD! LIZ ISN'T EVEN HERE YET!
JPM DAVPS 12-30
© 2006 PAWS, INC. All Rights Reserved.
www.garfield.com
STAY OUT OF THE DIP!
SHEESH
Distributed by Universal Press Syndicate
SOME PARTY THIS IS

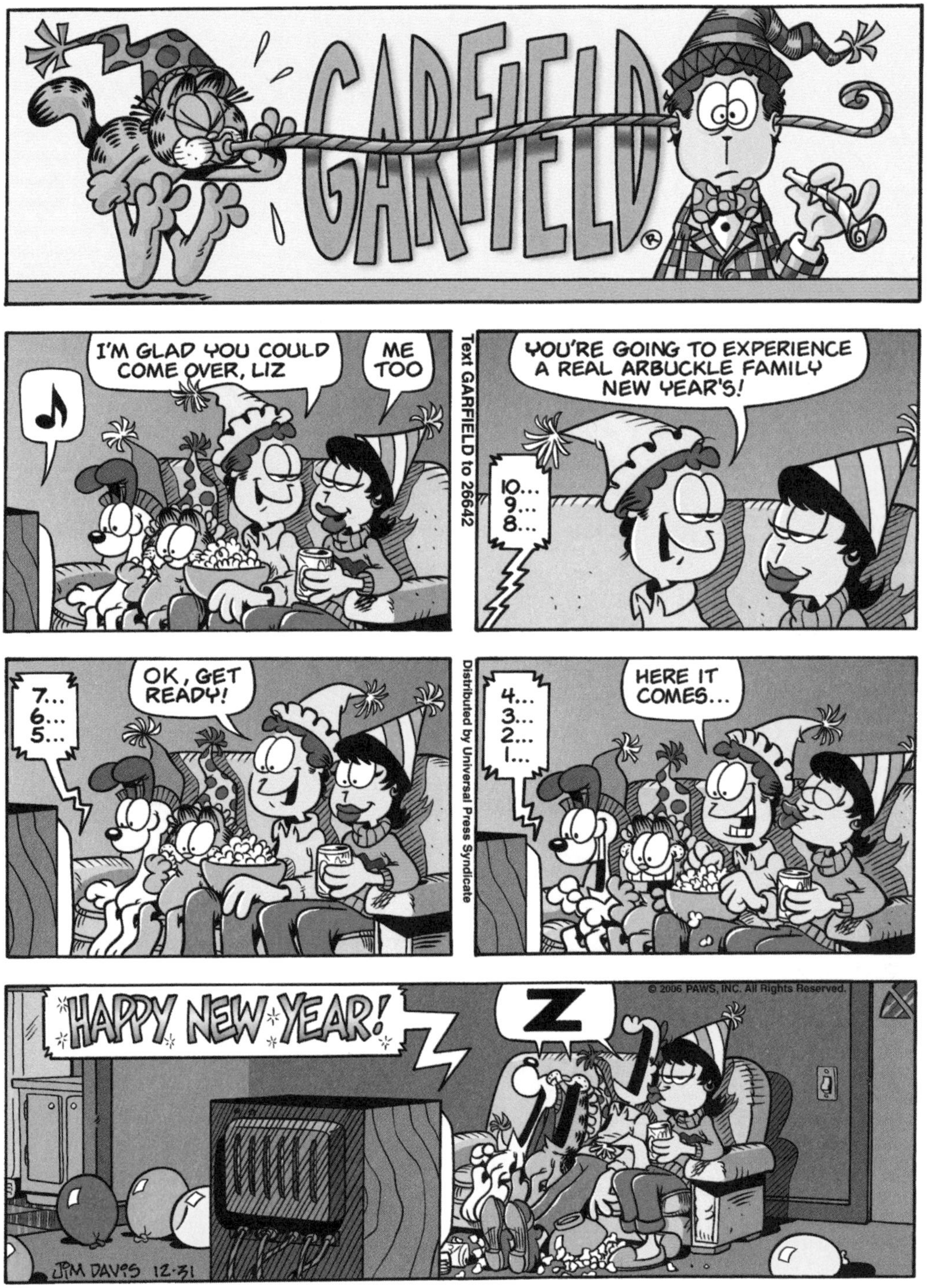
GARFIELD®
♪
I'M GLAD YOU COULD COME OVER, LIZ
ME TOO
YOU'RE GOING TO EXPERIENCE A REAL ARBUCKLE FAMILY NEW YEAR'S!
10... 9... 8...
Text GARFIELD to 26642
7... 6... 5...
OK, GET READY!
4... 3... 2... 1...
HERE IT COMES...
Distributed by Universal Press Syndicate
HAPPY NEW YEAR!
Z
© 2006 PAWS, INC. All Rights Reserved.
JIM DAVIS 12-31

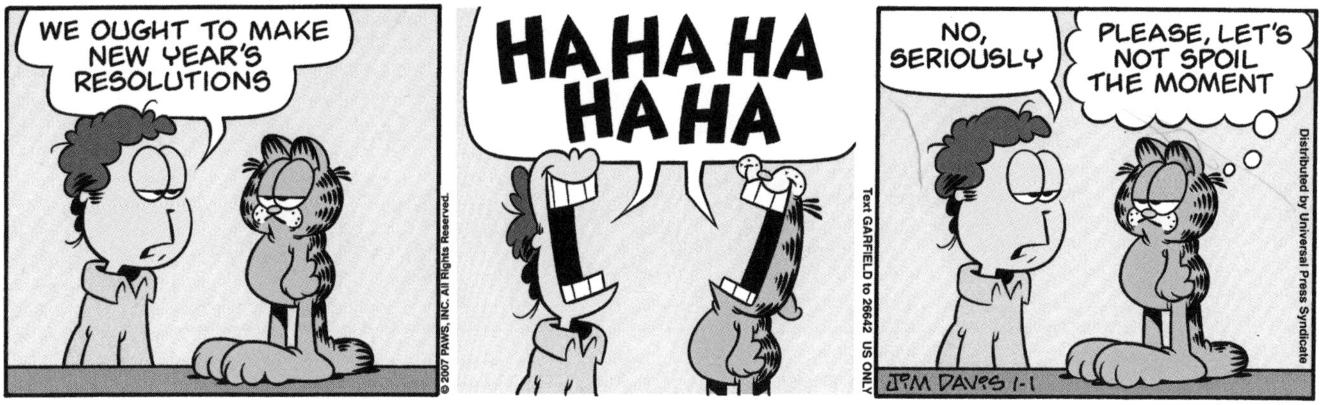
WE OUGHT TO MAKE NEW YEAR'S RESOLUTIONS
HAHAHA HAHA
NO, SERIOUSLY
PLEASE, LET'S NOT SPOIL THE MOMENT
© 2007 PAWS, INC. All Rights Reserved.
Text GARFIELD to 26642 US ONLY
Distributed by Universal Press Syndicate
JIM DAVIS 1-1

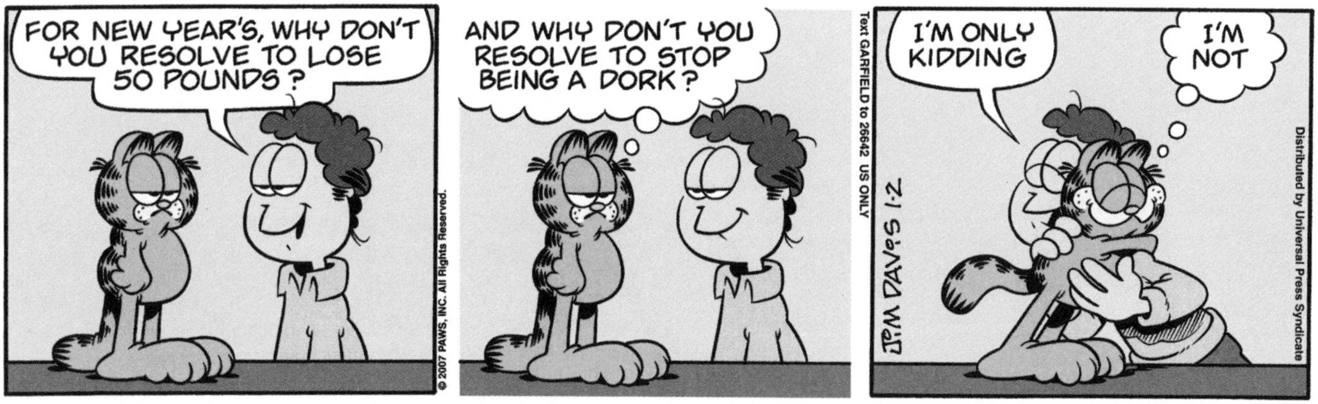
FOR NEW YEAR'S, WHY DON'T YOU RESOLVE TO LOSE 50 POUNDS?
AND WHY DON'T YOU RESOLVE TO STOP BEING A DORK?
I'M ONLY KIDDING
I'M NOT
© 2007 PAWS, INC. All Rights Reserved.
Text GARFIELD to 26642 US ONLY
Distributed by Universal Press Syndicate
JIM DAVIS 1-2

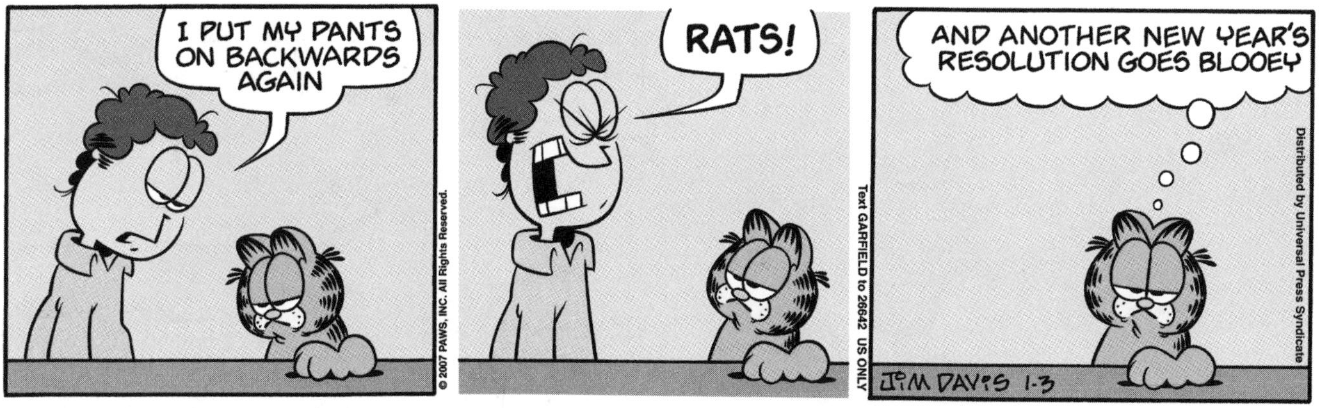
I PUT MY PANTS ON BACKWARDS AGAIN
RATS!
AND ANOTHER NEW YEAR'S RESOLUTION GOES BLOOEY
© 2007 PAWS, INC. All Rights Reserved.
Text GARFIELD to 26642 US ONLY
Distributed by Universal Press Syndicate
JIM DAVIS 1-3

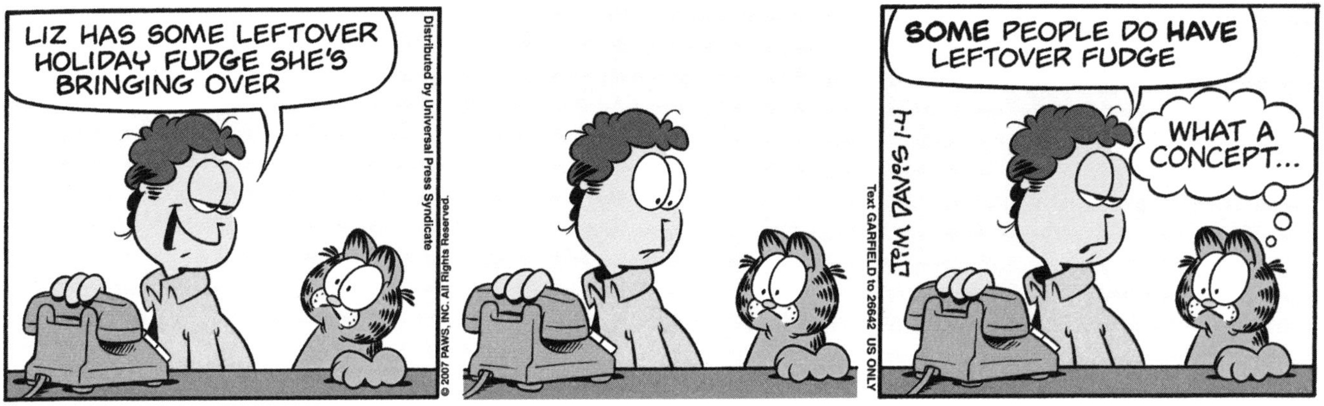
LIZ HAS SOME LEFTOVER HOLIDAY FUDGE SHE'S BRINGING OVER
Distributed by Universal Press Syndicate
© 2007 PAWS, INC. All Rights Reserved.
SOME PEOPLE DO HAVE LEFTOVER FUDGE
WHAT A CONCEPT...
JIM DAVIS 1-4
Text GARFIELD to 26642 US ONLY

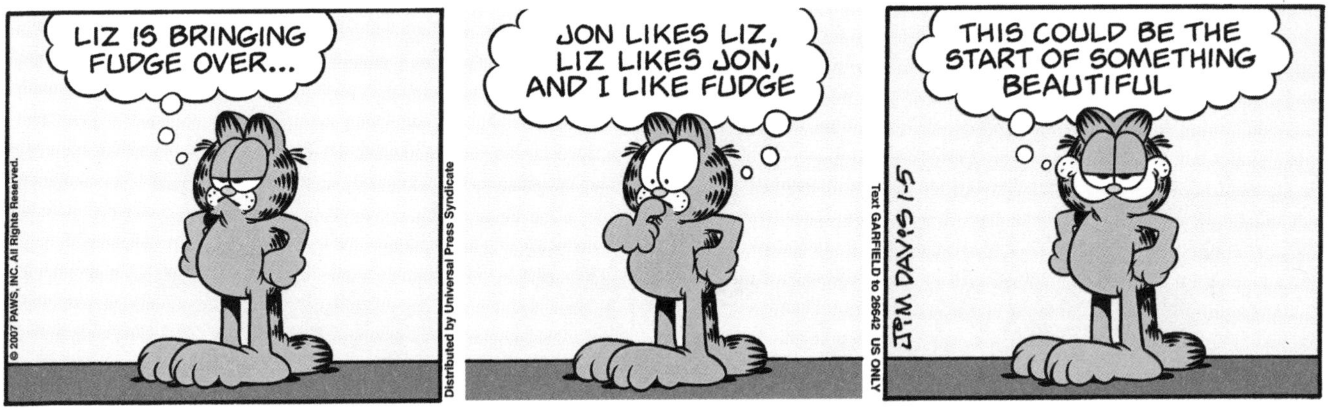
© 2007 PAWS, INC. All Rights Reserved.
LIZ IS BRINGING FUDGE OVER...
Distributed by Universal Press Syndicate
JON LIKES LIZ, LIZ LIKES JON, AND I LIKE FUDGE
JIM DAVIS 1-5
Text GARFIELD to 26642 US ONLY
THIS COULD BE THE START OF SOMETHING BEAUTIFUL

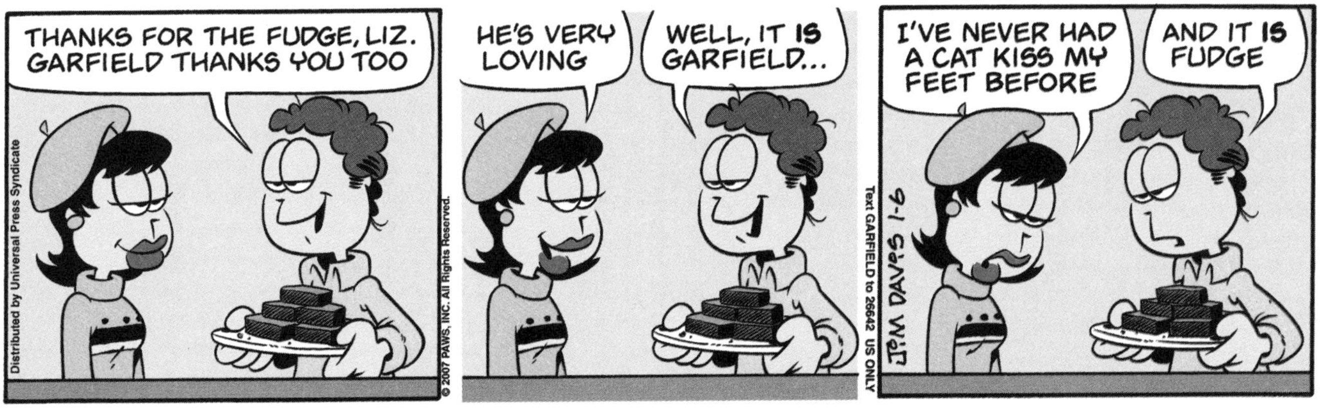
Distributed by Universal Press Syndicate
THANKS FOR THE FUDGE, LIZ. GARFIELD THANKS YOU TOO
© 2007 PAWS, INC. All Rights Reserved.
HE'S VERY LOVING
WELL, IT IS GARFIELD...
JIM DAVIS 1-6
Text GARFIELD to 26642 US ONLY
I'VE NEVER HAD A CAT KISS MY FEET BEFORE
AND IT IS FUDGE

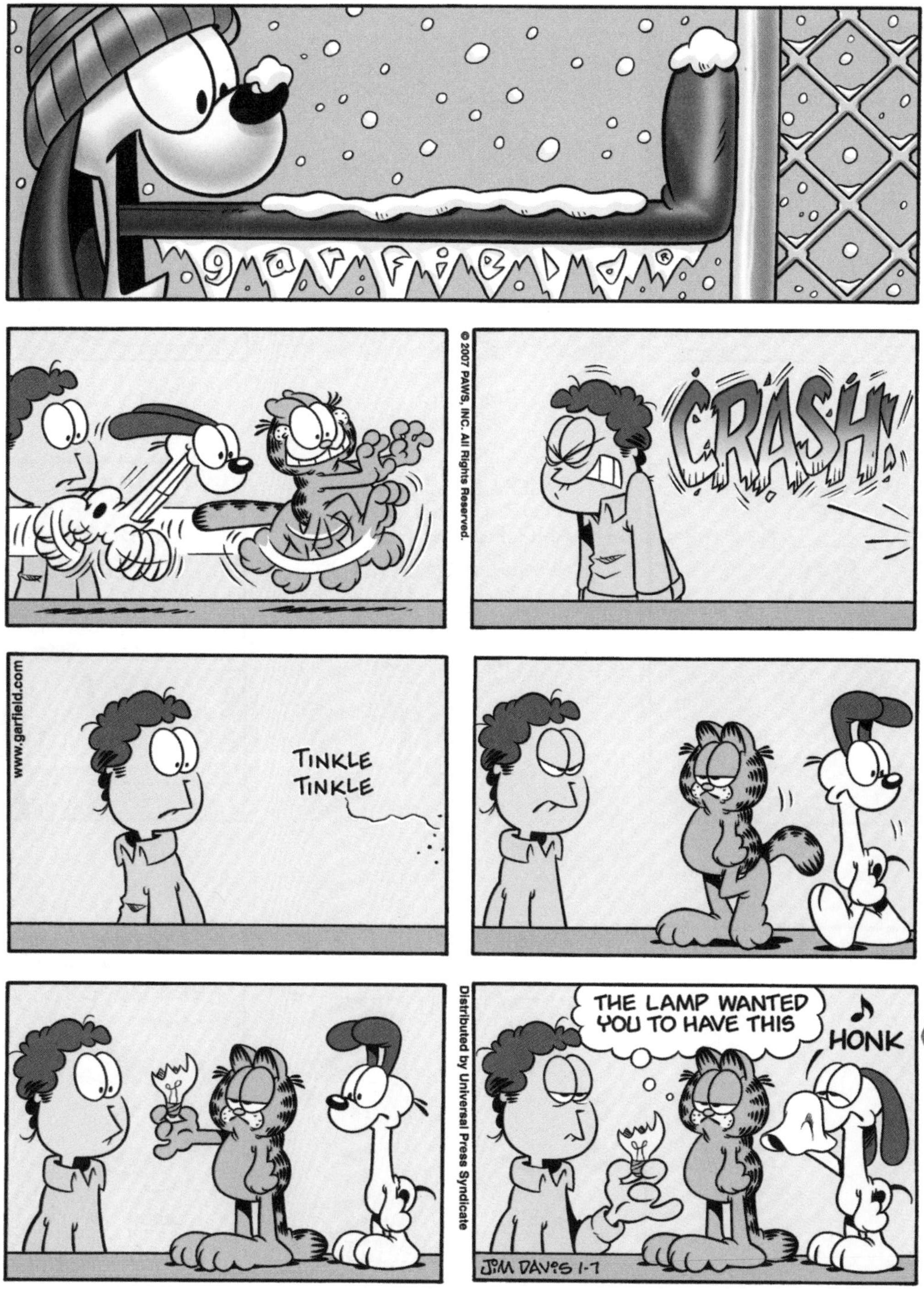
garfield®
© 2007 PAWS, INC. All Rights Reserved.
CRASH!
www.garfield.com
TINKLE
TINKLE
Distributed by Universal Press Syndicate
THE LAMP WANTED YOU TO HAVE THIS
HONK
JIM DAVIS 1-7

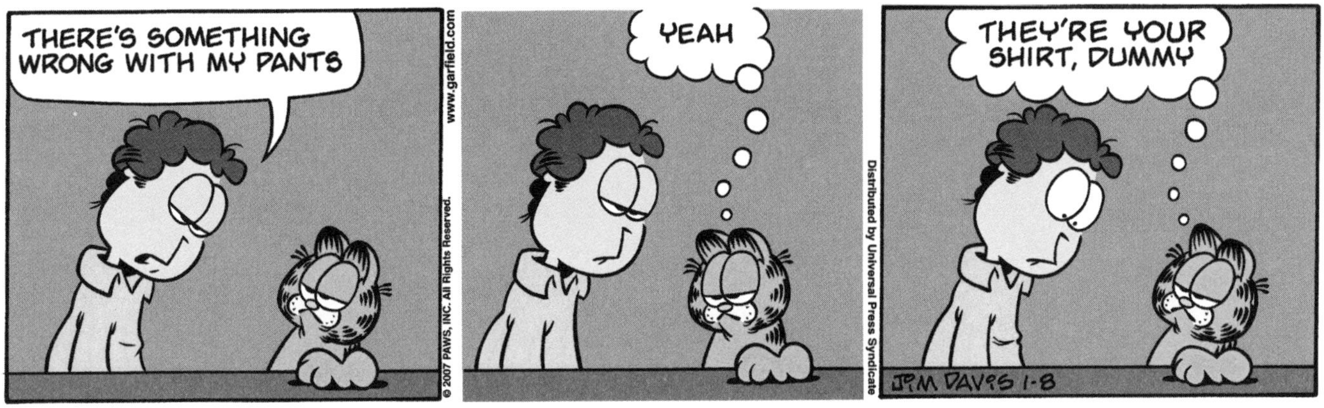
THERE'S SOMETHING WRONG WITH MY PANTS
YEAH
THEY'RE YOUR SHIRT, DUMMY
© 2007 PAWS, INC. All Rights Reserved.
www.garfield.com
Distributed by Universal Press Syndicate
JIM DAVIS 1-8

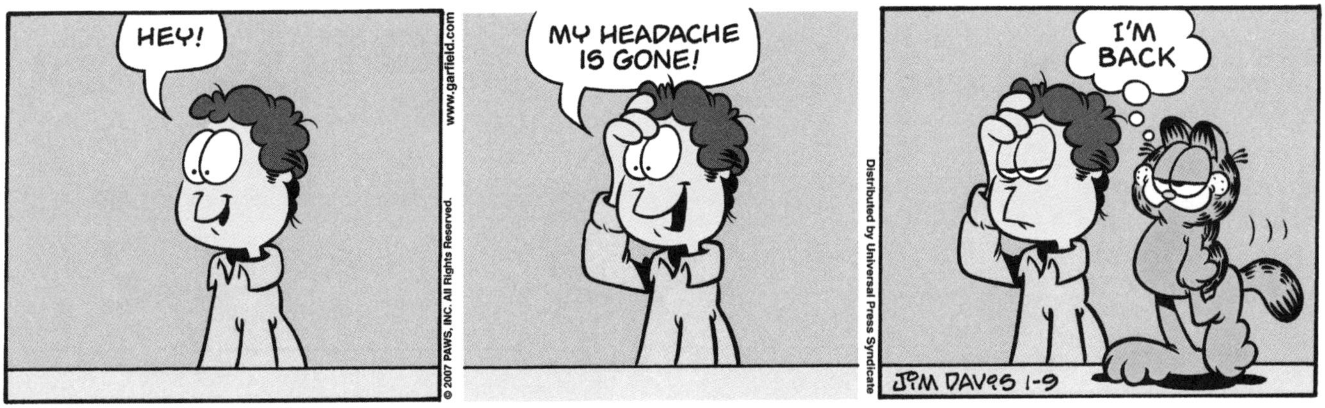
HEY!
MY HEADACHE IS GONE!
I'M BACK
© 2007 PAWS, INC. All Rights Reserved.
www.garfield.com
Distributed by Universal Press Syndicate
JIM DAVIS 1-9

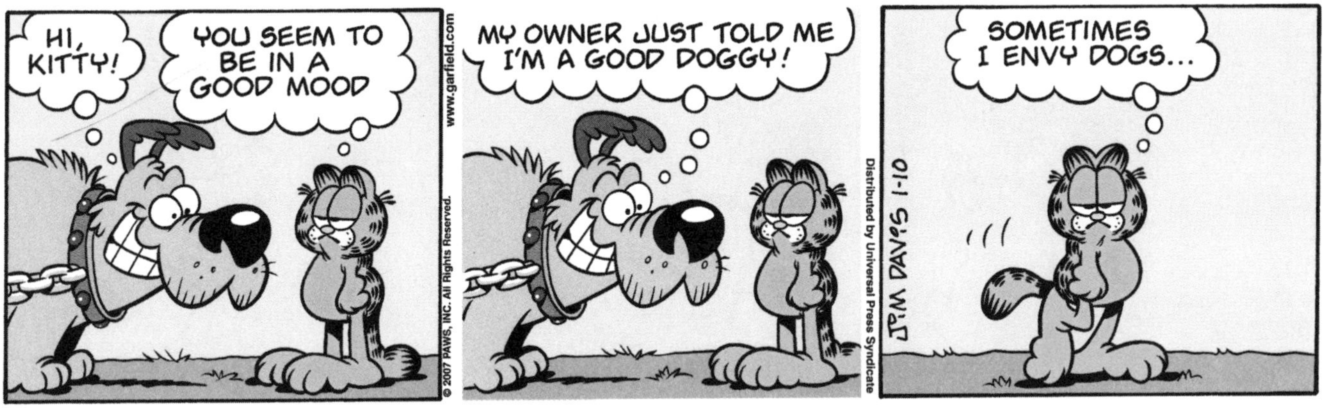
HI, KITTY!
YOU SEEM TO BE IN A GOOD MOOD
MY OWNER JUST TOLD ME I'M A GOOD DOGGY!
SOMETIMES I ENVY DOGS...
© 2007 PAWS, INC. All Rights Reserved.
www.garfield.com
Distributed by Universal Press Syndicate
JIM DAVIS 1-10

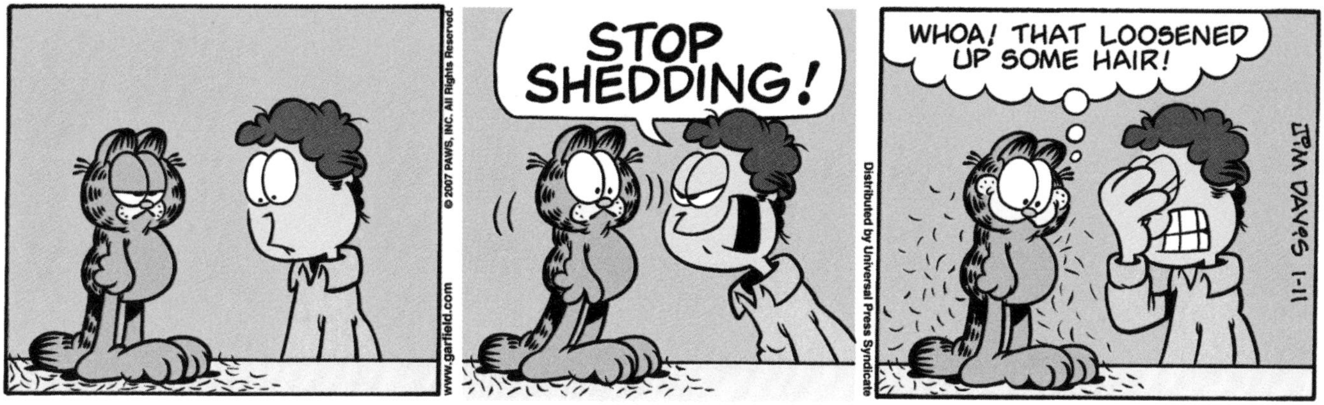
STOP SHEDDING!
WHOA! THAT LOOSENED UP SOME HAIR!
JIM DAVIS 1-11
© 2007 PAWS, INC. All Rights Reserved.
www.garfield.com
Distributed by Universal Press Syndicate

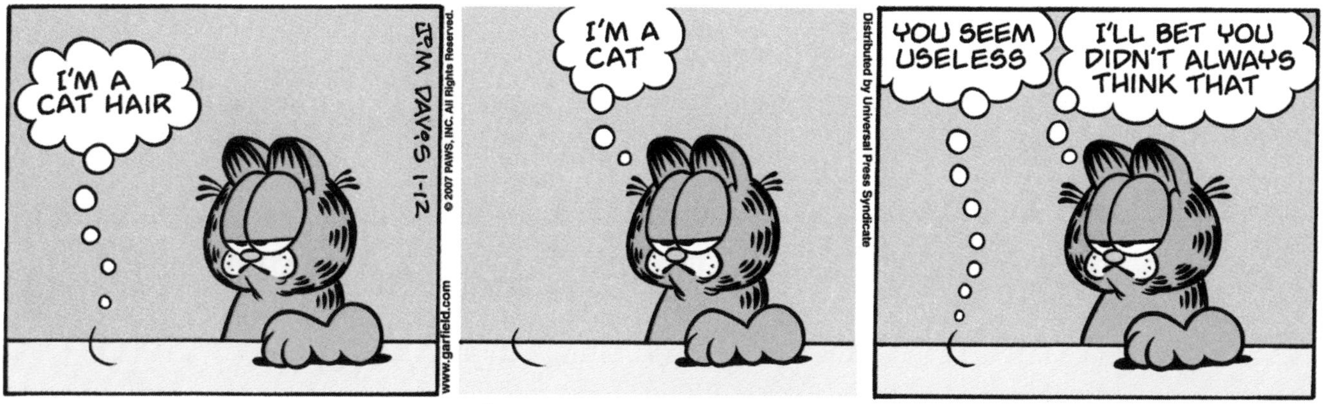
I'M A CAT HAIR
I'M A CAT
YOU SEEM USELESS
I'LL BET YOU DIDN'T ALWAYS THINK THAT
JIM DAVIS 1-12
© 2007 PAWS, INC. All Rights Reserved.
www.garfield.com
Distributed by Universal Press Syndicate

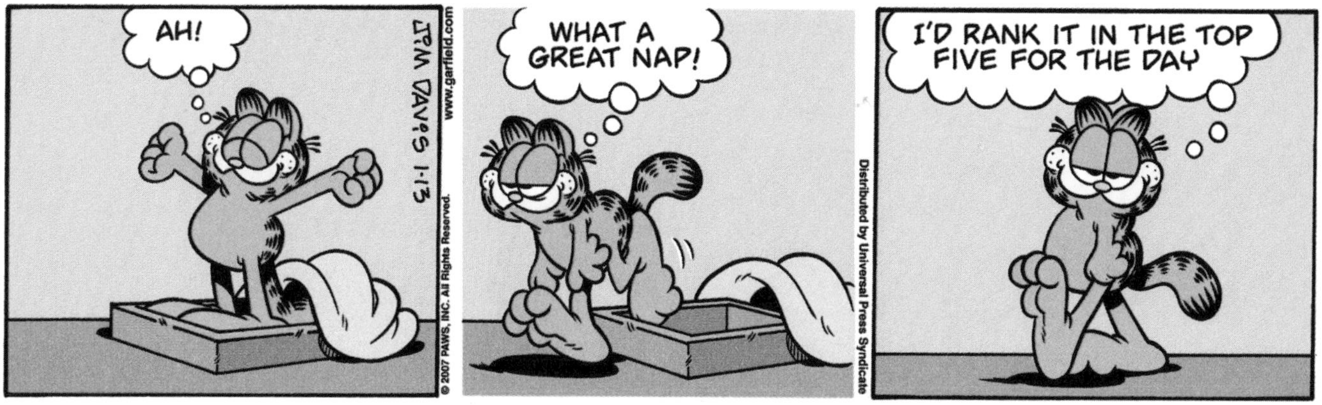
AH!
WHAT A GREAT NAP!
I'D RANK IT IN THE TOP FIVE FOR THE DAY
JIM DAVIS 1-13
www.garfield.com
© 2007 PAWS, INC. All Rights Reserved.
Distributed by Universal Press Syndicate

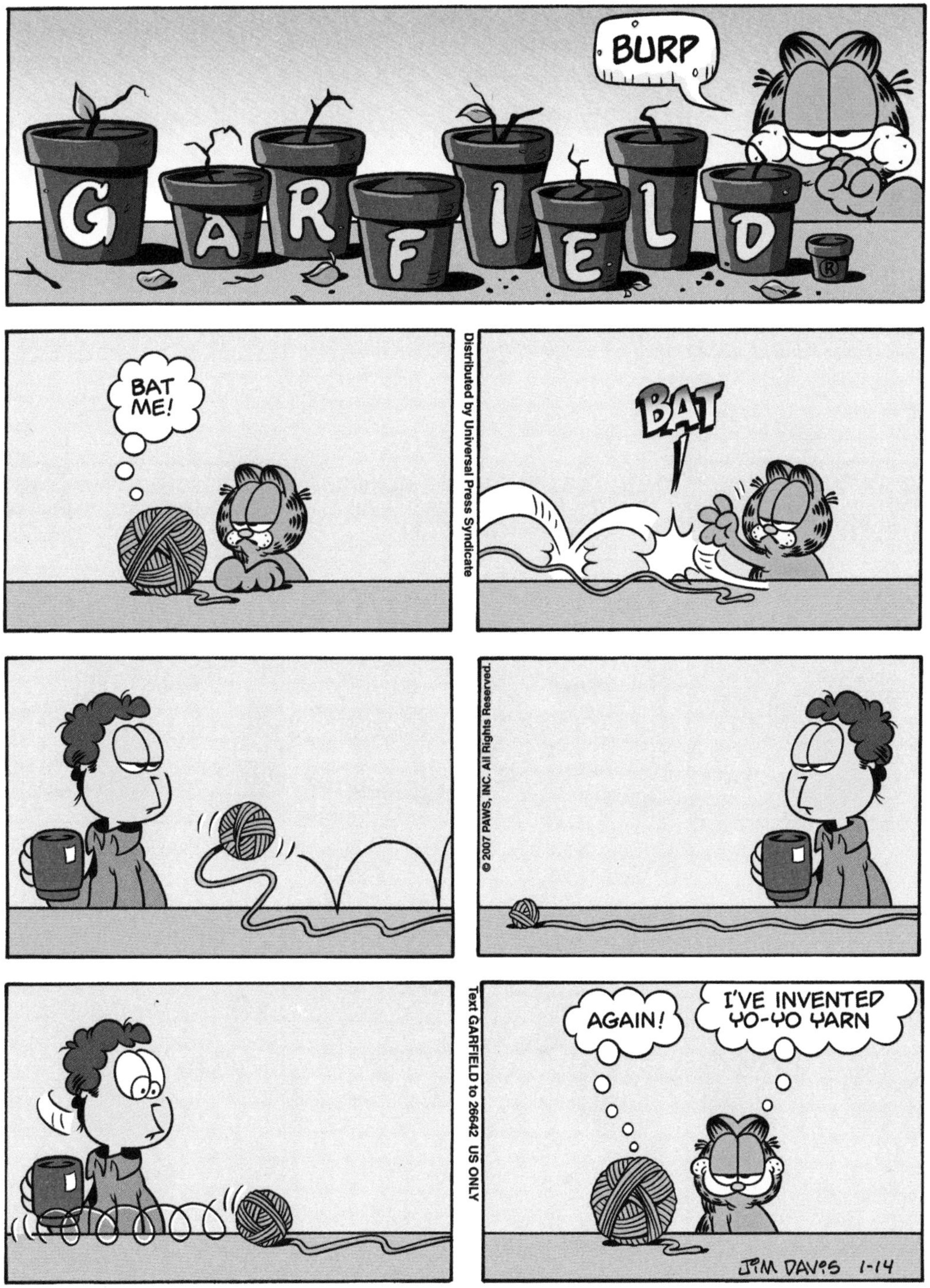
GARFIELD®
BURP
Distributed by Universal Press Syndicate
BAT ME!
BAT
© 2007 PAWS, INC. All Rights Reserved.
Text GARFIELD to 26642 US ONLY
AGAIN!
I'VE INVENTED YO-YO YARN
JIM DAVIS 1-14

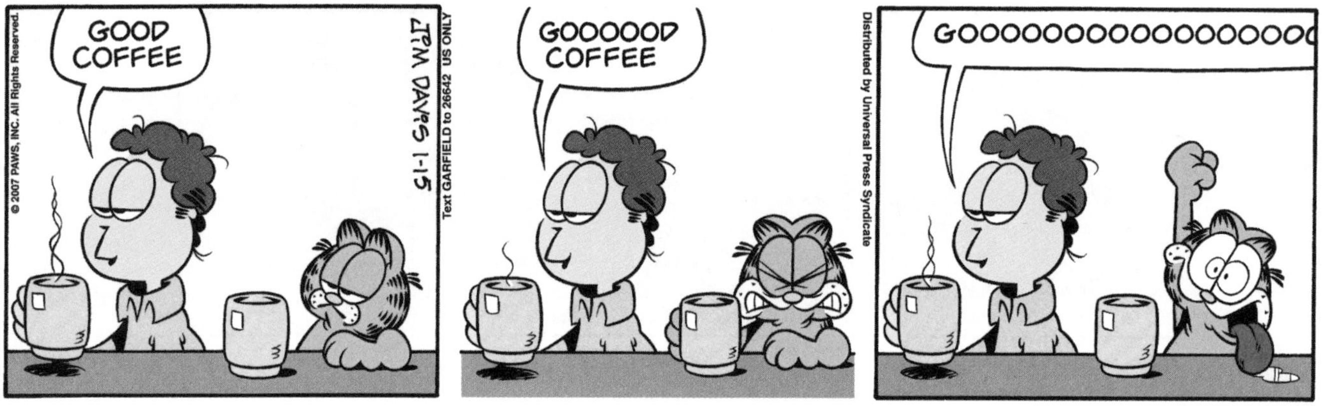
GOOD COFFEE
GOOOOOD COFFEE
GOOOOOOOOOOOOOOOOOO
© 2007 PAWS, INC. All Rights Reserved.
JIM DAVIS 1-15
Text GARFIELD to 26642 US ONLY
Distributed by Universal Press Syndicate

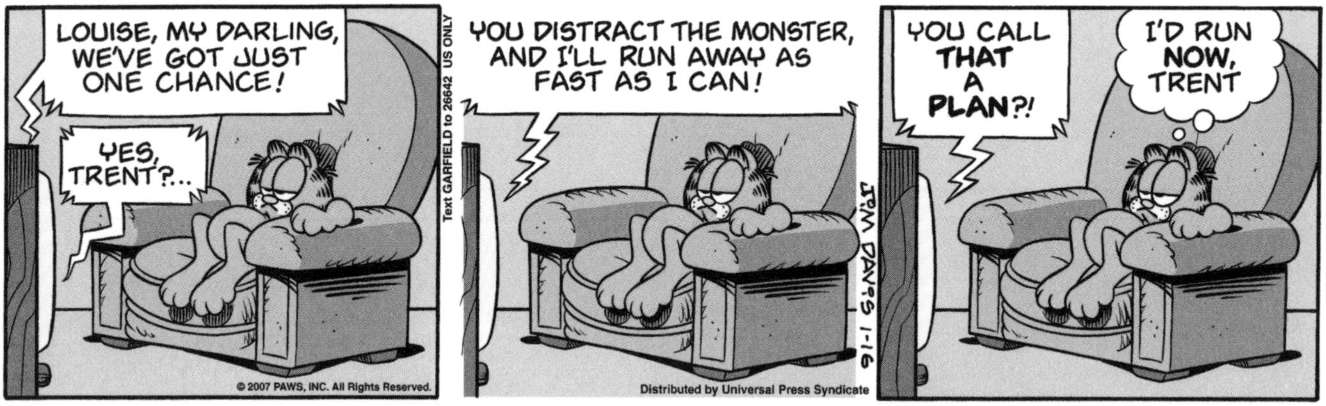
LOUISE, MY DARLING, WE'VE GOT JUST ONE CHANCE!
YES, TRENT?...
YOU DISTRACT THE MONSTER, AND I'LL RUN AWAY AS FAST AS I CAN!
YOU CALL **THAT** A **PLAN**?!
I'D RUN **NOW,** TRENT
© 2007 PAWS, INC. All Rights Reserved.
Text GARFIELD to 26642 US ONLY
JIM DAVIS 1-16
Distributed by Universal Press Syndicate

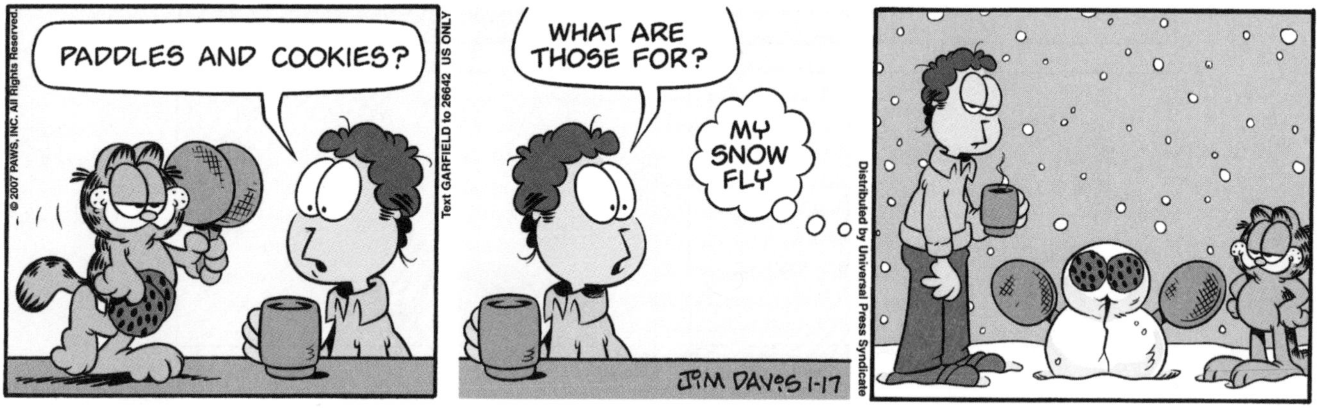
PADDLES AND COOKIES?
WHAT ARE THOSE FOR?
MY SNOW FLY
© 2007 PAWS, INC. All Rights Reserved.
Text GARFIELD to 26642 US ONLY
JIM DAVIS 1-17
Distributed by Universal Press Syndicate

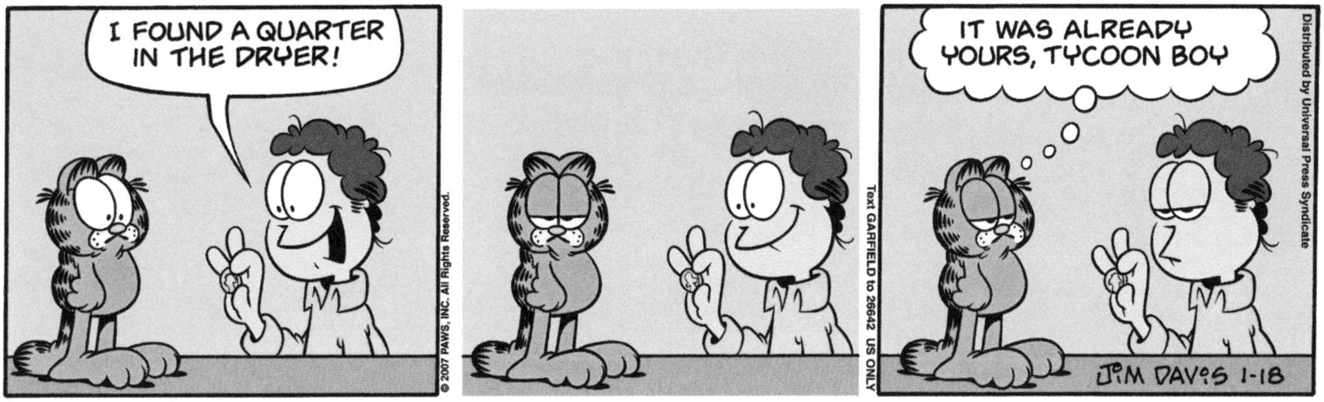
I FOUND A QUARTER IN THE DRYER!
IT WAS ALREADY YOURS, TYCOON BOY
© 2007 PAWS, INC. All Rights Reserved.
Text GARFIELD to 26642 US ONLY
Distributed by Universal Press Syndicate
JIM DAVIS 1-18

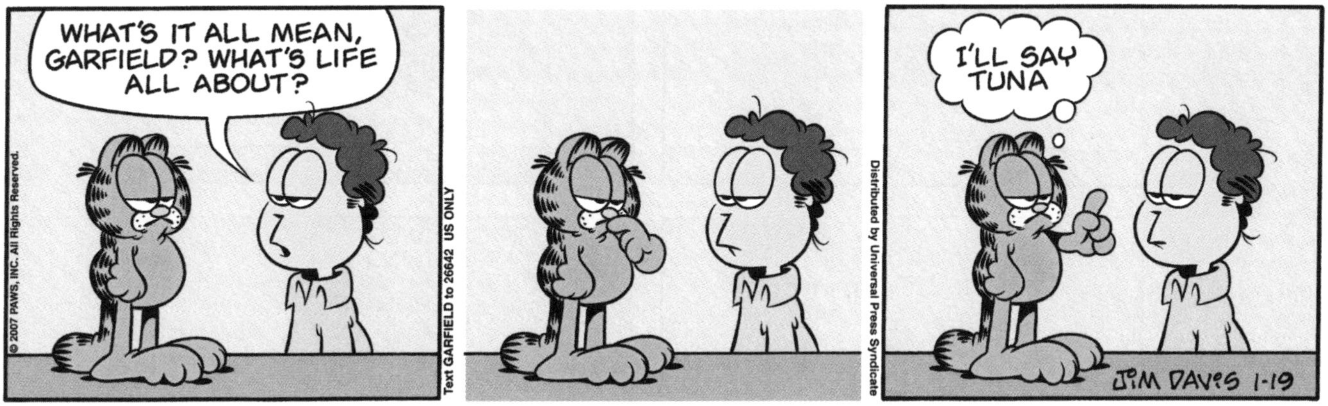
WHAT'S IT ALL MEAN, GARFIELD? WHAT'S LIFE ALL ABOUT?
I'LL SAY TUNA
© 2007 PAWS, INC. All Rights Reserved.
Text GARFIELD to 26642 US ONLY
Distributed by Universal Press Syndicate
JIM DAVIS 1-19

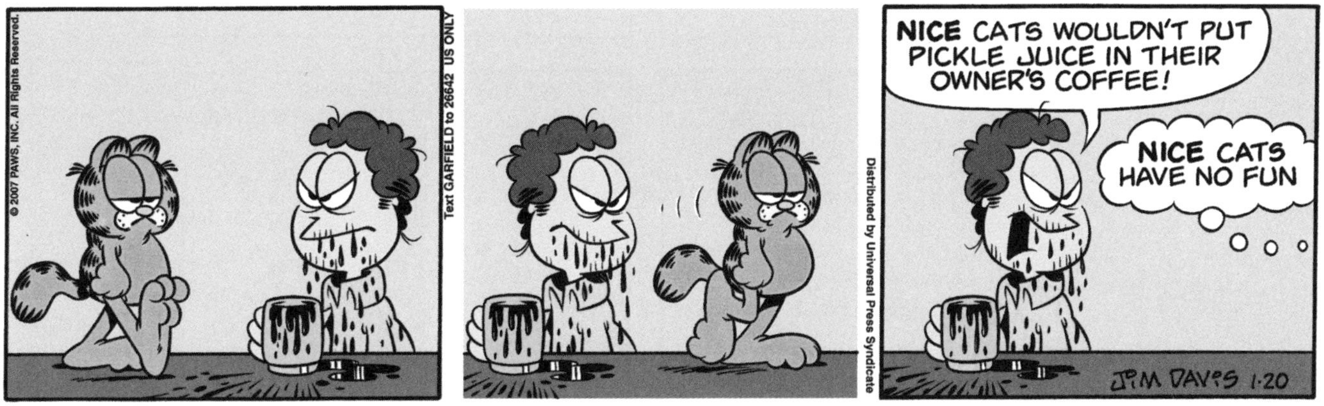
NICE CATS WOULDN'T PUT PICKLE JUICE IN THEIR OWNER'S COFFEE!
NICE CATS HAVE NO FUN
© 2007 PAWS, INC. All Rights Reserved.
Text GARFIELD to 26642 US ONLY
Distributed by Universal Press Syndicate
JIM DAVIS 1-20

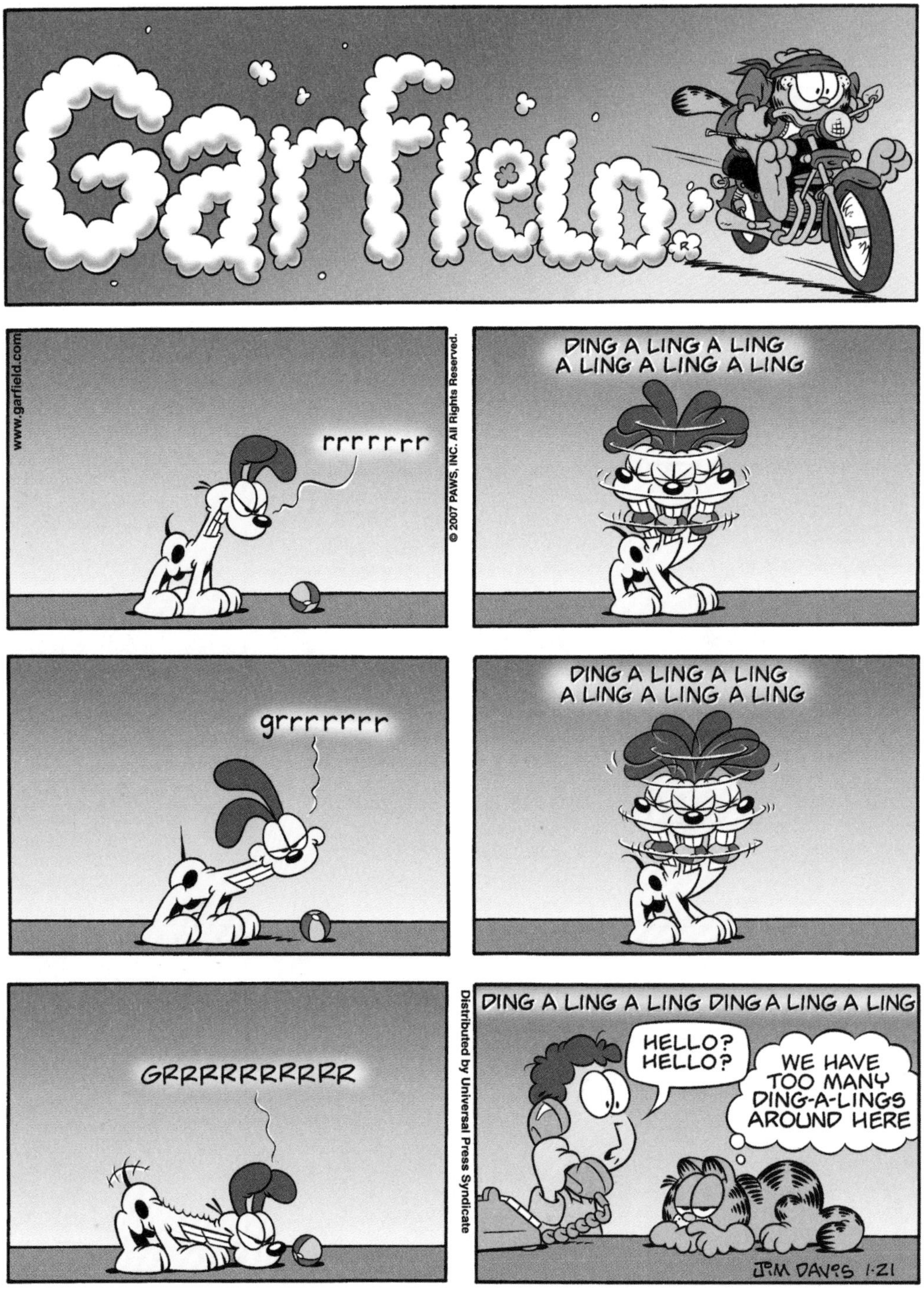
Garfield
www.garfield.com
© 2007 PAWS, INC. All Rights Reserved.
rrrrrrr
DING A LING A LING A LING A LING A LING
grrrrrrr
DING A LING A LING A LING A LING A LING
Distributed by Universal Press Syndicate
GRRRRRRRRRR
DING A LING A LING DING A LING A LING
HELLO? HELLO?
WE HAVE TOO MANY DING-A-LINGS AROUND HERE
JIM DAVIS 1·21

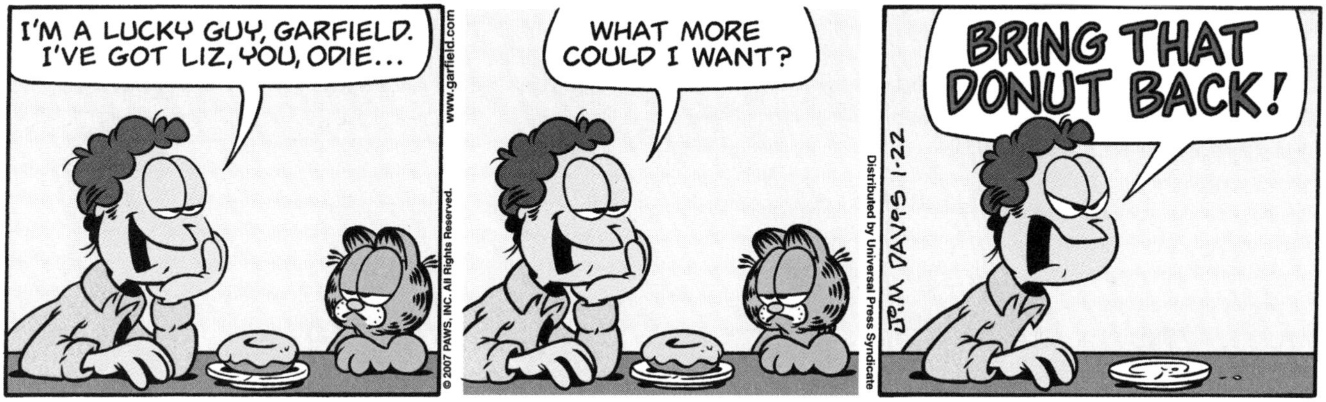
I'M A LUCKY GUY, GARFIELD. I'VE GOT LIZ, YOU, ODIE...
WHAT MORE COULD I WANT?
BRING THAT DONUT BACK!
JIM DAVIS 1-22
© 2007 PAWS, INC. All Rights Reserved. www.garfield.com
Distributed by Universal Press Syndicate

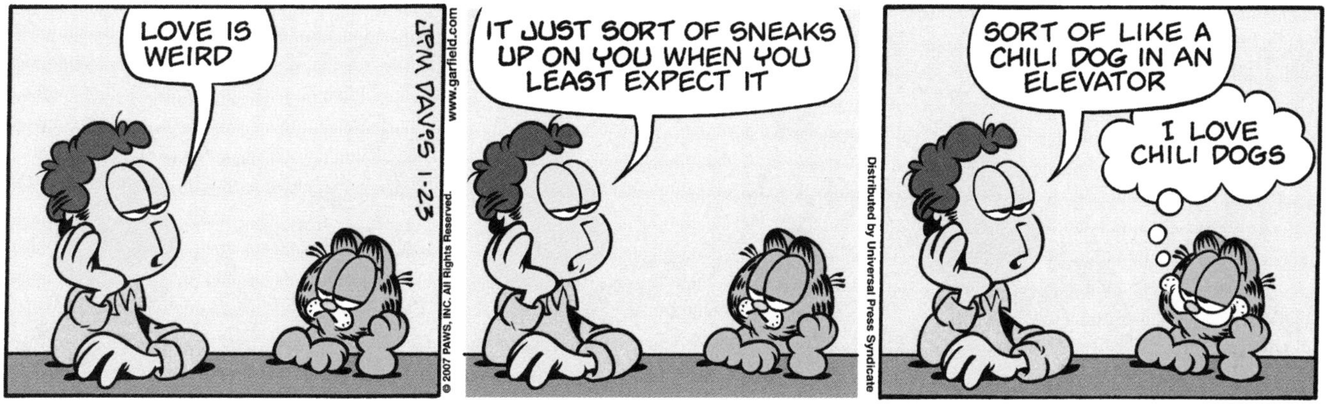
LOVE IS WEIRD
IT JUST SORT OF SNEAKS UP ON YOU WHEN YOU LEAST EXPECT IT
SORT OF LIKE A CHILI DOG IN AN ELEVATOR
I LOVE CHILI DOGS
JIM DAVIS 1-23
© 2007 PAWS, INC. All Rights Reserved. www.garfield.com
Distributed by Universal Press Syndicate

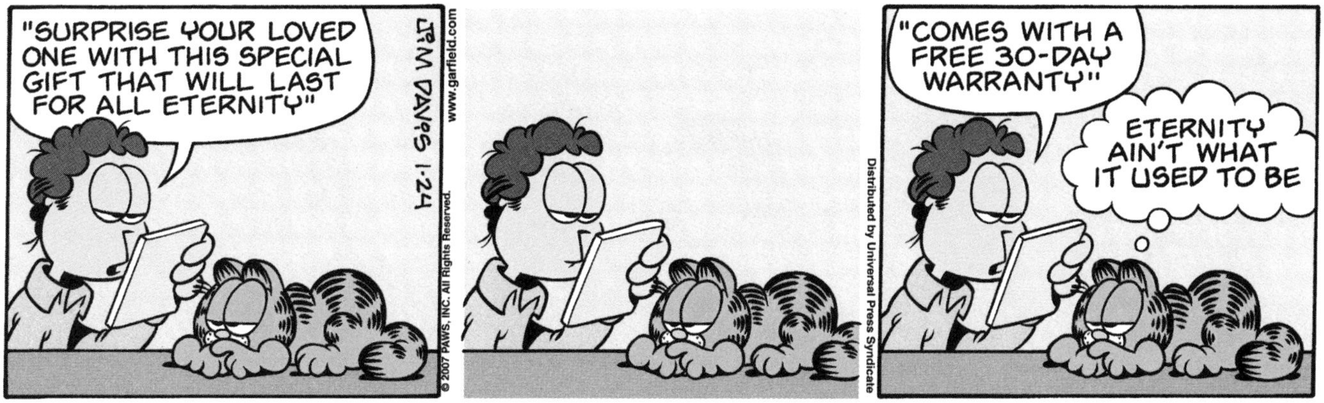
"SURPRISE YOUR LOVED ONE WITH THIS SPECIAL GIFT THAT WILL LAST FOR ALL ETERNITY"
"COMES WITH A FREE 30-DAY WARRANTY"
ETERNITY AIN'T WHAT IT USED TO BE
JIM DAVIS 1-24
© 2007 PAWS, INC. All Rights Reserved. www.garfield.com
Distributed by Universal Press Syndicate

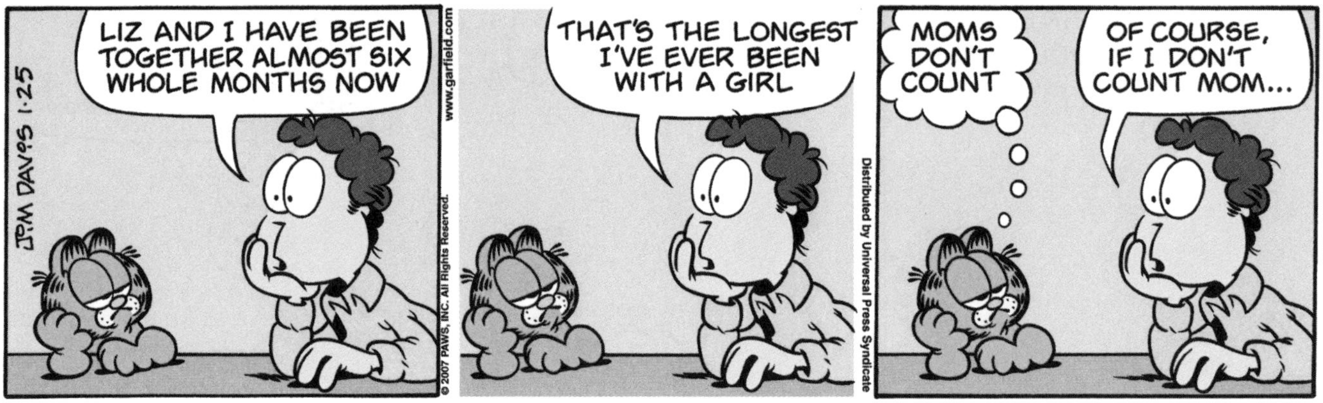
LIZ AND I HAVE BEEN TOGETHER ALMOST SIX WHOLE MONTHS NOW
THAT'S THE LONGEST I'VE EVER BEEN WITH A GIRL
MOMS DON'T COUNT
OF COURSE, IF I DON'T COUNT MOM...

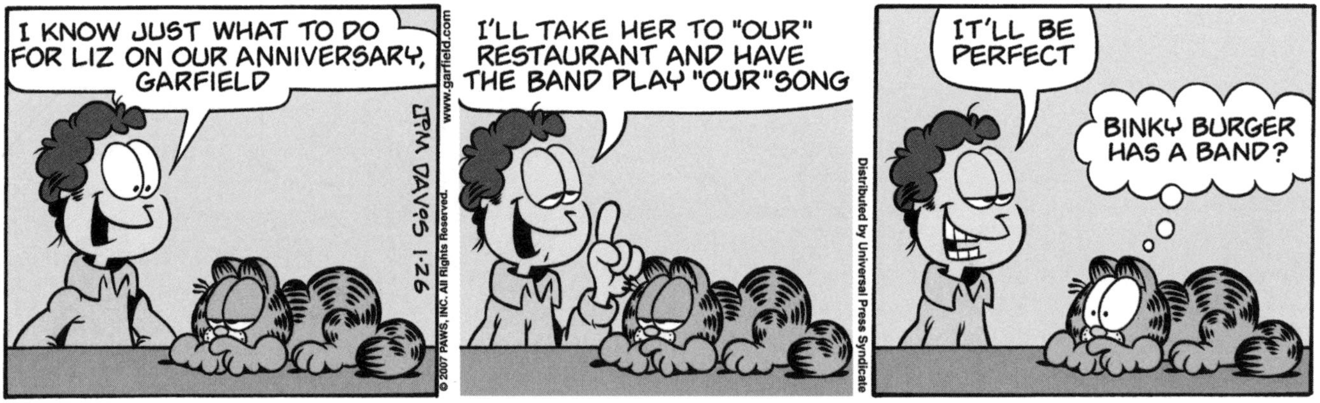
I KNOW JUST WHAT TO DO FOR LIZ ON OUR ANNIVERSARY, GARFIELD
I'LL TAKE HER TO "OUR" RESTAURANT AND HAVE THE BAND PLAY "OUR" SONG
IT'LL BE PERFECT
BINKY BURGER HAS A BAND?

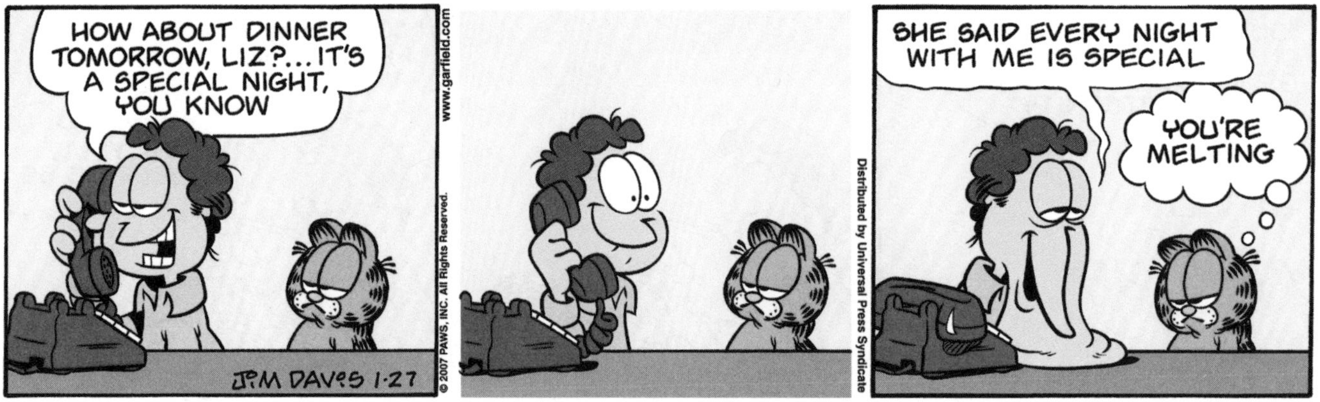
HOW ABOUT DINNER TOMORROW, LIZ?... IT'S A SPECIAL NIGHT, YOU KNOW
SHE SAID EVERY NIGHT WITH ME IS SPECIAL
YOU'RE MELTING

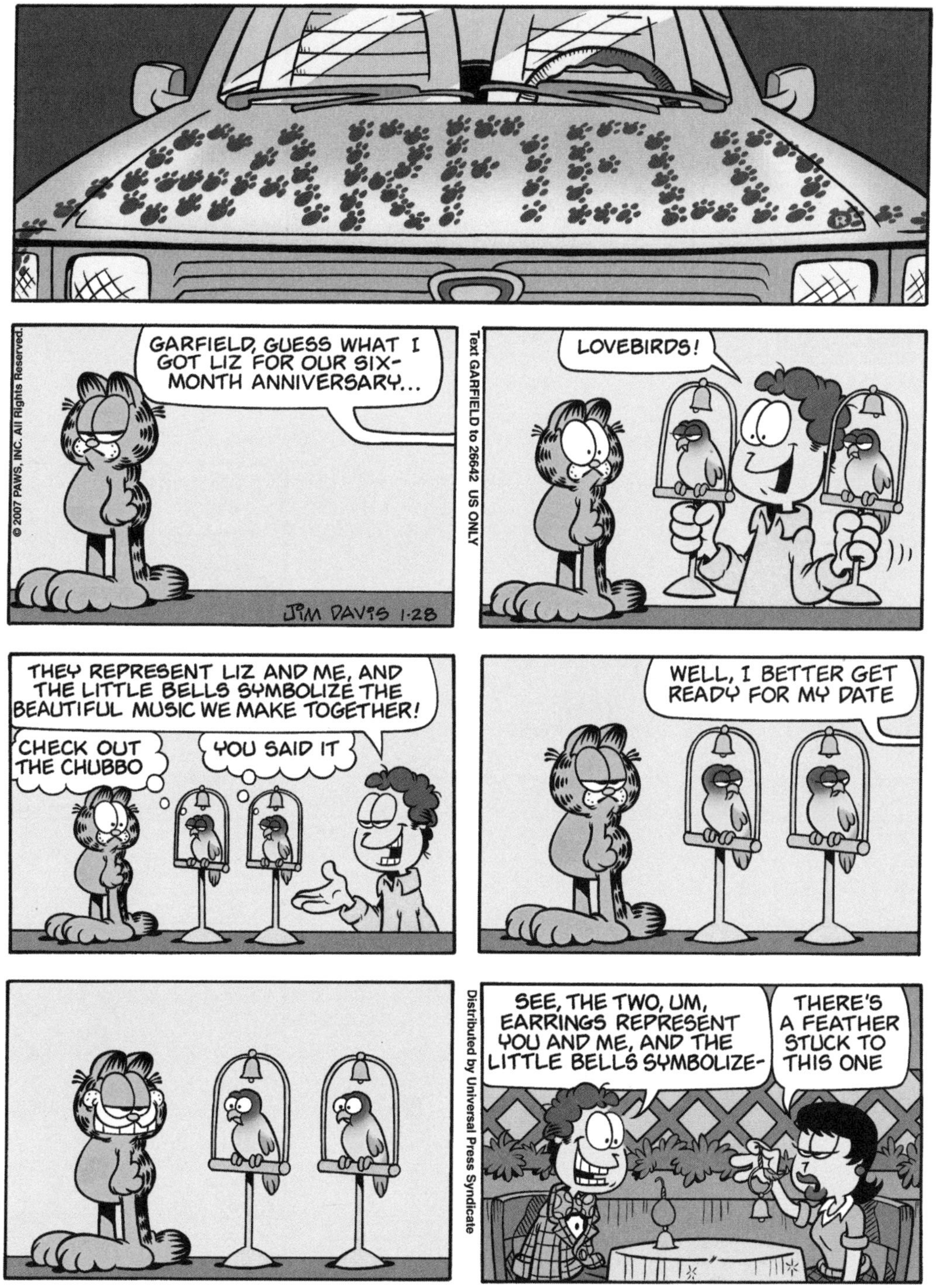
GARFIELD
GARFIELD, GUESS WHAT I GOT LIZ FOR OUR SIX-MONTH ANNIVERSARY...
© 2007 PAWS, INC. All Rights Reserved.
JIM DAVIS 1-28
LOVEBIRDS!
Text GARFIELD to 26642 US ONLY
THEY REPRESENT LIZ AND ME, AND THE LITTLE BELLS SYMBOLIZE THE BEAUTIFUL MUSIC WE MAKE TOGETHER!
CHECK OUT THE CHUBBO
YOU SAID IT
WELL, I BETTER GET READY FOR MY DATE
Distributed by Universal Press Syndicate
SEE, THE TWO, UM, EARRINGS REPRESENT YOU AND ME, AND THE LITTLE BELLS SYMBOLIZE-
THERE'S A FEATHER STUCK TO THIS ONE

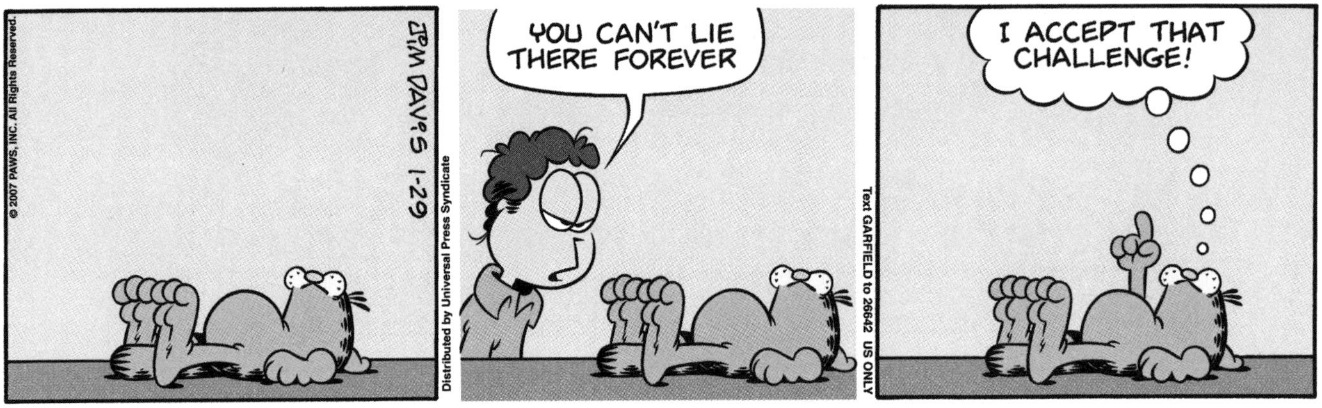
© 2007 PAWS, INC. All Rights Reserved.
JIM DAVIS 1-29
YOU CAN'T LIE THERE FOREVER
Distributed by Universal Press Syndicate
I ACCEPT THAT CHALLENGE!
Text GARFIELD to 26642 US ONLY

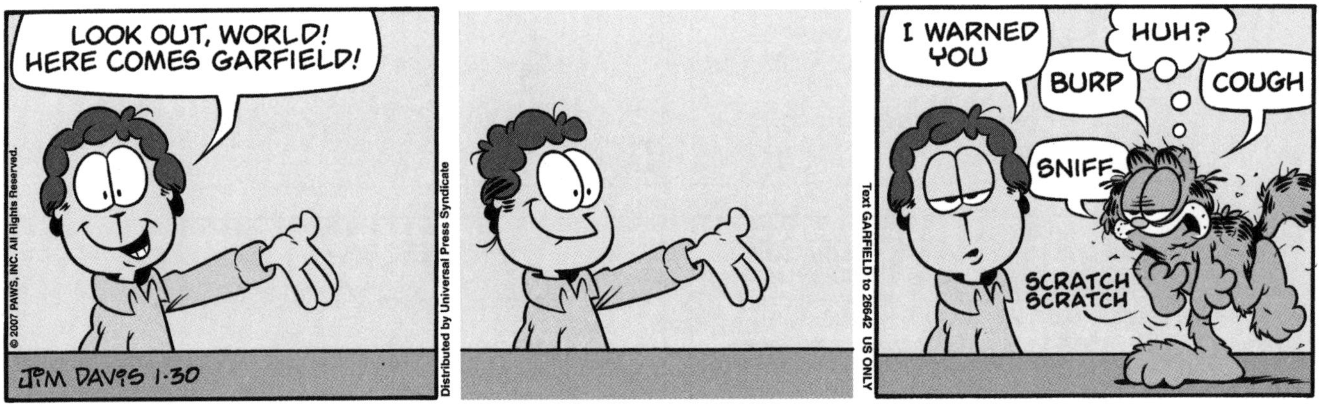
© 2007 PAWS, INC. All Rights Reserved.
LOOK OUT, WORLD! HERE COMES GARFIELD!
JIM DAVIS 1-30
Distributed by Universal Press Syndicate
I WARNED YOU
HUH?
BURP
COUGH
SNIFF
SCRATCH SCRATCH
Text GARFIELD to 26642 US ONLY

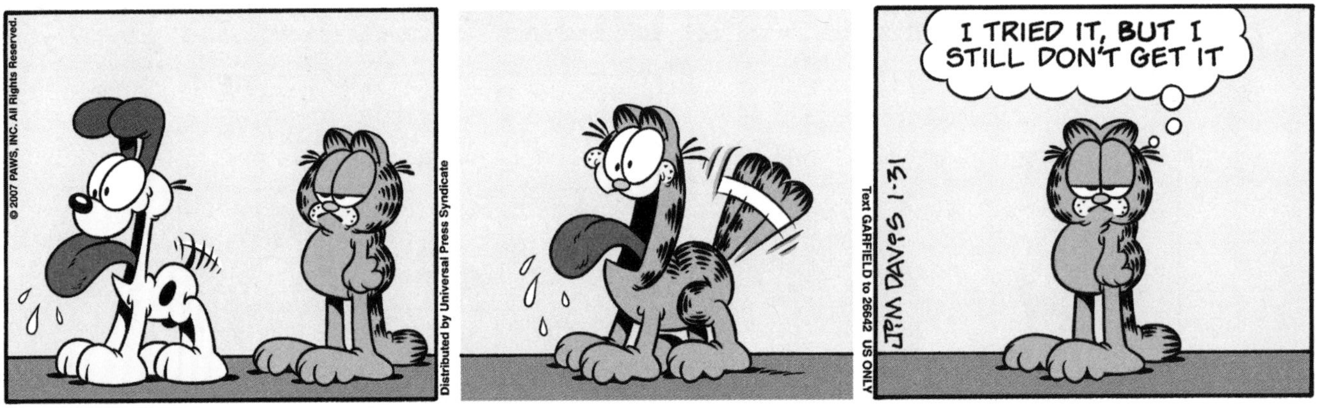
© 2007 PAWS, INC. All Rights Reserved.
Distributed by Universal Press Syndicate
I TRIED IT, BUT I STILL DON'T GET IT
JIM DAVIS 1-31
Text GARFIELD to 26642 US ONLY

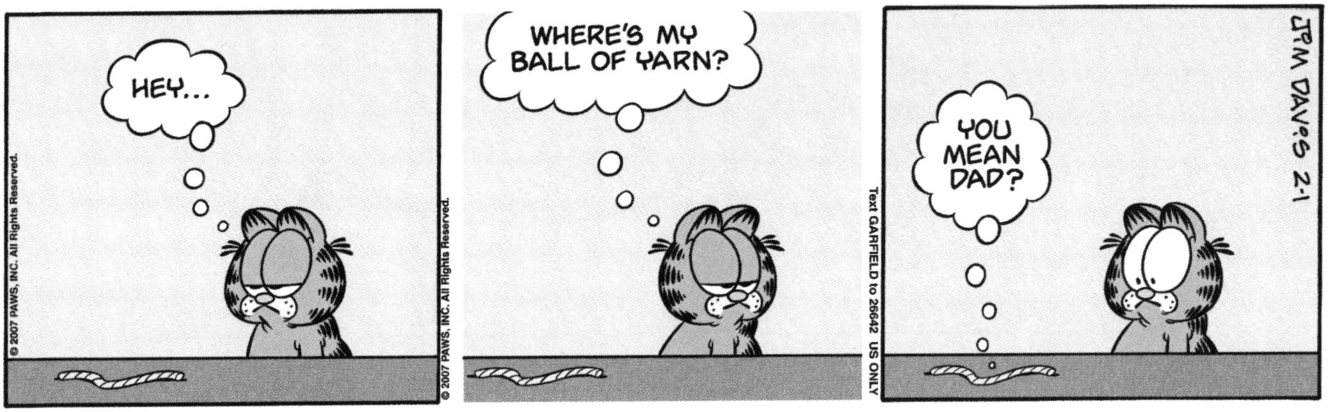
HEY...
WHERE'S MY BALL OF YARN?
YOU MEAN DAD?
© 2007 PAWS, INC. All Rights Reserved.
Text GARFIELD to 26642 US ONLY
JPM DAVIS 2-1

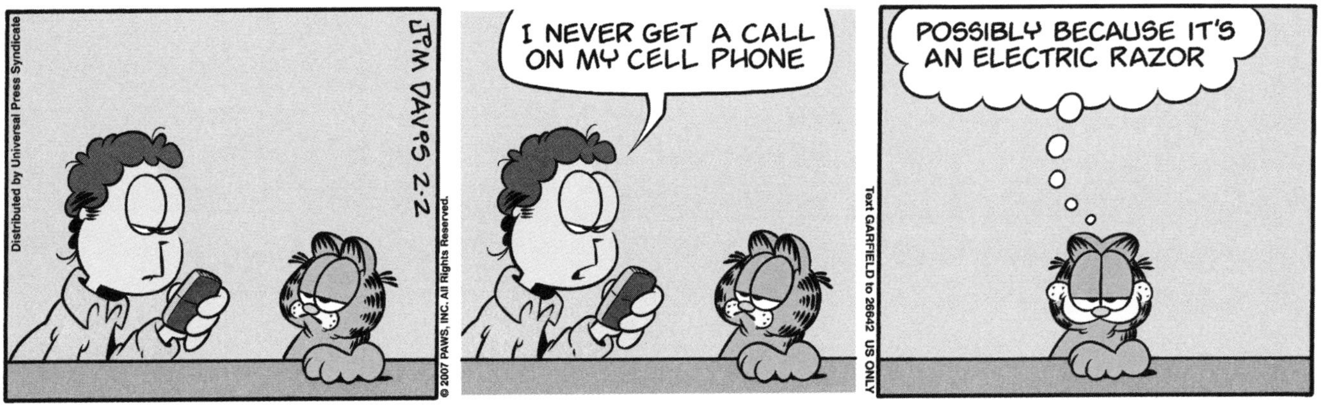
I NEVER GET A CALL ON MY CELL PHONE
POSSIBLY BECAUSE IT'S AN ELECTRIC RAZOR
Distributed by Universal Press Syndicate
© 2007 PAWS, INC. All Rights Reserved.
Text GARFIELD to 26642 US ONLY
JPM DAVIS 2-2

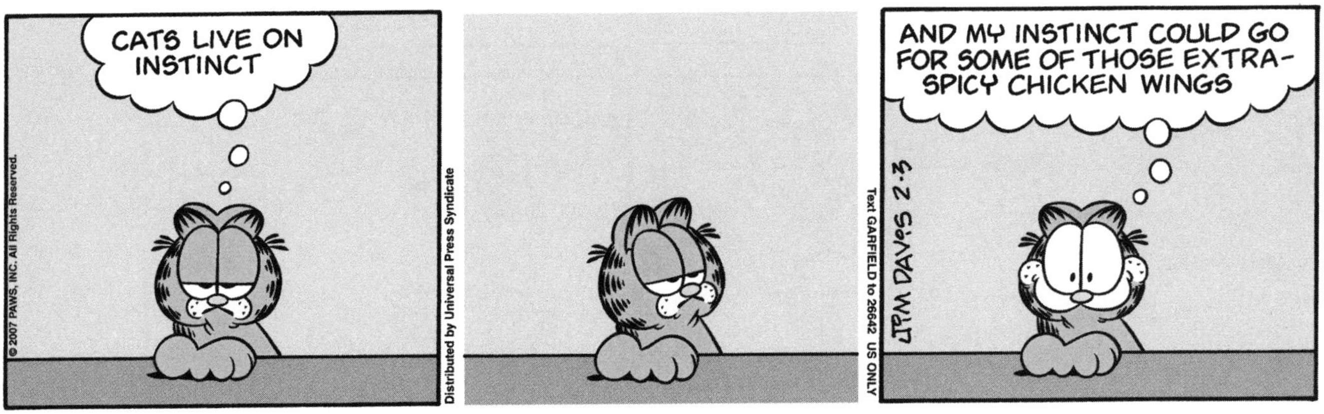
CATS LIVE ON INSTINCT
AND MY INSTINCT COULD GO FOR SOME OF THOSE EXTRA-SPICY CHICKEN WINGS
© 2007 PAWS, INC. All Rights Reserved.
Distributed by Universal Press Syndicate
Text GARFIELD to 26642 US ONLY
JPM DAVIS 2-3

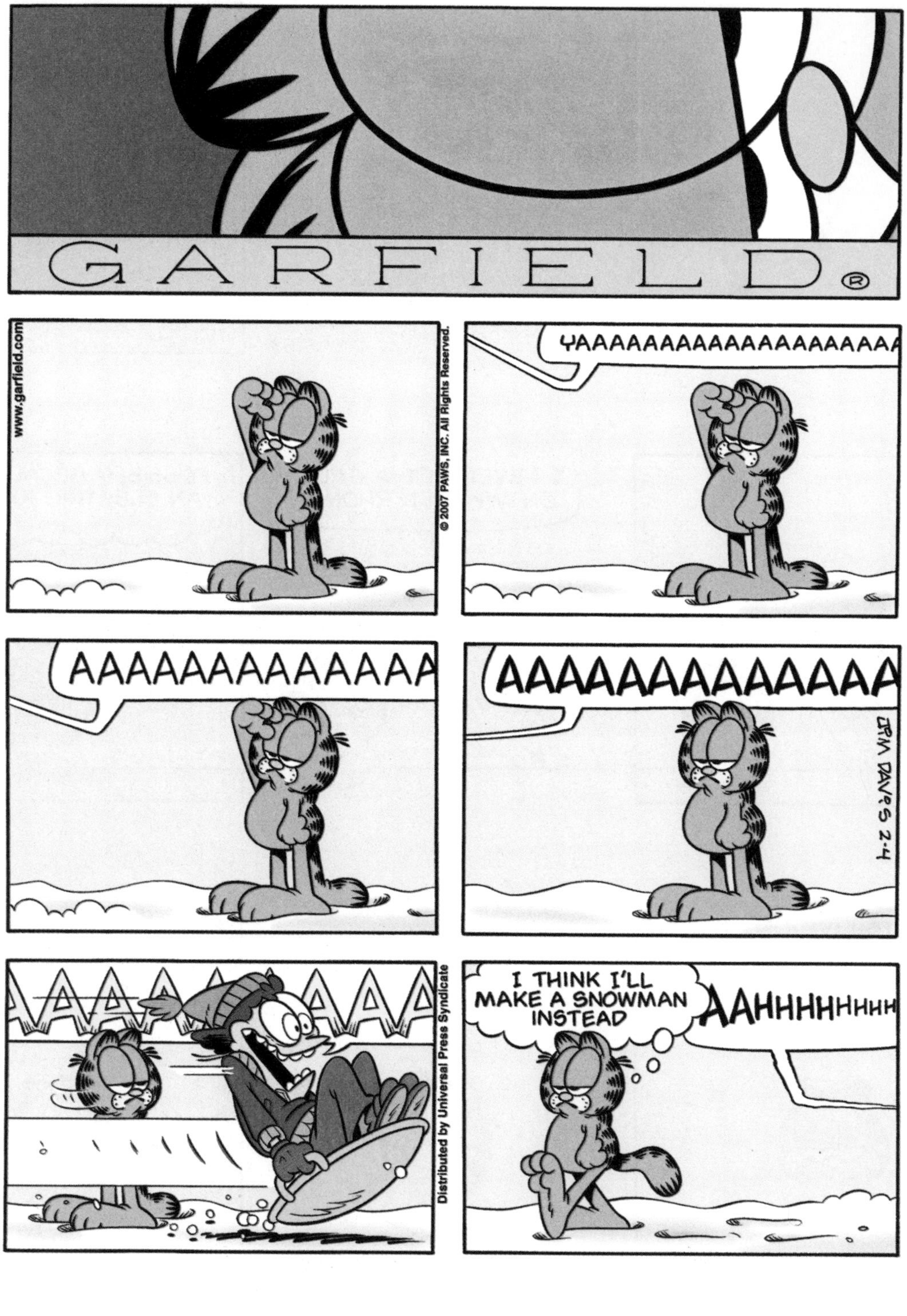
GARFIELD®
www.garfield.com
© 2007 PAWS, INC. All Rights Reserved.
YAAAAAAAAAAAAAAAAAAAA
AAAAAAAAAAAAAA
AAAAAAAAAAAAAA
JPM DAVIS 2-4
AAAAAAAAA
Distributed by Universal Press Syndicate
I THINK I'LL MAKE A SNOWMAN INSTEAD
AAHHHHHHHH

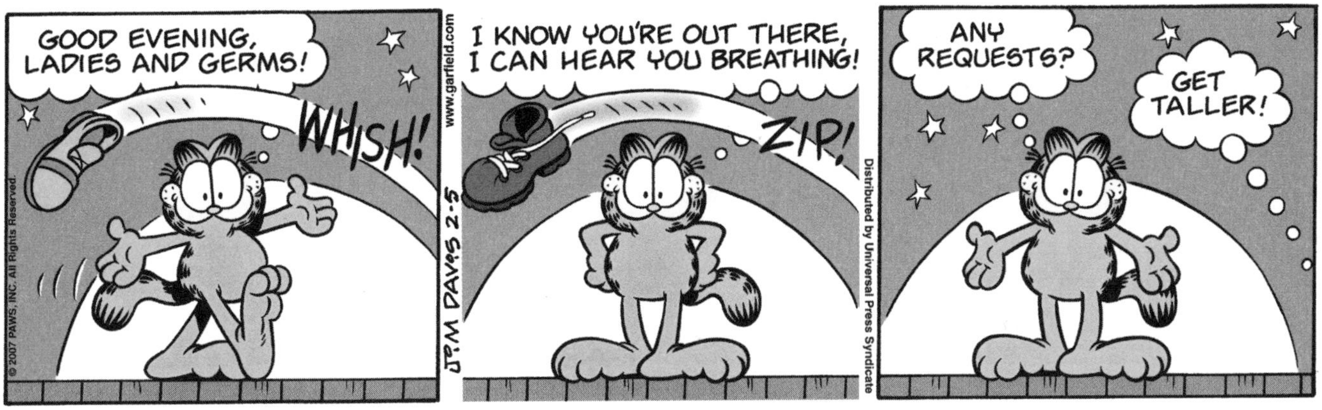
GOOD EVENING, LADIES AND GERMS!
WHISH!
© 2007 PAWS, INC. All Rights Reserved.
www.garfield.com
JIM DAVIS 2-5
I KNOW YOU'RE OUT THERE, I CAN HEAR YOU BREATHING!
ZIP!
Distributed by Universal Press Syndicate
ANY REQUESTS?
GET TALLER!

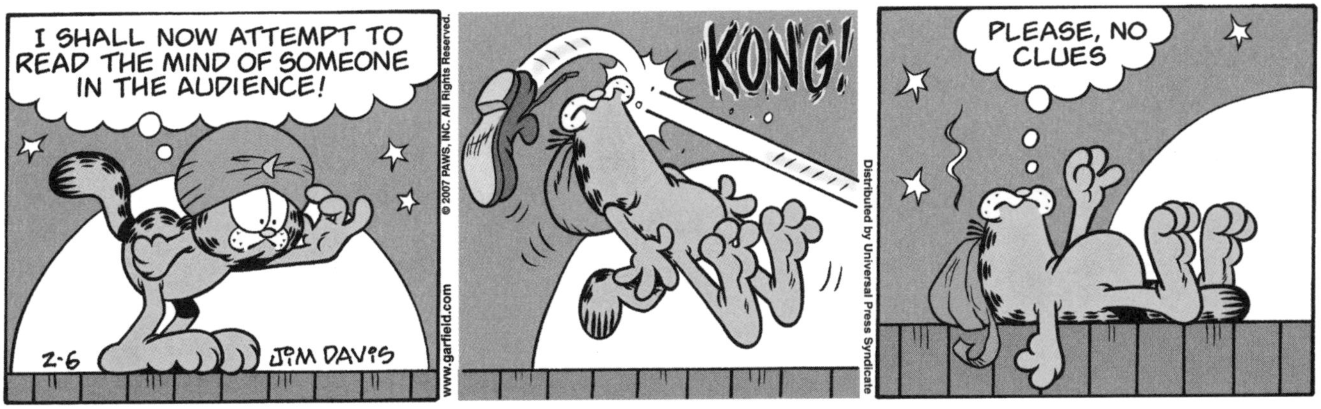
I SHALL NOW ATTEMPT TO READ THE MIND OF SOMEONE IN THE AUDIENCE!
2-6
JIM DAVIS
© 2007 PAWS, INC. All Rights Reserved.
www.garfield.com
KONG!
Distributed by Universal Press Syndicate
PLEASE, NO CLUES

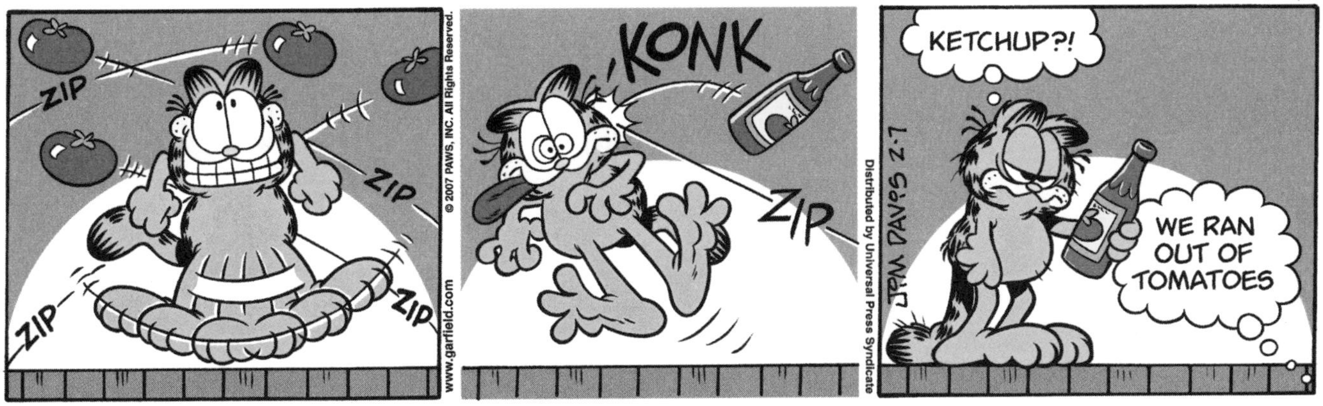
ZIP
ZIP
ZIP
ZIP
© 2007 PAWS, INC. All Rights Reserved.
www.garfield.com
KONK
ZIP
Distributed by Universal Press Syndicate
JIM DAVIS 2-7
KETCHUP?!
WE RAN OUT OF TOMATOES

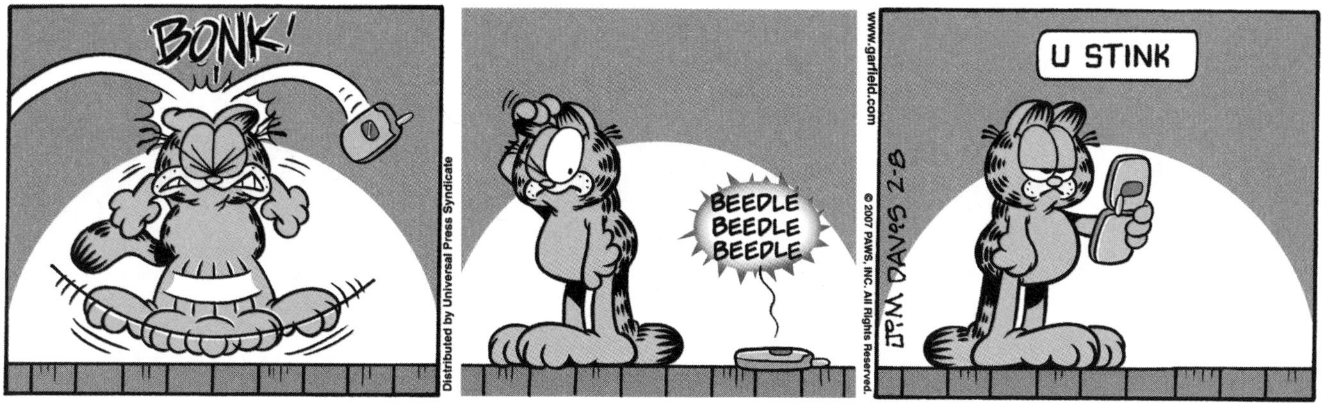
BONK!
Distributed by Universal Press Syndicate
BEEDLE BEEDLE BEEDLE
www.garfield.com
© 2007 PAWS, INC. All Rights Reserved.
JIM DAVIS 2-8
U STINK

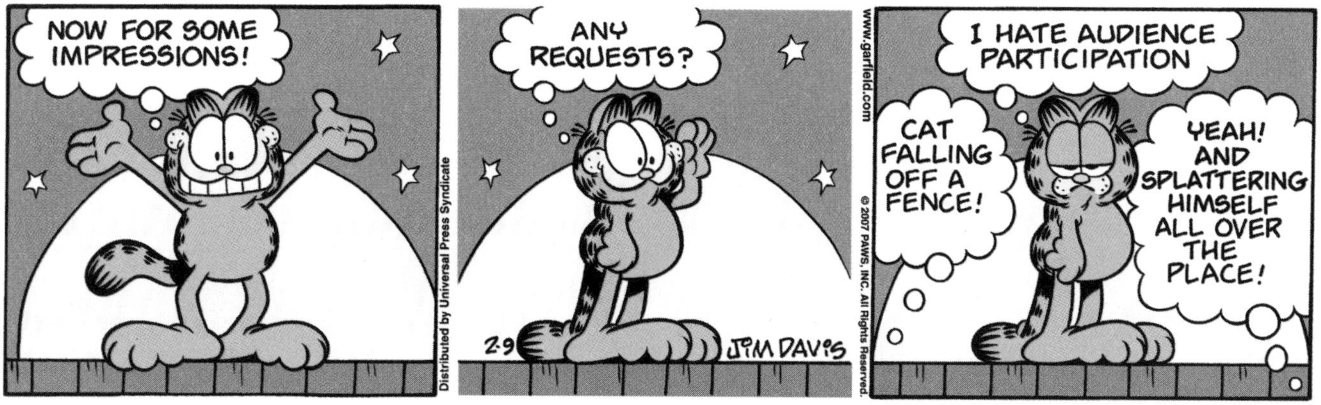
NOW FOR SOME IMPRESSIONS!
Distributed by Universal Press Syndicate
ANY REQUESTS?
2-9
JIM DAVIS
www.garfield.com
© 2007 PAWS, INC. All Rights Reserved.
I HATE AUDIENCE PARTICIPATION
CAT FALLING OFF A FENCE!
YEAH! AND SPLATTERING HIMSELF ALL OVER THE PLACE!

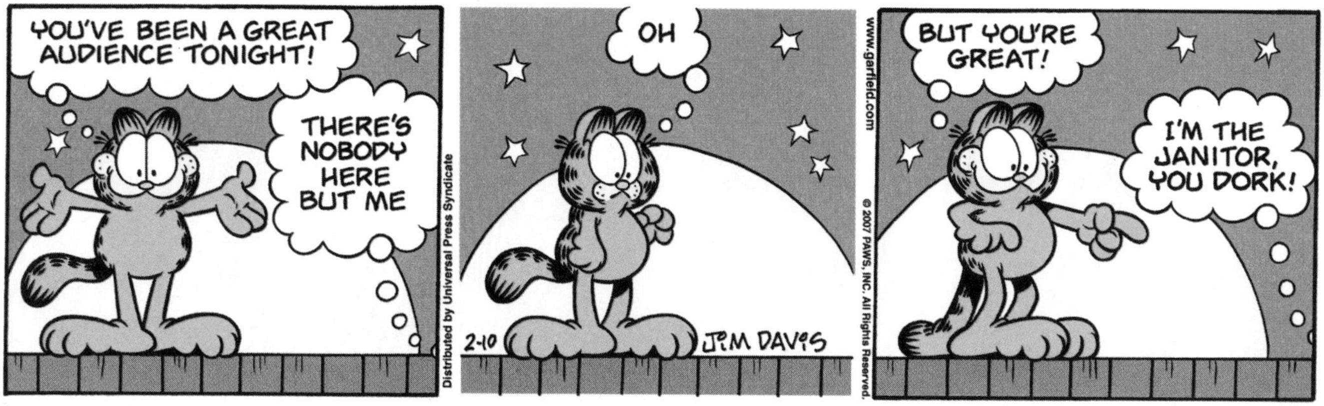
YOU'VE BEEN A GREAT AUDIENCE TONIGHT!
THERE'S NOBODY HERE BUT ME
Distributed by Universal Press Syndicate
OH
2-10
JIM DAVIS
www.garfield.com
© 2007 PAWS, INC. All Rights Reserved.
BUT YOU'RE GREAT!
I'M THE JANITOR, YOU DORK!

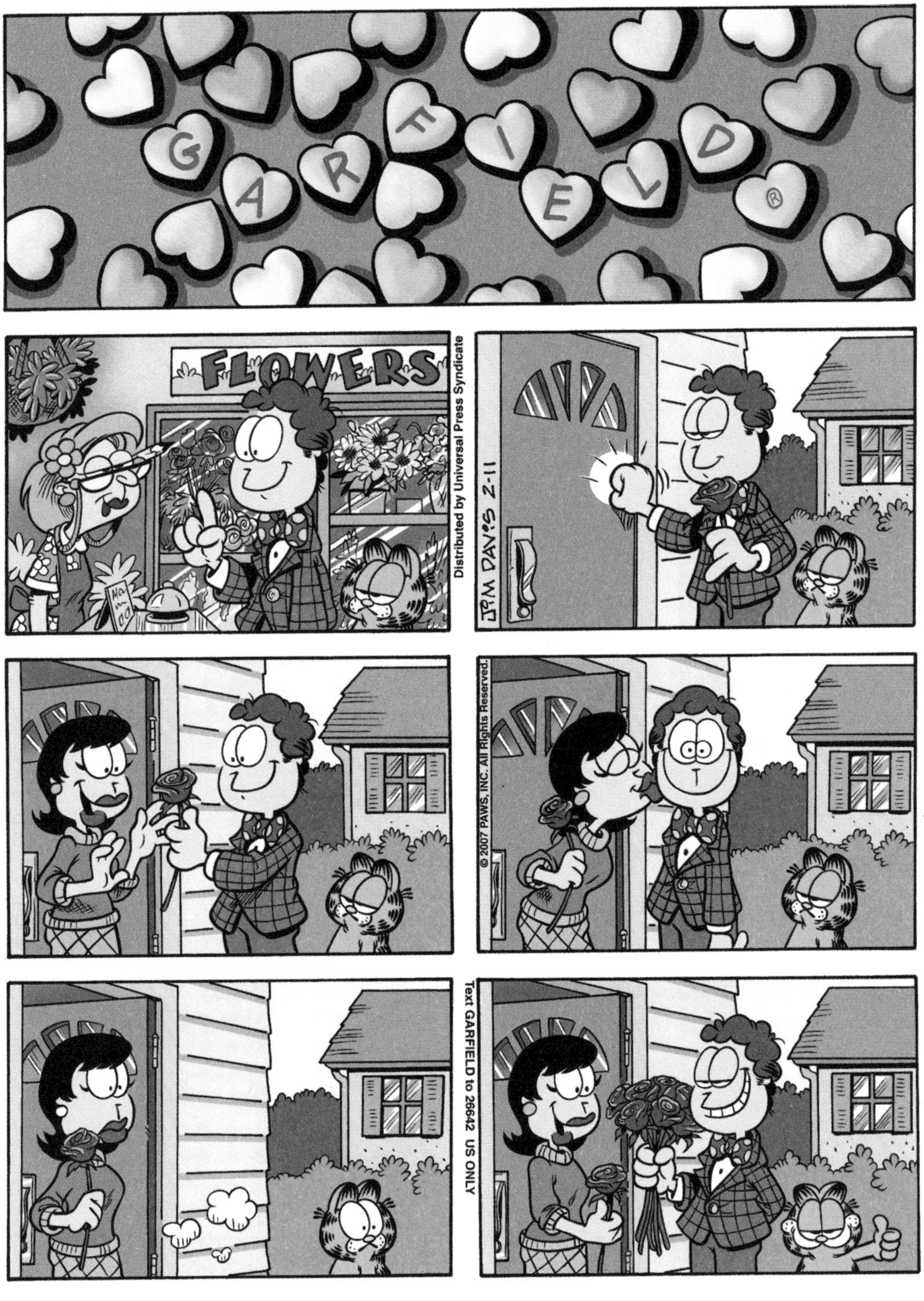
GARFIELD®
FLOWERS
JPM DAVIS 2-11
Distributed by Universal Press Syndicate
© 2007 PAWS, INC. All Rights Reserved.
Text GARFIELD to 26642 US ONLY

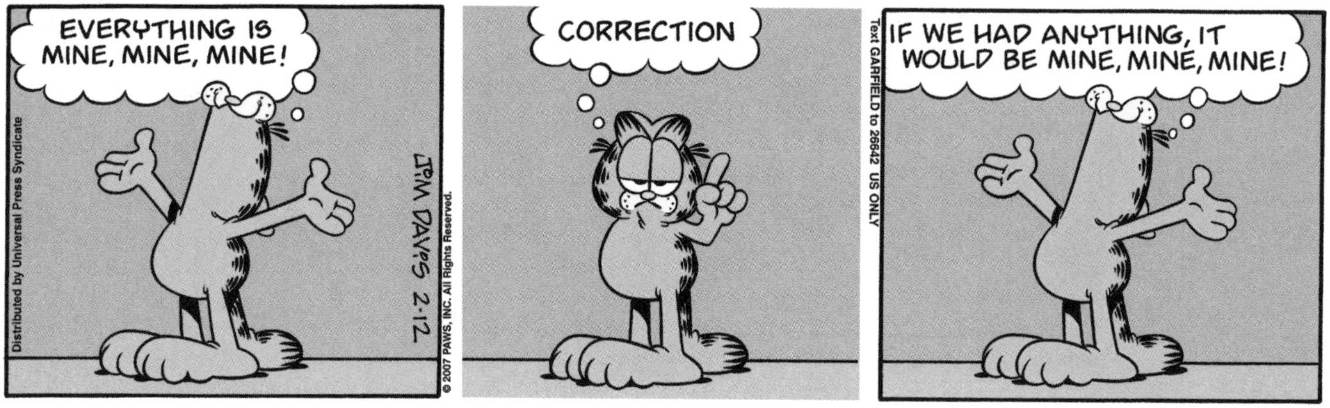
EVERYTHING IS MINE, MINE, MINE!
CORRECTION
IF WE HAD ANYTHING, IT WOULD BE MINE, MINE, MINE!
Distributed by Universal Press Syndicate
JIM DAVIS 2-12
© 2007 PAWS, INC. All Rights Reserved.
Text GARFIELD to 26642 US ONLY

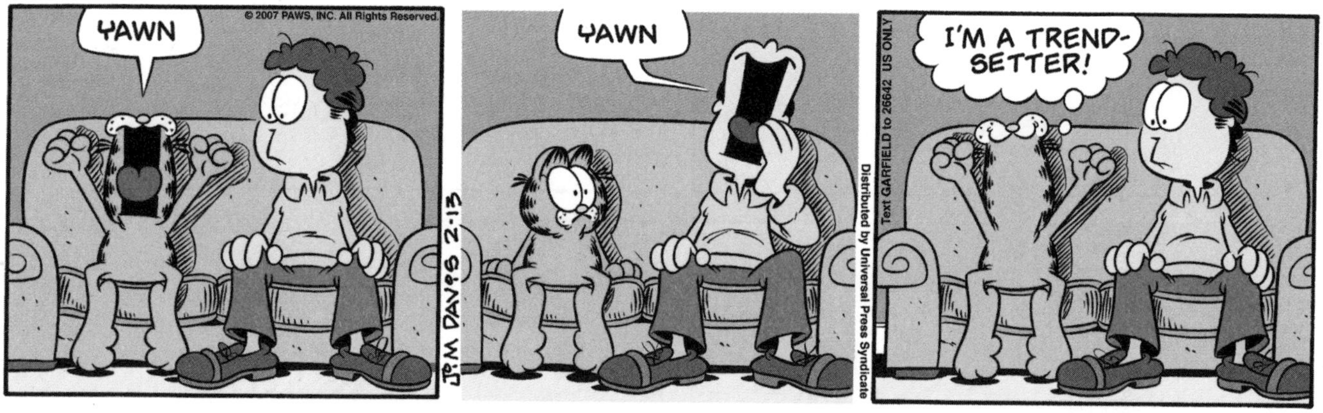
YAWN
YAWN
I'M A TREND-SETTER!
© 2007 PAWS, INC. All Rights Reserved.
JIM DAVIS 2-13
Distributed by Universal Press Syndicate
Text GARFIELD to 26642 US ONLY

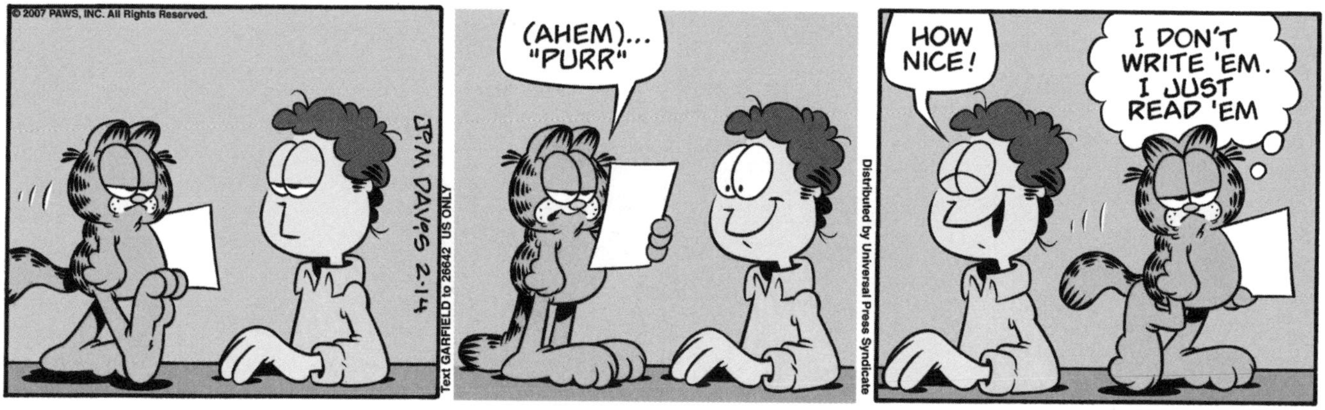
(AHEM)... "PURR"
HOW NICE!
I DON'T WRITE 'EM. I JUST READ 'EM
© 2007 PAWS, INC. All Rights Reserved.
JIM DAVIS 2-14
Text GARFIELD to 26642 US ONLY
Distributed by Universal Press Syndicate

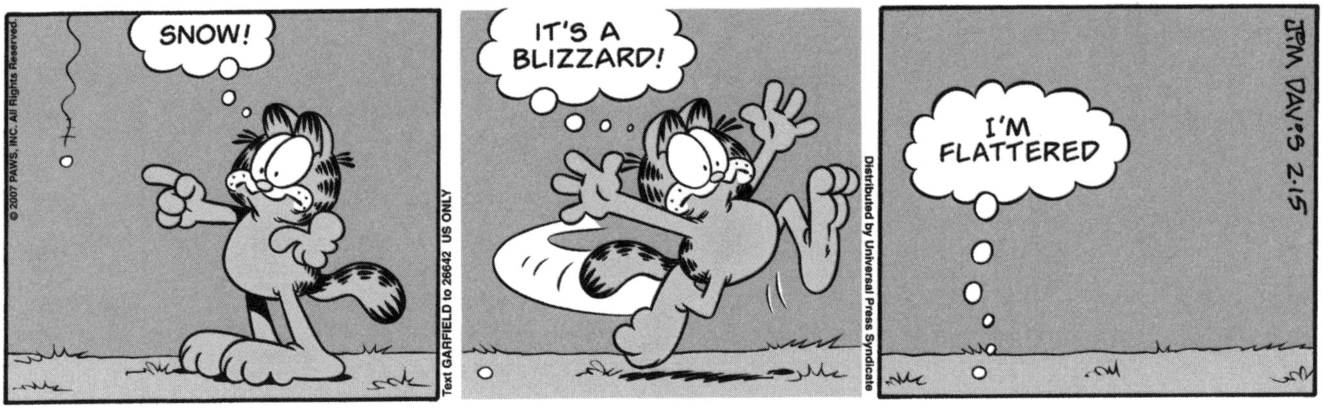
SNOW!
IT'S A BLIZZARD!
I'M FLATTERED
JIM DAVIS 2-15
© 2007 PAWS, INC. All Rights Reserved.
Text GARFIELD to 26642 US ONLY
Distributed by Universal Press Syndicate

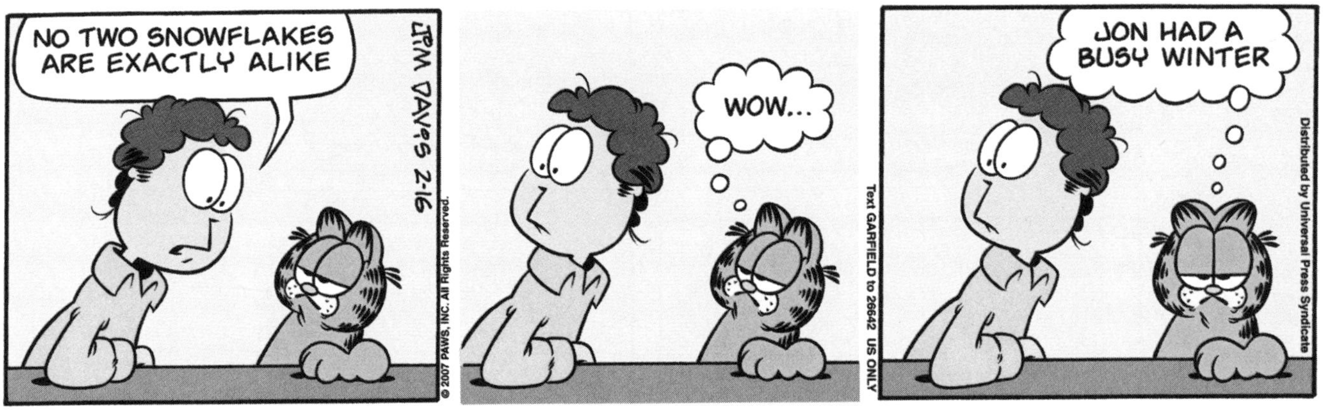
NO TWO SNOWFLAKES ARE EXACTLY ALIKE
JIM DAVIS 2-16
WOW...
JON HAD A BUSY WINTER
© 2007 PAWS, INC. All Rights Reserved.
Text GARFIELD to 26642 US ONLY
Distributed by Universal Press Syndicate

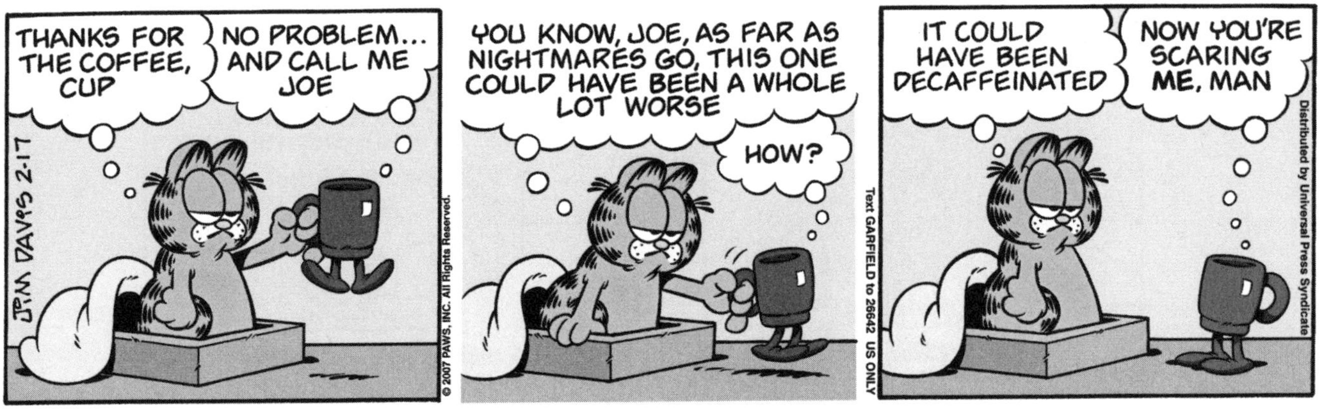
THANKS FOR THE COFFEE, CUP
NO PROBLEM... AND CALL ME JOE
JIM DAVIS 2-17
YOU KNOW, JOE, AS FAR AS NIGHTMARES GO, THIS ONE COULD HAVE BEEN A WHOLE LOT WORSE
HOW?
IT COULD HAVE BEEN DECAFFEINATED
NOW YOU'RE SCARING ME, MAN
© 2007 PAWS, INC. All Rights Reserved.
Text GARFIELD to 26642 US ONLY
Distributed by Universal Press Syndicate

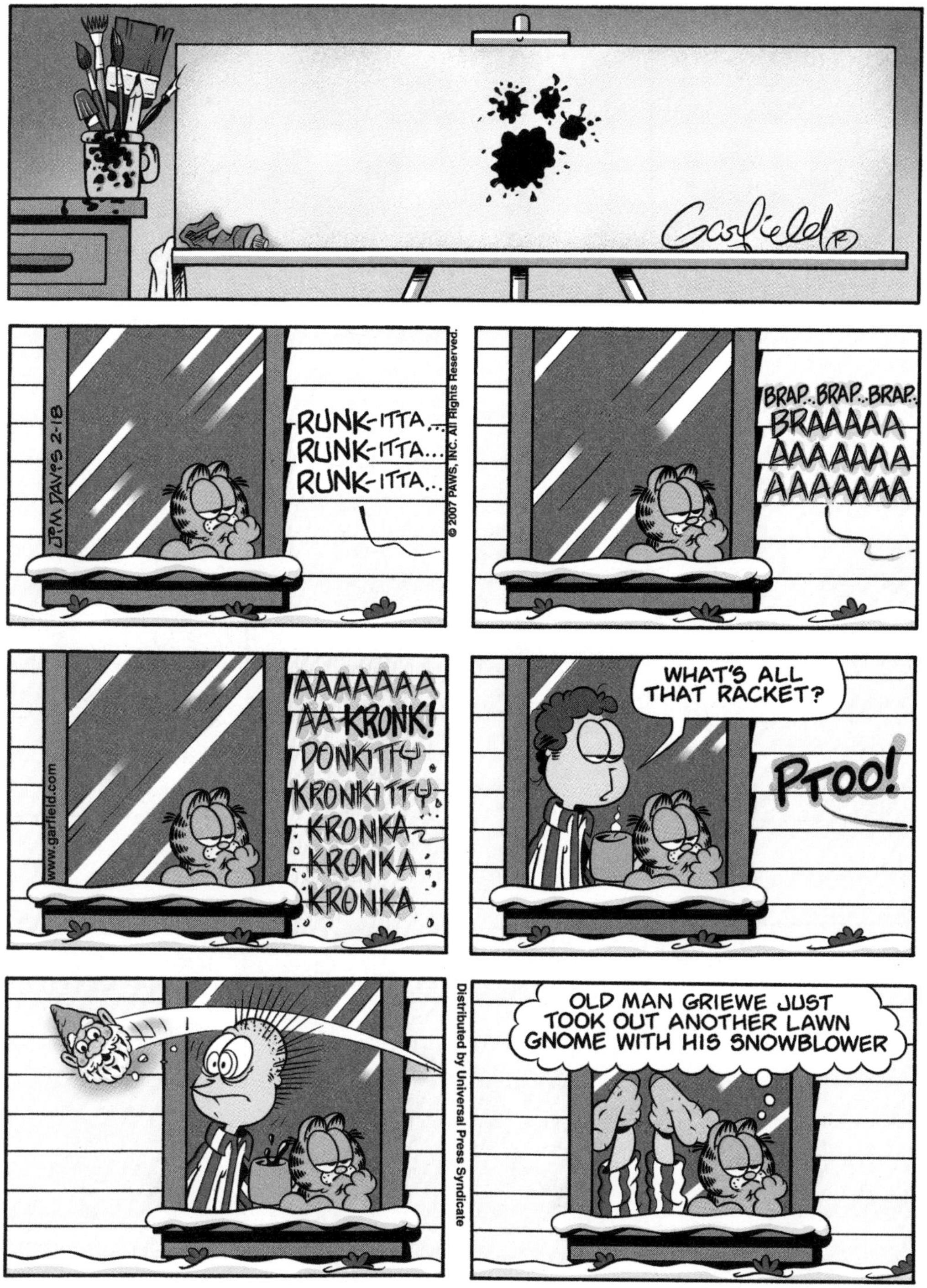
Garfield®
JPM DAVIS 2-18
RUNK-ITTA... RUNK-ITTA... RUNK-ITTA...
© 2007 PAWS, INC. All Rights Reserved.
BRAP..BRAP..BRAP.. BRAAAAAAAAAAAAAAAAAAAA
www.garfield.com
AAAAAAAAA KRONK! DONKITTY KRONKITTY KRONKA KRONKA KRONKA
WHAT'S ALL THAT RACKET?
PTOO!
Distributed by Universal Press Syndicate
OLD MAN GRIEWE JUST TOOK OUT ANOTHER LAWN GNOME WITH HIS SNOWBLOWER

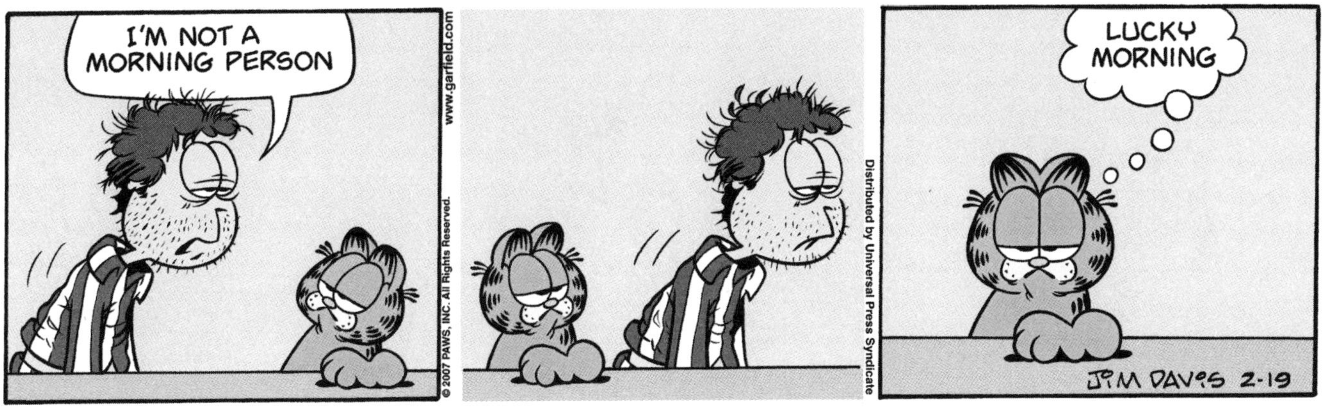
I'M NOT A MORNING PERSON
© 2007 PAWS, INC. All Rights Reserved. www.garfield.com
Distributed by Universal Press Syndicate
LUCKY MORNING
JIM DAVIS 2-19

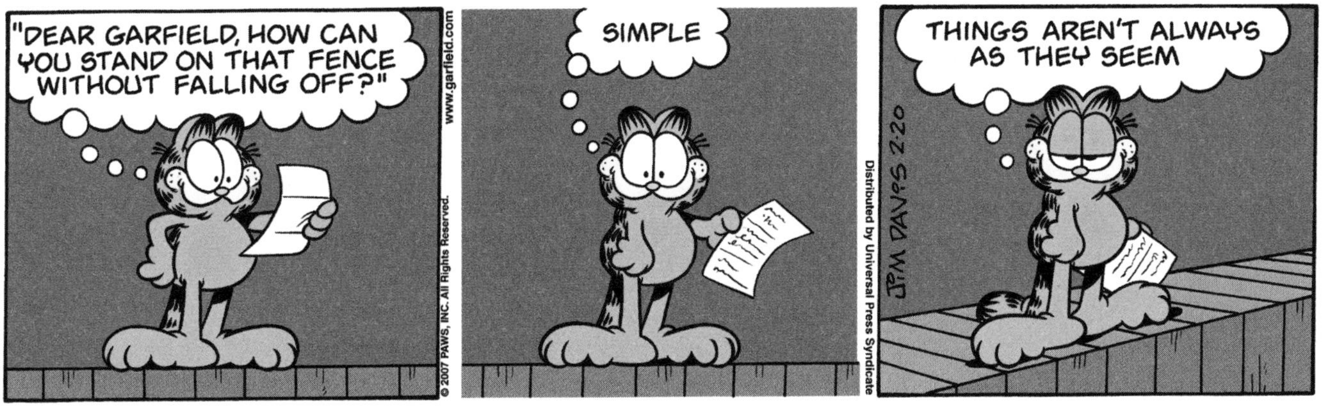
"DEAR GARFIELD, HOW CAN YOU STAND ON THAT FENCE WITHOUT FALLING OFF?"
© 2007 PAWS, INC. All Rights Reserved. www.garfield.com
SIMPLE
Distributed by Universal Press Syndicate
JIM DAVIS 2-20
THINGS AREN'T ALWAYS AS THEY SEEM

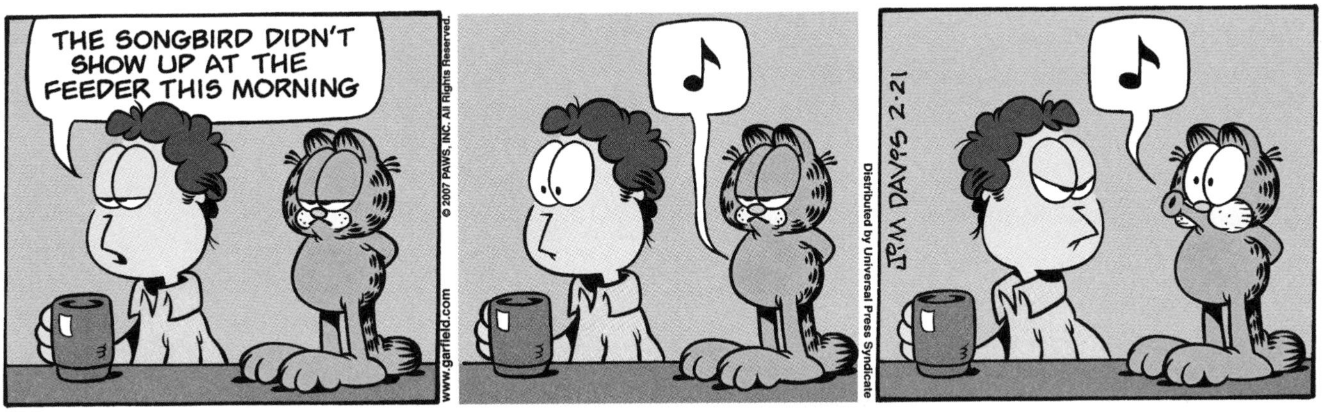
THE SONGBIRD DIDN'T SHOW UP AT THE FEEDER THIS MORNING
© 2007 PAWS, INC. All Rights Reserved. www.garfield.com
Distributed by Universal Press Syndicate
JIM DAVIS 2-21

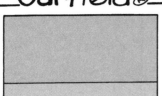

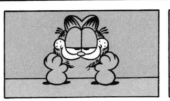

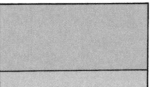

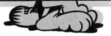

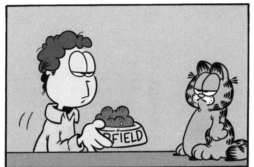

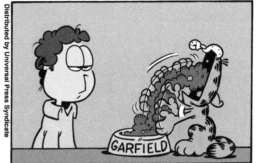

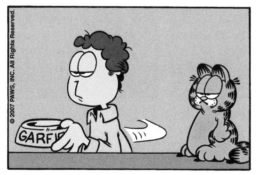

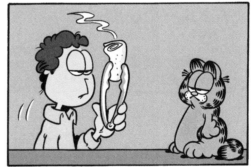

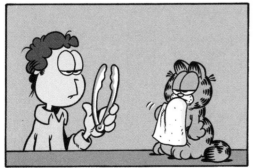

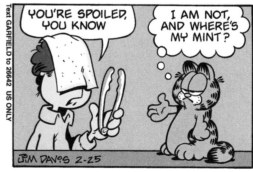

Garfield®
Distributed by Universal Press Syndicate
RFIELD
GARFIELD
© 2007 PAWS, INC. All Rights Reserved.
GARFI
Text GARFIELD to 26642 US ONLY
YOU'RE SPOILED, YOU KNOW
I AM NOT, AND WHERE'S MY MINT?
JIM DAVIS 2-25

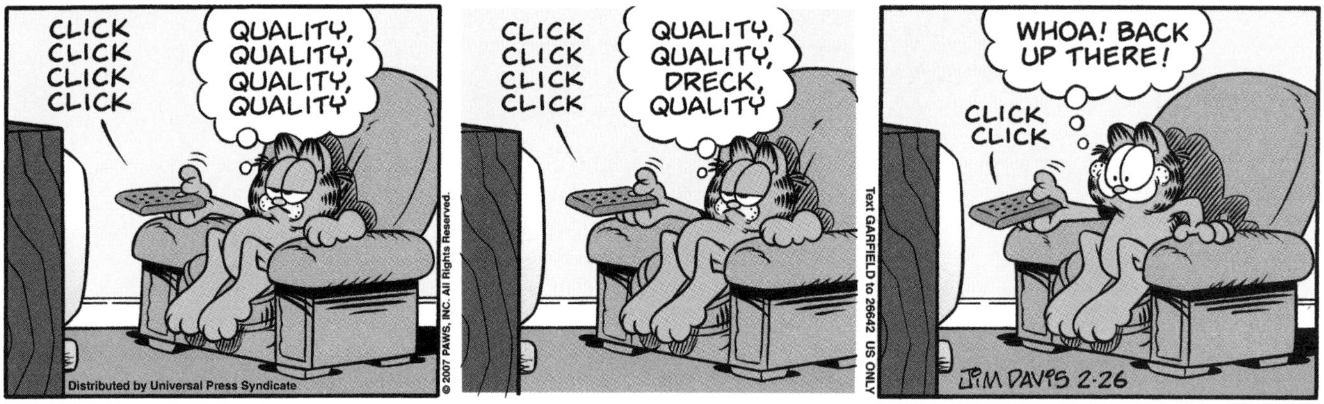
CLICK CLICK CLICK CLICK
QUALITY, QUALITY, QUALITY, QUALITY
CLICK CLICK CLICK CLICK
QUALITY, QUALITY, DRECK, QUALITY
WHOA! BACK UP THERE!
CLICK CLICK
JIM DAVIS 2-26

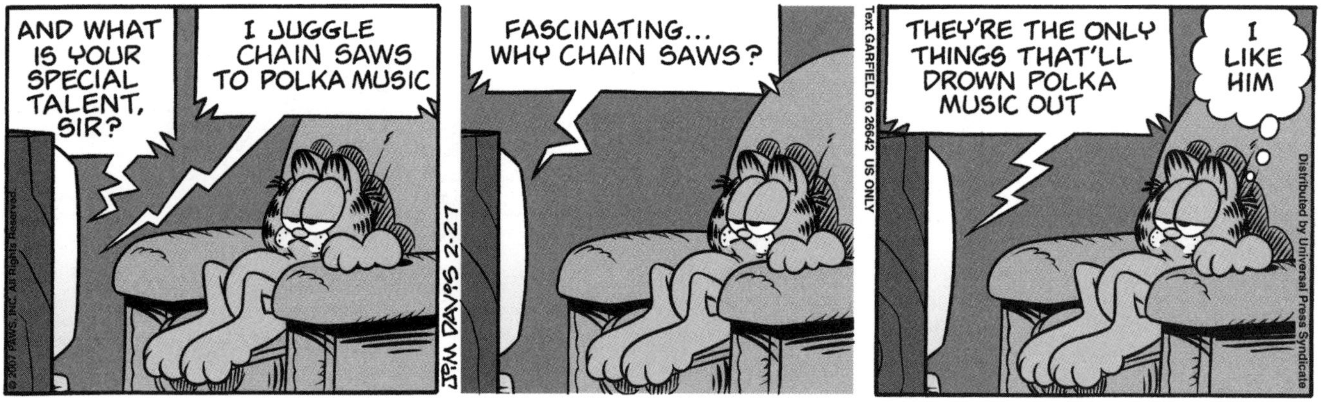
AND WHAT IS YOUR SPECIAL TALENT, SIR?
I JUGGLE CHAIN SAWS TO POLKA MUSIC
FASCINATING... WHY CHAIN SAWS?
THEY'RE THE ONLY THINGS THAT'LL DROWN POLKA MUSIC OUT
I LIKE HIM
JIM DAVIS 2-27

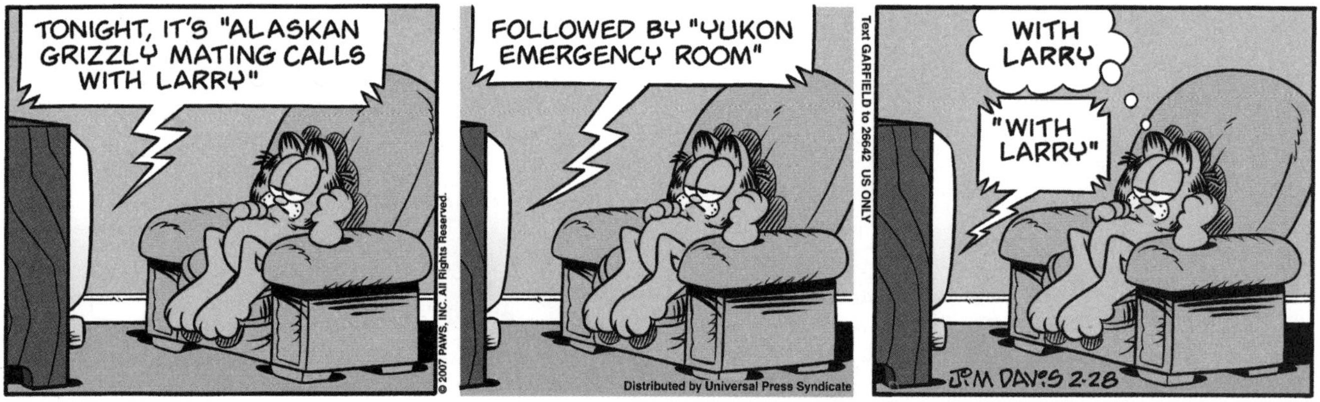
TONIGHT, IT'S "ALASKAN GRIZZLY MATING CALLS WITH LARRY"
FOLLOWED BY "YUKON EMERGENCY ROOM"
WITH LARRY
"WITH LARRY"
JIM DAVIS 2-28

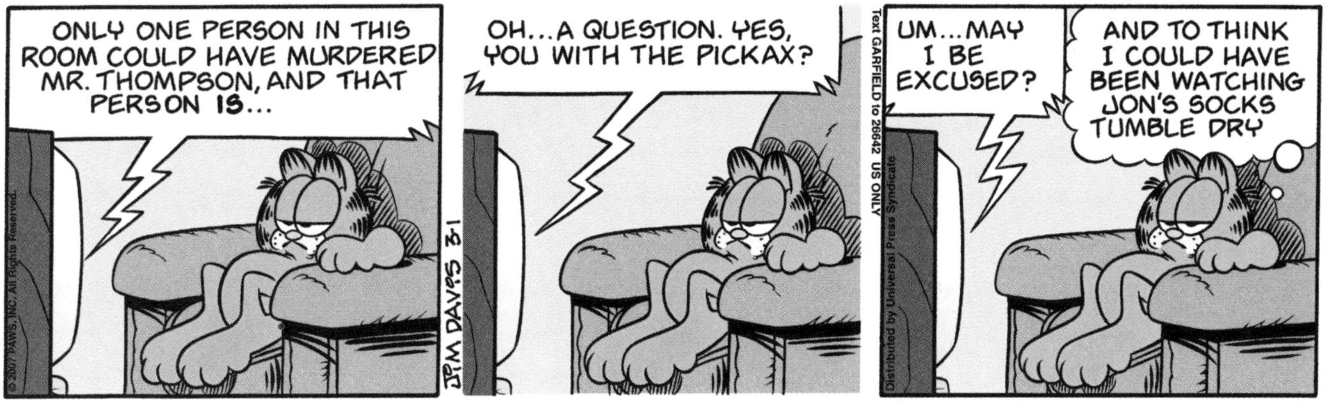
ONLY ONE PERSON IN THIS ROOM COULD HAVE MURDERED MR. THOMPSON, AND THAT PERSON IS...
OH... A QUESTION. YES, YOU WITH THE PICKAX?
UM... MAY I BE EXCUSED?
AND TO THINK I COULD HAVE BEEN WATCHING JON'S SOCKS TUMBLE DRY
JIM DAVIS 3-1
© 2007 PAWS, INC. All Rights Reserved.
Text GARFIELD to 26642 US ONLY
Distributed by Universal Press Syndicate

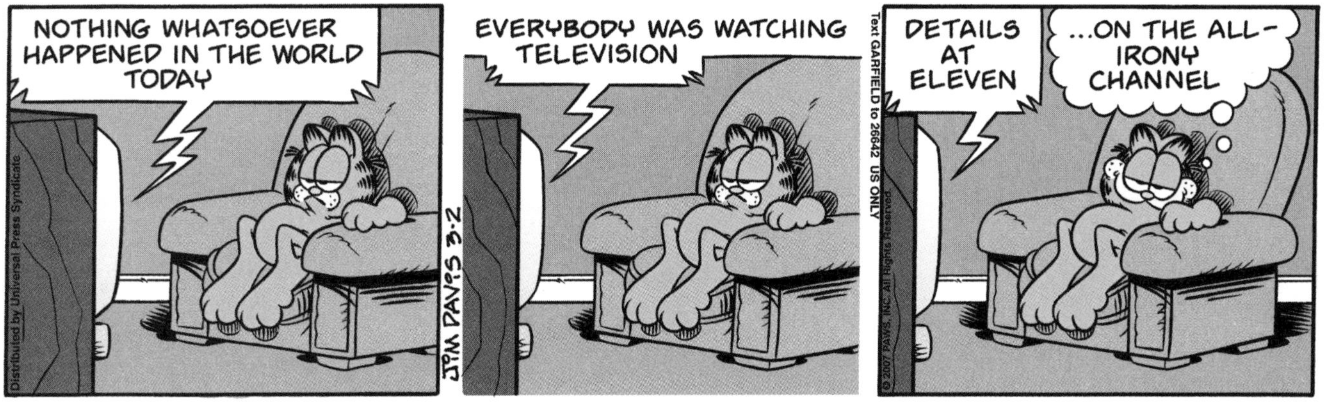
NOTHING WHATSOEVER HAPPENED IN THE WORLD TODAY
EVERYBODY WAS WATCHING TELEVISION
DETAILS AT ELEVEN
...ON THE ALL-IRONY CHANNEL
JIM DAVIS 3-2
Distributed by Universal Press Syndicate
Text GARFIELD to 26642 US ONLY
© 2007 PAWS, INC. All Rights Reserved.

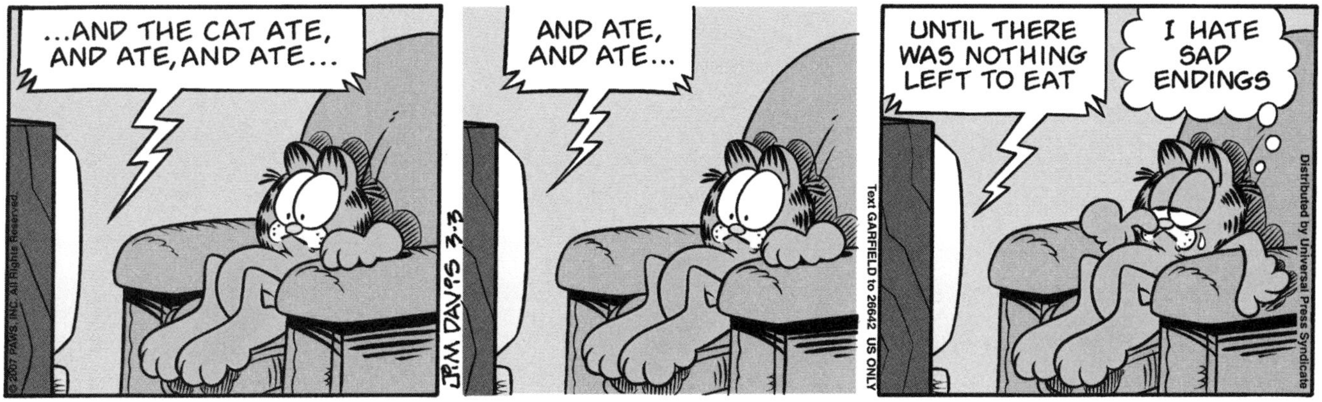
...AND THE CAT ATE, AND ATE, AND ATE...
AND ATE, AND ATE...
UNTIL THERE WAS NOTHING LEFT TO EAT
I HATE SAD ENDINGS
JIM DAVIS 3-3
© 2007 PAWS, INC. All Rights Reserved.
Text GARFIELD to 26642 US ONLY
Distributed by Universal Press Syndicate

GARFIELD FROM THE TRASH BIN

WARNING!

This page contains gross gags, crass cartoons, sick sketches, and truly tasteless trash that may cause brain damage, liver damage, foot fungus, painful earwax buildup, multiple personalities, bulging eyes, decreased night vision, dizziness, confusion, atypical facial pain, itching without a rash, itching with a rash, splotchy complexion, excessive thirst, insomnia, bloating, and really, really bad breath.

READ AT YOUR OWN RISK!

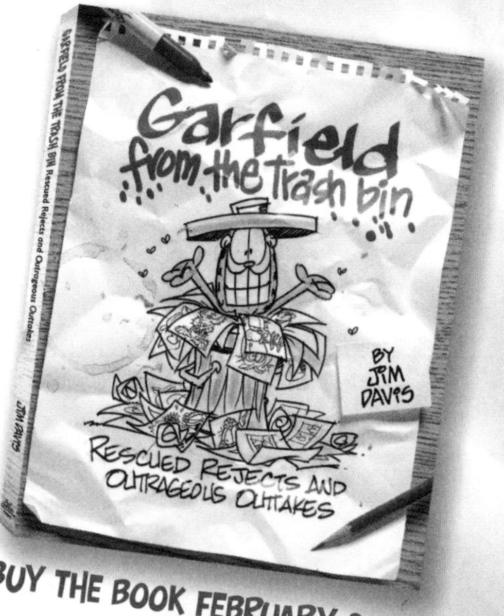
Garfield from the trash bin
BY JIM DAVIS
RESCUED REJECTS AND OUTRAGEOUS OUTTAKES

BUY THE BOOK FEBRUARY 2010!

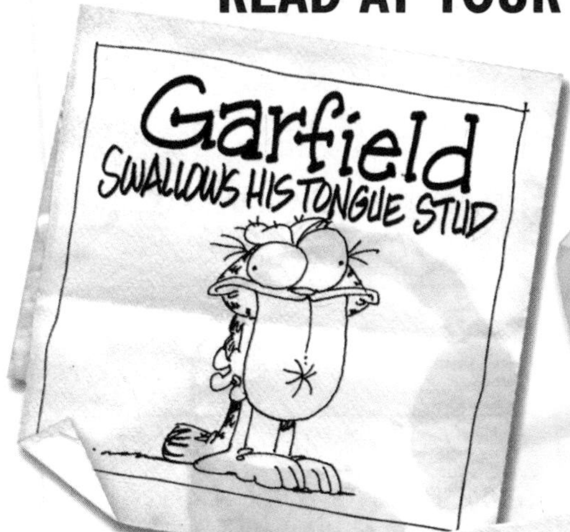
Garfield
SWALLOWS HIS TONGUE STUD

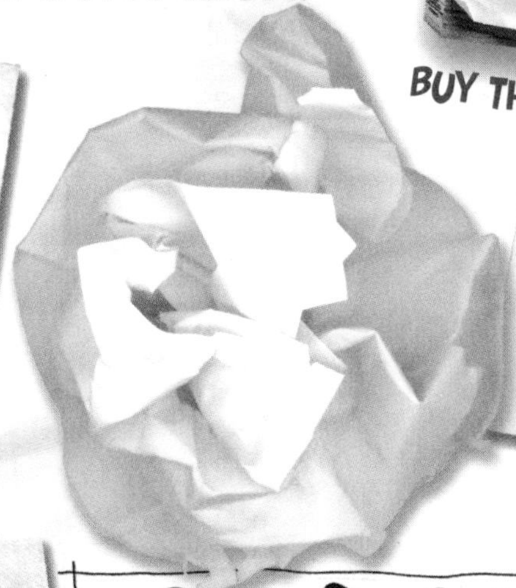

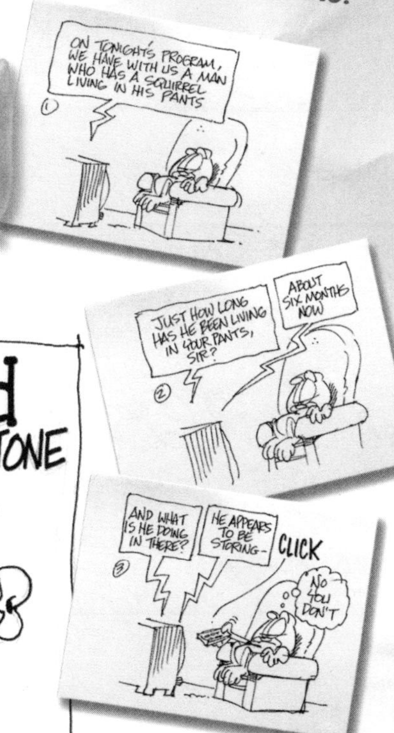
ON TONIGHT'S PROGRAM, WE HAVE WITH US A MAN WHO HAS A SQUIRREL LIVING IN HIS PANTS
JUST HOW LONG HAS HE BEEN LIVING IN YOUR PANTS, SIR?
ABOUT SIX MONTHS NOW
AND WHAT IS HE DOING IN THERE?
HE APPEARS TO BE STORING-
CLICK
NO YOU DON'T

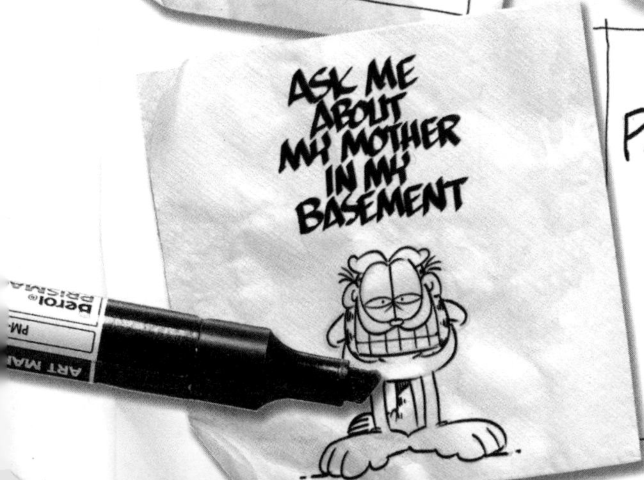
ASK ME ABOUT MY MOTHER IN MY BASEMENT

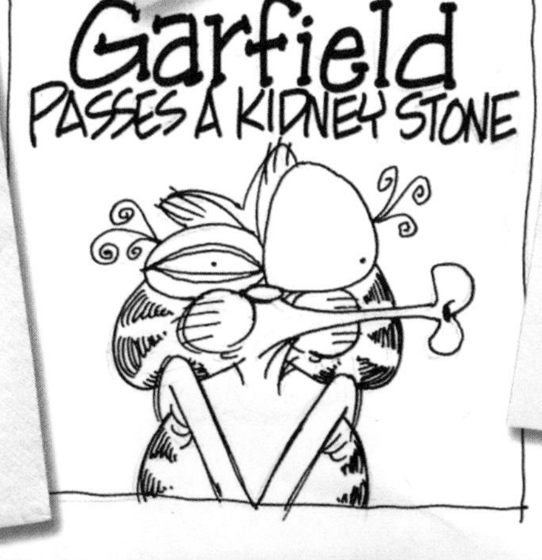
Garfield
PASSES A KIDNEY STONE

It's a party online—and YOU'RE invited!

GARFIELD.COM

News
Get the latest scoop on everyone's favorite media darling!

Fun & Games
Tons of arcade fun for everyone. Wanna play?

Comics
Read the daily comic or browse the vault for a blast from the past!

PostCards
Stay connected! Send animated greetings to all your online buds.

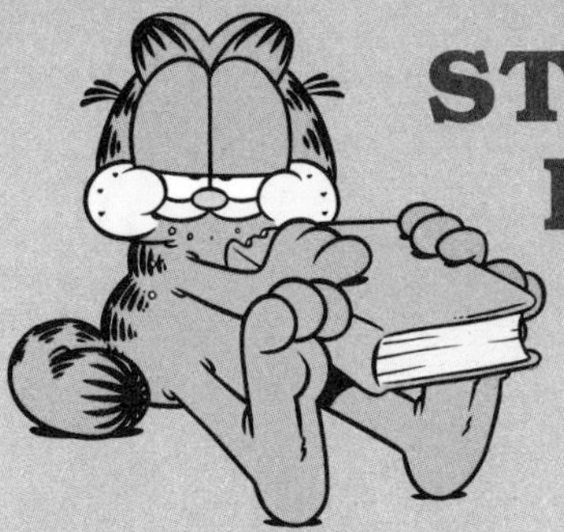

STRIPS, SPECIALS, OR BESTSELLING BOOKS . . . GARFIELD'S ON EVERYONE'S MENU.

Don't miss even one episode in the Tubby Tabby's hilarious series!

GARFIELD AT LARGE ....(#1) 978-0-345-44382-3
GARFIELD GAINS WEIGHT ....(#2) 978-0-345-44975-7
GARFIELD BIGGER THAN LIFE ....(#3) 978-0-345-45027-2
GARFIELD WEIGHS IN ....(#4) 978-0-345-45205-4
GARFIELD TAKES THE CAKE ....(#5) 978-0-345-44978-8
GARFIELD EATS HIS HEART OUT ....(#6) 978-0-345-46459-0
GARFIELD SITS AROUND THE HOUSE ....(#7) 978-0-345-46463-7
GARFIELD TIPS THE SCALES ....(#8) 978-0-345-46909-0
GARFIELD LOSES HIS FEET ....(#9) 978-0-345-46467-5
GARFIELD MAKES IT BIG ....(#10) 978-0-345-46468-2
GARFIELD ROLLS ON ....(#11) 978-0-345-47561-9
GARFIELD OUT TO LUNCH ....(#12) 978-0-345-47562-6
GARFIELD FOOD FOR THOUGHT ....(#13) 978-0-345-47563-3
GARFIELD SWALLOWS HIS PRIDE ....(#14) 978-0-345-91386-9
GARFIELD WORLDWIDE ....(#15) 978-0-345-91754-6
GARFIELD ROUNDS OUT ....(#16) 978-0-345-49169-5
GARFIELD CHEWS THE FAT ....(#17) 978-0-345-49170-1
GARFIELD GOES TO WAIST ....(#18) 978-0-345-49173-2
GARFIELD HANGS OUT ....(#19) 978-0-345-49174-9
GARFIELD TAKES UP SPACE ....(#20) 978-0-345-37029-7
GARFIELD SAYS A MOUTHFUL ....(#21) 978-0-345-37368-7
GARFIELD BY THE POUND ....(#22) 978-0-345-37579-7
GARFIELD KEEPS HIS CHINS UP ....(#23) 978-0-345-37959-7
GARFIELD TAKES HIS LICKS ....(#24) 978-0-345-38170-5
GARFIELD HITS THE BIG TIME ....(#25) 978-0-345-38332-7
GARFIELD PULLS HIS WEIGHT ....(#26) 978-0-345-38666-3
GARFIELD DISHES IT OUT ....(#27) 978-0-345-39287-9
GARFIELD LIFE IN THE FAT LANE ....(#28) 978-0-345-39776-8
GARFIELD TONS OF FUN ....(#29) 978-0-345-40386-5
GARFIELD BIGGER AND BETTER ....(#30) 978-0-345-40770-2
GARFIELD HAMS IT UP ....(#31) 978-0-345-41241-6
GARFIELD THINKS BIG ....(#32) 978-0-345-41671-1
GARFIELD THROWS HIS WEIGHT AROUND ....(#33) 978-0-345-42749-6
GARFIELD LIFE TO THE FULLEST ....(#34) 978-0-345-43239-1
GARFIELD FEEDS THE KITTY ....(#35) 978-0-345-43673-3
GARFIELD HOGS THE SPOTLIGHT ....(#36) 978-0-345-43922-2
GARFIELD BEEFS UP ....(#37) 978-0-345-44109-6
GARFIELD GETS COOKIN' ....(#38) 978-0-345-44582-7
GARFIELD EATS CROW ....(#39) 978-0-345-45201-6
GARFIELD SURVIVAL OF THE FATTEST ....(#40) 978-0-345-46458-3
GARFIELD OLDER AND WIDER ....(#41) 978-0-345-46462-0
GARFIELD PIGS OUT ....(#42) 978-0-345-46466-8
GARFIELD BLOTS OUT THE SUN ....(#43) 978-0-345-46615-0
GARFIELD GOES BANANAS ....(#44) 978-0-345-91346-3
GARFIELD LARGE & IN CHARGE ....(#45) 978-0-345-49172-5
GARFIELD SPILLS THE BEANS ....(#46) 978-0-345-49177-0
GARFIELD GETS HIS JUST DESSERTS ....(#47) 978-0-345-91387-6
GARFIELD WILL EAT FOR FOOD ....(#48) 978-0-345-49176-3

DVD TIE-INS

GARFIELD AS HIMSELF 978-0-345-47805-4
GARFIELD HOLIDAY CELEBRATIONS 978-0-345-47930-3
GARFIELD TRAVEL ADVENTURES 978-0-345-48087-3

AND DON'T MISS...

GARFIELD AT 25: IN DOG YEARS I'D BE DEAD 978-0-345-45204-7
GARFIELD'S JOKE ZONE/INSULTS 978-0-345-46263-3
GARFIELD FAT CAT 3-PACK/ VOL. 1 978-0-345-46455-2
GARFIELD FAT CAT 3-PACK/ VOL. 2 978-0-345-46465-1
GARFIELD FAT CAT 3-PACK/ VOL. 3 978-0-345-48088-0
GARFIELD FAT CAT 3-PACK/ VOL. 4 978-0-345-49171-8
GARFIELD FAT CAT 3-PACK/ VOL. 13 978-0-345-46460-6
GARFIELD FAT CAT 3-PACK/ VOL. 14 978-0-345-49175-6
SEASON'S EATINGS: A VERY MERRY GARFIELD CHRISTMAS 978-0-345-47560-2
GARFIELD'S GUIDE TO EVERYTHING 978-0-345-46461-3
ODIE UNLEASHED! 978-0-345-46464-4
GARFIELD'S BOOK OF CAT NAMES 978-0-345-48516-8
THE GARFIELD JOURNAL 978-0-345-46469-9
LIGHTS, CAMERA, HAIRBALLS!: GARFIELD AT THE MOVIES 978-0-345-49134-3
30 YEARS OF LAUGHS AND LASAGNA 978-0-345-50379-4
GARFIELD MINUS GARFIELD 978-0-345-51387-8

New larger, full-color format! (#1–#19)